SLAVE NARRATIVES

Volume IV
Georgia Narratives, Part 4

By
United States.
Work Projects Administration

Copyright © 2024 by BLACKLEGACYPRESS.ORG

All rights reserved. No part of this publication may be reproduced or transmitted in any form or by any means electronic or mechanical, including information storage and retrieval systems without permission in writing from the publisher, except for student research using the appropriate citations.

ISBN: 978-1-63652-205-0

SLAVE NARRATIVES

A Folk History of Slavery in the United States.
From Interviews with Former Slaves

**UNITED STATES.
WORK PROJECTS ADMINISTRATION**

TYPEWRITTEN RECORDS PREPARED BY
THE FEDERAL WRITERS' PROJECT
1936-1938
ASSEMBLED BY
THE LIBRARY OF CONGRESS PROJECT
WORK PROJECTS ADMINISTRATION
FOR THE DISTRICT OF COLUMBIA
SPONSORED BY THE LIBRARY OF
CONGRESS

WASHINGTON 1941

VOLUME IV
GEORGIA NARRATIVES
PART 4

Prepared by
The Federal Writers' Project of
The Works Progress Administration
For the State of Georgia

CONTENTS

Georgia Telfair	1
Cordelia Thomas	9
Ike Thomas	21
Jane Mickens Toombs	25
Phil Towns	33
Neal Upson	45
John F. Van Hook	67
Addie Vinson	91
Emma Virgel	107
Rhodus Walton	115
William Ward	121
William Ward	127
Lula Washington	131
Green Willbanks	135
Eliza Williamson	147
Frances Willingham	151
Adeline Willis	161
Uncle Willis	169
Cornelia Winfield	181
George Womble	185
Henry Wright	203
Dink Walton Young	217
Mammy Dink	223
Combined Interviews	225
[Adeline]	227
[Eugene]	229

[Mary]	231
[Rachel]	232
[Laura]	233
[Matilda]	234
[Easter]	236
[Carrie]	237
[Malinda]	238
[Amelia]	239
Ellen Campbell	241
Rachel Sullivan	247
Eugene Wesley Smith	253
Willis Bennefield	259
Mrs. Emmaline Heard	271
Mrs. Rosa Millegan And Mr. Jasper Millegan	278
Camilla Jackson	281
Mrs. Anna Grant	284
Mrs. Emmaline Heard	286
Folklore	293
Conjuration	303
Folk Remedies And Superstition	315
Mistreatment Of Slaves	323
Slavery	341
Housing Conditions	343
Food	346
Types Of Work	348
Education	352
Religion	354
Discipline	358

Overseers	366
Amusements	373
Slave Sales	377
War Memories	383
Freedom	387
Folk Lore	391
Interesting Customs	393
Dress	394
Number Of Slaves	395
Bibliography	396
Work, Play, Food, Clothing, Marriage, Etc.	397

PLANTATION LIFE AS VIEWED BY AN EX-SLAVE
GEORGIA TELFAIR, Age 74
Box 131, R.F.D. #2
Athens, Ga.

Written by:
Miss Grace McCune
Athens, Ga.

Edited by:
Mrs. Sarah H. Hall
Athens, Ga.

and
Mrs. Leila Harris
Augusta, Ga.
[Date Stamp: APR 29 1938]

GEORGIA TELFAIR

"Yes chile, I'll be glad to tell you de story of my life, I can't tell you much 'bout slav'ry 'cause I wuz jus' six months old when freedom come, but I has heared quite a lot, and I will tell you all I kin 'member 'bout everythin." Said old "Aunt" Georgia Telfair, who lives with her son to whom her devotion is quite evident. Both "Aunt" Georgia and the little home show the excellent care that is given them.

"My pa," she said, "wuz Pleasant Jones, an' he b'longed to Marse Young L.G. Harris. Dey lived at de Harris place out on Dearing Street. Hit wuz all woods out dar den, an' not a bit lak Dearing Street looks now.

"Rachel wuz my ma's name. Us don' know what her

las' name wuz 'cause she wuz sold off when she wuz too little to 'member. Dr. Riddin' (Redding) bought her an' his fambly always jus' called her Rachel Riddin'. De Riddin' place wuz whar Hancock Avenue is now, but it wuz all in woods 'roun' dar, jus' lak de place whar my pa wuz. Atter dey wuz married ma had to stay on wid de Riddin' fambly an' her chilluns b'longed to de Riddin's 'cause dey owned her. Miss Maxey Riddin' wuz my brudder's young Missus, an' I wuz give to her sister, Miss Lula Riddin', for to be her own maid, but us didn't git to wuk for 'em none 'cause it wuz jus' at dis time all de slaves got sot free. Atter dat my pa tuk us all wid him an' went to farm on de old Widderspoon (Witherspoon) place.

"It wuz 'way off in de woods. Pa cut down trees an' built us a log cabin. He made de chimbly out of sticks an' red mud, an' put iron bars crost de fireplace to hang pots on for to bile our vittuls an' made ovens for de bakin'. De bes' way to cook 'tatoes wuz to roas' 'em in de ashes wid de jackets on. Dey ain' nothin' better tastin' dan ash-roasted 'tatoes wid good home-made butter to eat wid 'em. An 'us had de butter, 'cause us kep' two good cows. Ma had her chickens an' tukkeys an' us raised plenty of hogs, so we nebber wuz widout meat. Our reg'lar Sunday breakfas' wuz fish what pa cotch out of de crick. I used to git tired out of fish den, but a mess of fresh crick fish would sho' be jus' right now.

"Us always kep' a good gyardan full of beans, corn, onions, peas an' 'taters, an' dey warn't nobody could beat us at raisin' lots of greens, 'specially turnips an' colla'd greens. Us saved heaps of dry peas an' beans, an' dried lots of peaches an' apples to cook in winter. When de wind wuz a howlin an' de groun' all kivvered wid snow, ma would make dried fruit puffs for us, dat sho' did hit de spot.

"When I wuz 'bout eight years old, dey sont me to school. I had to walk from Epps Bridge Road to Knox School. Dey calls it Knox Institute now. I toted my blue back speller in one han' and my dinner bucket in de other. Us wore homespun dresses wid bonnets to match. De bonnets wuz all made in one piece an' had drawstrings on de back to make 'em fit, an' slats in de brims to make 'em stiff an' straight. Our dresses wuz made long to keep our legs warm. I don't see, for to save me, how dey keeps dese young-uns from freezin' now since dey let 'em go 'roun' mos' naked.

"Our brush arbor church wuz nigh whar Brooklyn Mount Pleasant Church is now, an' us went to Sunday School dar evvy Sunday. It warn't much of a church for looks, 'cause it wuz made out of poles stuck in de groun' an' de roof wuz jus' pine limbs an' brush, but dere sho' wuz some good meetin's in dat old brush church, an' lots of souls foun' de way to de heb'enly home right dar.

"Our reg'lar preacher wuz a colored man named Morrison, but Mr. Cobb preached to us lots of times. He wuz a white gemman, an' he say he could a sot all night an' lissen long as us sung dem old songs. Some of 'em I done clar forgot, but de one I lak bes' goes sorter lak dis:

> 'I want to be an angel
> An' wid de angels stan'
> A crown upon my forehead
> And a harp widin my han'.'

"Another tune wuz 'Roll, Jordan Roll.' Little chillun wuz larnt to sing, 'How Sweetly do de Time Fly, When

I Please my Mother,' an' us chillun sho' would do our best a singin' dat little old song, so Preacher Cobb would praise us.

"When I jined de church dere wuz 35 of us baptized de same day in de crick back of de church. While Preacher Brown wuz a baptizin' us, a big crowd wuz standin' on de bank a shoutin' an' singin', 'Dis is de healin' Water,' an', 'Makin' for de Promise Lan! Some of 'em wuz a prayin' too. Atter de baptizin' wuz done dey had a big dinner on de groun's for de new members, but us didn't see no jugs dat day. Jus' had plenty of good somethin' t'eat.

"When us warn't in school, me an' my brudder wukked in de fiel' wid pa. In cotton plantin' time, pa fixed up de rows an' us drap de seeds in 'em. Nex' day us would rake dirt over 'em wid wooden rakes. Pa made de rakes hisse'f. Dey had short wooden teef jus' right for to kivver de seed. Folkses buys what dey uses now an' don't take up no time makin' nothin' lak dat.

"In dem days 'roun' de house an' in de fiel' boys jus' wo' one piece of clo'es. It wuz jus' a long shirt. Dey didn't know nothin' else den, but I sho' would lak to see you try to make boys go 'roun' lookin' lak dat now.

"Dey hired me out to Mr. Jack Weir's fambly when I wuz 'bout fo'teen years old to do washin', ironin', an' cleanin' up de house, an' I wukked for 'em 'til I married. Dey lemme eat all I wanted dere at de house an' paid me in old clo'es, middlin' meat, sirup, 'tatoes, an' wheat flour, but I never did git no money for pay. Not nary a cent.

"Us wukked mighty hard, but us had good times too. De bigges' fun us had wuz at candy pullin's. Ma cooked de candy in de wash pot out in de yard. Fust she poured in some home-made sirup, an' put in a heap of brown sugar from de old sirup barrel an' den she biled it down to whar if you drapped a little of it in cold water it got hard quick. It wuz ready den to be poured out in greasy plates an' pans. Us greased our han's wid lard to keep de candy from stickin' to 'em, an' soon as it got cool enough de couples would start pullin' candy an' singin'. Dat's mighty happy music, when you is singin' an' pullin' candy wid yo' bes' feller. When de candy got too stiff an' hard to pull no mo', us started eatin', an' it sho' would evermo' git away from dar in a hurry. You ain't nebber seed no dancin', what is dancin', lessen you has watched a crowd dance atter dey et de candy what dey done been pullin'.

"Quiltin's wuz a heap of fun. Sometimes two or three famblies had a quiltin' together. Folkses would quilt some an' den dey passed 'roun' de toddy. Some would be cookin' while de others wuz a quiltin' an' den when supper wuz ready dey all stopped to eat. Dem colla'd greens wid cornpone an' plenty or gingercakes an' fruit puffs an' big ole pots of coffee wuz mighty fine eatin's to us den.

"An' dere warn't nothin' lackin' when us had cornshuckin's. A gen'ral of de cornshuckin' wuz appointed to lead off in de fun. He sot up on top of de big pile of corn an' hysted de song. He would git 'em started off singin' somethin' lak, 'Sallie is a Good Gal,' an' evvybody kept time shuckin' an' a singin'. De gen'ral kept singin' faster an' faster, an' shucks wuz jus' flyin'. When pa started passin' de jug 'roun' dem Niggers sho' nuff begun to sing loud an' fas' an' you wuz 'bliged for to 'low Sallie mus' be a Good Gal, de way de shucks wuz comin' off of dat corn so fas'. Dey kep' it up 'til de corn wuz all shucked, an' ma hollered, 'Supper ready!' Den dey made tracks for de kitchen, an' dey didn't stop eatin' an' drinkin' dat hot coffee long as dey could swallow. Ain't nobody fed 'em no better backbones, an' spareribs, turnip greens, 'tato pies, an' sich lak dan my ma set out for 'em. Old time ways lak dat is done gone for good now. Folkses ain't lak dey used to be. Dey's all done got greedy an' don't keer 'bout doin' nothin' for nobody else no more.

"Ma combed our hair wid a Jim Crow comb, or cyard, as some folkses called 'em. If our hair wuz bad nappy she put some cotton in de comb to keep it from pullin' so bad, 'cause it wuz awful hard to comb.

"Evvybody tried to raise plenty of gourds, 'cause dey wuz so handy to use for dippers den. Water wuz toted from de spring an' kept in piggins. Don't spec' you ebber did see a piggin. Dats a wooden bucket wid wire hoops 'roun' it to keep it from leakin'. De wash place wuz nex' to de spring. Pa fixed us up a big old stump whar us had to battle de clo'es wid a battlin' stick. It tuk a sight of battlin' to git de dirt out sometimes.

"If you turned a chunk over in de fire, bad luck wuz sho' to come to you. If a dog howled a certain way at night, or if a scritch owl come in de night, death wuz on de way to you, an' you always had to be keerful so maybe bad spirits would leave you alone.

"Pa built us a new kitchen, jus' lak what de white folkses had dem days. It sot out in de back yard, a little piece of a way from our house. He made it out of logs an' put a big old chimbly wid a big fireplace at one end. Benches wuz built 'roun' de sides for seats. Dere warn't no floor in it, but jus' dirt floor. Dat wuz one gran' kitchen an' us wuz mighty proud of it. [HW: p.4]

"My w'ite folkses begged me not to leave 'em, when I told 'em I wuz gwine to marry Joe Telfair. I'd done been wukkin' for 'em nigh on to six years, an' wuz mos' twenty years old. Dey gimme my weddin' clo'es, an' when I seed dem clo'es I wuz one proud Nigger, 'cause dey wuz jus' lak I wanted. De nightgown wuz made out of white bleachin' an' had lots of tucks an' ruffles an' it even had puff sleeves. Sho' 'nough it did! De petticoat had ruffles an' puffs plum up to de wais' ban'. Dere wuz a cosset kiver dat wuz cut to fit an' all fancy wid tucks an' trimmin', an' de drawers, dey sho' wuz pretty, jus' full of ruffles an' tucks 'roun' de legs. My dress wuz a cream buntin', lak what dey calls serge dese days. It had a pretty lace front what my ma bought from one of de Moss ladies. When I got all dressed up I wuz one mo' gran' lookin' bride.

"Us got married in de new kitchen an' it wuz plum full, 'cause ma had done axed 76 folkses to de weddin'. Some of 'em wuz Joe's folkses, an' us had eight waiters: four gals, an' four boys. De same Preacher Brown what baptized me, married us an' den us had a big supper. My Missus, Lula Weir, had done baked a great big pretty cake for me an' it tasted jus' as good as it looked. Atter us et all us could, one of de waiters called de sets for us to dance de res' of de night. An' sich dancin' as us did have! Folkses don't know how to dance dat good no mo'. Dat wuz sho' nuff happy dancin'. Yes Ma'am, I ain't nebber gonna forgit what a gran' weddin' us had.

"Next day us moved right here an' I done been here ever since. Dis place b'longed to Joe's gran'ma, an' she willed it to him. Us had 15 chillun, but ain't but five of 'em livin' now, an' Joe he's been daid for years. Us always made a good livin' on de farm, an' still raises mos' of what us needs, but I done got so po'ly I can't wuk no more.

"I'se still tryin' to live right an' walk de narrow way, so as I kin go to Heb'en when I dies. I'se gwine to pray for you an' ax de Lawd to bless you, for you has been so good an' patient wid me, an' I'se sho' thankful my son sont you to see me. You done helped me to feel lots better. Good-bye, an' God bless you, an' please Ma'am, come back to see me again."

PLANTATION LIFE

CORDELIA THOMAS, Age 80
130 Berry Street
Athens, Ga.

Written by:
Grace McCune [HW: (white)]
Athens

Edited by:
Sarah H. Hall
Athens

Leila Harris
Augusta

and

John N. Booth
District Supervisor
Federal Writers' Project
Residencies 6 & 7

CORDELIA THOMAS

A long, hot walk over rough, hilly roads brought the visitor to Cordelia's place just after the noon hour of a sweltering July day, and the shade of the tall water oaks near the little cabin was a most welcome sight. The house stood only a few feet from a spur of railroad track but the small yard was enclosed by a luxurious green hedge. Roses predominated among the many varieties of flowers in evidence on the otherwise drab premises.

A dilapidated porch across the front of the residence had no roof and the floorboards were so badly rotted that it did not seem quite safe to walk from the steps to the front door where Cordelia stood waiting. "Come right in, Missy," she invited, "but be keerful not to fall through dat old porch floor." The tall, thin Negress was clad in a faded but scrupulously clean blue dress, a white apron, and a snowy headcloth crowned by a shabby black hat. Black brogans completed her costume. Cordelia led the way to the rear of a narrow hall. "Us will be cooler back here," she explained. Sunlight poured through gaping holes in the roof, and the coarse brown wrapping paper pasted on the walls was splattered and streaked by rain. The open door of Cordelia's bedroom revealed a wooden bed, a marble-topped bureau, and a washstand of the Victorian period. A rocker, two straight chairs, a small table, and a trunk completed the furnishings of the room and left but little space for its occupant to move about.

"I'se jus' a mite tired," Cordelia stated, "'cause I jus' got back from de courthouse whar dem welfare 'omans done gimme a sack o' flour and some other bundles what I ain't opened up yit, but I knows dey's got somepin in 'em to holp me, 'cause dem folks is sho' been mighty good to me since my rheumatiz is been so bad I couldn't wuk enough to make a livin'. De doctor, he say I got de blood presser. I don't rightly know jus' what dat is, but it looks lak somepin's a-pressin' right down in my haid 'til I feels right foolish, so I reckon he's right 'bout it a-bein de blood presser. When I gits down on my knees it takes a long time for me to git straight up on my feet again. De Lord, He's done been wid me all dese years, and old Cordelia's goin' to keep right on kneelin' 'fore Him and praisin' Him often 'til He 'cides de time has come for her to go home to Heben.

"I was borned on Marse Andrew Jackson's plantation down in 'Conee (Oconee) County, twixt here and High Shoals. Marse Andy, he owned my Mammy, and she was named Em'ly Jackson. Bob Lowe was my Daddy, and he b'longed to Marse Ike Lowe. The Lowe plantation was nigh whar Marse Andy's was, down der in 'Conee County. 'Cause neither one of deir marsters wouldn't sell one of 'em to de other marster, Mammy had to stay on de Jackson plantation and Daddy was kept right on wukin' on de Lowe place atter dey had done got married. Marse Bob, he give Daddy a ticket what let him go to see Mammy evvy Wednesday and Sadday night, and dem patterollers couldn't bother him long as he kept dat ticket. When dey did find a slave off his marster's plantation widout no ticket, it was jus' too bad, for dat meant a beatin' what most kilt him. Mammy said dey didn't never git my Daddy, 'cause he allus had his ticket to show.

"I don't ricollect much 'bout days 'fore de big war ended 'cause I was so little den, but many's de time I heared Mammy and Daddy and de other old folks tell 'bout dem times. Us chillun had de bestes' time of anybody dem days, 'cause dey didn't 'low us to do nothin' but jus' eat all us could and play de rest of de time. I don't know how it was on other places, but dat was de way us was raised on our old marster's plantation.

"De cracks of de log cabins whar de slaves lived was chinked wid red mud to keep out de cold and rain. Dere warn't no glass in de windows, dey jus' had plank shutters what dey fastened shut at night. Thin slide blocks kivvered de peepholes in de rough plank doors. Dey had to have dem peepholes so as dey could see who was at de door 'fore dey opened up. Dem old stack chimblies what was made out of sticks and red clay, was all time gittin' on fire. Dem old home-made beds had high posties and us called 'em 'teesters.' To take de place of springs, what hadn't never been seen 'round dar in dem days, dey wove heavy cords lengthways and crostways. Over dem cords dey laid a flat mat wove out of white oak splints and on dat dey put de homespun bed ticks stuffed wid wheat straw. Dey could have right good pillows if dey was a mind to pick de scrap cotton and fix it up, but dere warn't many of 'em keered dat much 'bout no pillows.

"Slaves didn't do no cookin' on our place 'cause Marster fed evvybody up at de big house. Missy, I ain't never gwine to forgit dat big old fireplace up dar. Dey piled whole sticks of cord wood on it at one time, wid little sticks crossways under 'em and, let me tell you, dat was a fire what would cook anything and evvything. De pots hung on swingin' racks, and dere was big ovens, little ovens, long-handled fryin' pans, and heavy iron skillets wid tight, thick lids. It sho' was a sight de way us chillun used to make 'way wid dem ash-roasted 'taters and dat good, fresh butter. Us chillun had to eat supper early 'cause all chillun had to be in bed 'fore dark. It warn't lak dese days. Why Missy, chilluns now stays up 'most all night runnin' 'round dese parts.

"Marster was sho' good 'bout seein' dat his Niggers had plenty to eat and wear. For supper us et our bread and milk wid wooden spoons out of wooden bowls, but for dinner dey give us veg'ables, corn pone, and 'taters. Marster raised all de sorts of veg'ables what dey knowed anything 'bout in dem days, and he had big old fields of wheat, rye, oats, and corn, 'cause he 'lowed dat stock had to eat same as folkses. Dere was lots of chickens, turkeys, cows, hogs, sheep, and some goats on dat plantation so as dere would allus be plenty of meat for evvybody.

"Our Marster evermore did raise de cotton—lots of it to sell, and plenty for clothes for all de folkses, white and black, what lived on his place. All de cloth was homemade 'cept de calico for de best Sunday dresses. Chillun had to spin de thread and deir mammies wove de cloth. 'Fore de end of de war, whilst I was still so little I had to stand on a box to reach de spinnin' wheel good, I could spin six reels a day.

"Chillun was happy when hog-killin' time come. Us warn't 'lowed to help none, 'cept to fetch in de wood to keep de pot bilin' whar de lard was cookin'. Our Mist'ess allus had de lard rendered in de bigges' washpot, what dey sot on rocks in de fireplace. Us didn't mind gittin' de wood for dat, 'cause when dem cracklin's got done, dey let us have all us could eat and, jus' let me tell you, Missy, you ain't never had nothin' good 'less you has et a warm skin cracklin' wid a little salt. One time when dey was renderin' lard, all us chillun was crowdin' 'round close as us could git to see which one could git a cracklin' fust. Mist'ess told us to stand back 'fore somebody got burnt; den Mammy said she was gwine to take de hides off our backs 'bout gittin' so close to dat fire, and 'bout dat time somebody 'hind me gimme a quick push; and in de fire I went. Marster grabbed me 'most time I hit dem red coals, but one hand and arm was burnt so bad I had to wear it in a sling for a long time. Den Marster laid down de law and told us what he would do if he cotch us chillun hangin' 'round de fire whar dey was cookin' lard again.

"Folkses said our Marster must have a powerful sweet tooth on account of he kept so many bee hives. When bees swarmed folkses rung bells and beat on tin pans to git 'em settled. Veils was tied over deir haids to keep de bees from gittin' to deir faces when dey went to rob de hives. Chillun warn't never 'lowed to be nowhar nigh durin' dat job. One day I sneaked out and got up close to see how dey done it, and dem bees got all over me. Dey stung me so bad I couldn't see for days and days. Marster, he jus' fussed and said dat gal, Cordelia, she was allus whar she didn't b'long. Missy, I ain't never wanted to fool wid no more bees, and I don't even lak honey no more.

"Slaves all went to church wid deir white folkses 'cause dere warn't no Nigger churches dem days. All de preachin' was done by white preachers. Churches warn't nigh and convenient dem days lak dey is now and dey was such a fur piece from de plantations dat most of de folkses stayed all day, and dem meetin' days was big days den. De cooks was told to fix de bestes' dinners dey could git up, and chillun was made to know dey had better mind what dey was 'bout when dey was in de meetin' house or it was gwine to be made mighty hot for 'em when dey got back home. Dat was one thing our Marster didn't 'low no foolin' 'bout. His Niggers had to be-have deyselfs at de meetin' house. 'Long 'bout August when craps was laid by, dey had brush arbor meetin's. White folks brought deir slaves and all of 'em listened to a white preacher from Watkinsville named Mr. Calvin Johnson. Dere was lots of prayin' and shoutin' at dem old brush arbor 'vival meetin's.

"Dey had campmeetin's too. De old Freeman place was whar dey had some of dem fust campmeetin's, and

Hillsboro, Mars Hill, and Bethabara was some of de other places whar Marster tuk us to campmeetin's. Missy, you jus' don't know nothin' 'bout 'citement if you ain't never been to one of dem old-time campmeetin's. When folkses would git 'ligion dey would holler and shout a-testifyin' for de Lord. Atter de meetin' dey dammed up de crick and let it git deep enough for de baptizin'. Dey dipped de white folkses fust, and den de Niggers. You could hear 'em singin' a mile away dem old songs lak: *On Jordan's Stormy Banks I Stand,*—*Roll, Jordan Roll,*—*All God's Chilluns is a-goin' Home,* and—*Whar de Livin' Waters Flow.* I jus' can't 'member half of dem good old songs 'cause my mem'ry ain't good as it used to be." Here Cordelia paused. She seemed oblivious to all around her for several minutes, and then she suddenly smiled. "Lordy, Missy," she began, "if I could jus' call back dem days wid our good old Marster to look atter us and see dat us had what us needed to eat and wear and a good comf'table cabin to live in, wouldn't dis be a happy old 'oman? Lots of de other old folks would lak it too, 'cause our white folkses day sho' did take good keer of deir slaves.

"Did you ever hear of dem logrollin's? On our place dey spent 'bout two whole days cookin' and gittin' ready. Marster axed evvybody from fur and nigh, and dey allus come 'cause dey knowed he was gwine to give 'em a good old time. De way dey rolled dem logs was a sight, and de more good corn liquor Marster passed 'round, de faster dem logs rolled. Come night-time, Marster had a big bonfire built up and sot lots of pitchpine torches 'round so as dere would be plenty of light for 'em to see how to eat dat fine supper what had done been sot out for 'em. Atter supper, dey danced nigh all de rest of de night. Mammy used to tell us 'bout de frolics next day, 'cause us chillun was made to go to bed at sundown. Come day, go day, no matter what might happen, growin' chillun had to be in bed at deir reg'lar time, but Mammy never forgot to tell us all 'bout de good times next day.

"Mammy said dem cornshuckin's meant jus' as much fun and jollification as wuk. Dey gathered Marster's big corn crap and 'ranged it in long, high piles, and sometimes it tuk sev'ral days for dem cornshuckers to git it all shucked, but evvybody stayed right dar on de job 'til it was finished. At night, dey wukked by de light of big fires and torches, den dey had de big supper and started dancin'. Dey stopped so often to swig dat corn liquor Marster pervided for 'em dat 'fore midnight folkses started fallin' out and drappin' down in de middle of de dance ring. De others would git 'em by de heels and drag 'em off to one side 'til dey come to and was ready to drink more liquor and dance again. Dat was de way dey went on de rest of de night.

"Corpses! Buryin's! Graveyards! Why, Miss, dere warn't nigh so many folkses a-dyin' all de time dem days as dere is now. Folkses lived right and was tuk better keer of and dere warn't so much reason for 'em to die out den. When somebody did die, folkses come from miles and miles around to de buryin'. Dey give de slaves de same sort of funerals de white folkses had. De corpses was washed good all over wid hot water and home-made soap, den dey was dressed and laid out on de coolin' boards 'til de cyarpenter man had time to make up de coffins. Lordy, Missy, ain't you never seed no coolin' board? I 'spects dey is all gone now though. Dey looked a good deal lak ironin' boards, only dey had laigs to stand on. Lots of times dey didn't dress de corpses, but jus' wropped 'em in windin' sheets. Dem home-made, pine coffins didn't look so bad atter dey got 'em painted up and lined nice. Dey driv de wagon what had de corpse on it right slow to de graveyard. De preacher talked a little and prayed; den atter de mourners had done sung somepin on de order of *Harps [HW: Hark?] From De Tomb*, dey shovelled in de dirt over de coffin whilst de preacher said comfortin' words to de fambly of de daid. Evvy plantation had its own graveyard wid a fence around it, and dere was a place in it for de slaves 'nigh whar deir white folks was buried.

"Honey, didn't you never hear tell of Dr. Frank Jackson? He was sho' a grand doctor. Dr. Jackson made up his own medicines and toted 'em 'round wid him all de time. He was close kin to our Marse Andy Jackson's fambly. All dem Jacksons down in 'Conee was good white folks.

"Us stayed on wid Old Marster for a little while atter de war was over, and den right away Mammy died and Daddy hired me out to Mrs. Sidney Rives (Reaves?). I 'spects one reason she was so mighty good to me was 'cause I was so little den. I was nigh grown when I left her to wuk for Dr. Palmer's fambly. All his chillun was little den and I was deir nuss. One of de best of his chillun was little Miss Eunice. She is done growed to be a school teacher and dey tells me she is still a-teachin'. It warn't long atter my Daddy died dat I left de Palmers and started wukkin' for Mr. Dock Dorsey's fambly. If dere ever was a good Christian 'oman in dis here old world it was Miss Sallie Dorsey, Mr. Dock Dorsey's wife. She had been Miss Sallie Chappell 'fore she married Mr. Dorsey. Miss Sallie tried to git evvybody what stayed 'round her to live right too, and she wanted all her help to go to church reg'lar. If Miss Sallie and Marse Dock Dorsey was livin' now, dey would pervide for Old 'Delia jus' lak dey used to do. All deir chillun was nice. Miss Fannie and Miss Sue, dey was extra good gals, but somehow I jus' can't call back de names of dem other ones now. Dey all had to be good wid de sort of mammy and daddy dey had. Miss Sallie, she was sick a long time 'fore she died, and dey let me wait on her. Missy, I tell you de gospel truth, I sho' did love dat 'oman. Not long 'fore she passed on to Heben, she told her husband dat atter she was gone, she wanted him to marry up wid her cousin, Miss Hargrove, so as he would have somebody to help him raise up her chillun, and he done 'zactly what she axed him to. All of my own white folkses has done died out, and Old 'Delia won't be here much longer. One of de Thorntons here—I forgits which one—married up wid my young Mist'ess, Rebecca Jackson. Her gal got married up wid Dr. Jago, a horse-doctor. A insurance man named Mr. Speer married into de Jackson fambly too. He moved his fambly from here to de mountains on account of his son's health, and I jus' los' track of 'em den.

"Lordy, Chile! What you want to know 'bout my weddin' for, nowhow? Dere ain't never gwine to be no more weddin's lak dey had back dere in dem times 'cause folkses thinks dey got to have too much nowadays. When folkses got married den dey was a-thinkin' 'bout makin' sho' 'nough homes for deyselfs, and gittin' married meant somepin sort of holy. Mammy said dat most times when slaves got married dey jus' jumped backwards over a broomstick whilst deir Marster watched and den he pernounced dat dey was man and wife. Now dey is got to go to de courthouse and pay out good money for a license and den go git a preacher or somebody lak a jestice jedge to say de marriage words over 'em.

"Me and Solomon Thomas had to go buy us a license too, but us didn't mind 'bout 'puttin out 'dat money cause us was so much in love. I wore a pretty white dress and a breakfast shawl, and atter us had done went to de preacher man's house and got married, us come right on here to dis very house what had b'longed to Solomon's daddy 'fore it was Solomon's. Us built two more rooms on de house, but all de time Solomon lived us tried to keep de place lookin' a good deal lak it was de day us got married.

"Atter Solomon died, I sold off most of de land to de railroad for de right of way for dat dere track what you sees out dere, and it sho' has made plenty of wuk for me to keep dat soot what dem engines is all time a-spittin' out cleaned off my things in de house. It draps down through dem big holes overhead, and I can't git hold of no money to have de roof patched up.

"Me and Solomon, us had 11 chillun, but dey is all daid out but three. One of my boys is in Baltimore and another boy lives in Louisiana somewhar. My gal, Delia, she stays over in de Newtown part of Athens here. She would love to help her old Mammy, but my Delia's got chillun of her own and she can't git nothin' to do 'cept a little washin' for de white folkses, and she ain't able to pervide what her own household needs to eat. Dem boys of mine is done got so fur off dey's done forgot all 'bout deir old Mammy.

"When us fust got married, Solomon wukked at Mr. Orr's cotton house, and he stayed dere a long time 'fore he went to wuk for Mr. Moss and Mr. Levy. All dem white folks was good to me and Solomon. I kept on wukkin' for de Dorseys 'til us had so many chillun I had to stay home and look atter 'em. Solomon got sick and he lay dere sufferin' a long, long time, but Mr. Moss and Mr. Levy seed dat he didn't want for nothin'. Even atter Solomon died dem good white mens kept on comin' out now and den to see if me and Solomon's chillun had what us needed.

"Solomon, my Solomon, he went out of dis here world, in dat dere room whar you sees dat old bed, and dat is perzactly whar I wants to be when de Blessed Lord lays his hands on me and tells me to come on Home to Glory. I wants to be toted out of dat room, through dis hall and on out to de graveyard jus' lak my man was. I knows dat evvything would be done nice jus' lak I wants it if Mr. Moss and Mr. Levy was a-livin' 'cause dey was both Masons, and members of de Masons is all done swore a oath to look atter deir own folkses. Dey said Solomon and his fambly was lak deir own folkses, Mr. Moss and Mr. Levy did. Most of de folkses, both white and black, dat I has knowed and loved has done gone on over de Jordan, out of dis world of trouble, and it will be happy days for all of us when us meets again in de place 'of many mansions' whar dere won't be nothin' for none of us to pester ourselfs 'bout no more.

"All of my life, I'se had a great desire to travel, jus' to go evvywhar, but atter all dese years of busy livin' I 'spects all de trav'lin' I'll ever do will be on de road to Glory. Dat will be good enough for me 'cause I got so many more of 'em I loves over dar dan is left here."

As the visitor passed out of earshot of Cordelia's cabin the last words she heard from the old Negress were: "Good-bye again, Missy. Talkin' to you has been a heap of consolation to me."

[HW: Dist-2
Ex Slave #105]
Alberta Minor
Re-search Worker

FOLKLORE
EX-SLAVE—IKE THOMAS
Heidt Bridges Farm near Rio Georgia
Interviewed

September 4, 1936
[Date Stamp: MAY 8 1937]

[TR: This interview contained many handwritten edits; where text was transposed or meaning was significantly changed, it has been noted.]

IKE THOMAS

Ike Thomas was born near Monticello in Jasper County on the Thomas plantation. His mother and father were sold when he was a little boy, and "Missus" Thomas, in picking her house boy, took Ike to raise for a carriage boy. She picked her little niggers by the way they wore their hats. If they set them on the back of their heads, they grew up to be "high-minded", but if they pulled them over their eyes, they'd grow up to be "sneaky and steal".

Mrs. Thomas let him sleep on a trundle bed pulled out at night and put under her bed in the day and fed him under the table. She'd put a piece of meat in a biscuit and hand it down to him and warned him if they had company not to holler when he was thru so he'd touch her on the knee but his mouth was so big and he'd eat so fast that he "jes kep' on teching her on the knee."

During the war, when they got word the Yankees were coming, Mrs. Thomas would hide her "little niggers" sometimes in the wardrobe back of her clothes, sometimes between the mattresses, or sometimes in the cane brakes. After the Yankees left, she'd ring a bell and they would know they could come out of hiding. (When they first heard the slaves were free, they didn't believe it so they just stayed on with their "white folks".) [HW: Transpose to page 3.]

If the negroes were mean or ran away, they would be chased by hounds and brought back for punishment.

When still a young man, Ike ran away with a negro couple coming in a buggy to Blanton Mill near Griffin and worked for Mr. William Blanton until he died. After he had been here a while, he got married. His wife's people had the wedding supper and party. He was a fiddler so had to fiddle most all night then the next day his "white folks" gave him the food for the wedding dinner that he had at his own house.

Ike says every seven [HW: 7] years the locusts come and its sure to be a short crop that "God sends all sorts of cusses" (curses) sometimes its the worms that eat the cotton or the corn or the bugs that eat the wheat. He doesn't believe in "hants" or "conjurin'". It seems Sid Scott was a "mean nigger", [HW: and] everyone was afraid of [HW: him]. He was cut in two by the saw mill and after his funeral whenever anyone pass his house at night that could hear his "hant" going "rat-a-tat-tat-bang, bang, bang" like feet running.

One night when Ike was coming home from "fiddlin'" at a white folks party, he had to pass Scott's house. Now they kept the cotton seed in half of the house and the other half was empty. When Ike got close, he made a racket and sure enough the noise started. "The moon was about an hour up" and he saw these funny white things run out from under the house and scatter. It scared him at first but he looked and looked and saw they were sheep that [HW: having] found a hole into the cotton seed would go in at night to eat.

Before the war the negroes had a big celebration on the 4th of July, a big barbecue, ball game, wrestling matches, lots of music and singing. They had to have a pass from their Masters to attend and pay to get in. The "patta-roll" came by to see your pass and if you didn't have one, they'd whip you and send you home. [HW: When the Negroes first heard that they were free, they didn't believe it so they just stayed on with their white folks.]

After he came to Blanton's, the Negroes could come and go as they pleased for they were free. Ike has been a member of several "Societies" but something has always happened to the President and Secretary or they ran off with the money so now he just has a sick and accident policy.

Ike will be 94 years old next month. His hair is white, his eyes blurred with age, but he's quite active tho' he does walk with a stick.

[HW: Dist 1
Ex-Slave #107]

JANE MICKENS TOOMBS OF WASHINGTON-WILKES
Age approx. 82

by
Minnie Branham Stonestreet
Washington-Wilkes
GEORGIA
[Date Stamp: JAN 26 1937]
[Date Stamp: MAY 8 1937]

JANE MICKENS TOOMBS

A story of happiness and contentment on a big plantation where there were "a heap of us slaves" is told by Jane Mickens Toombs who said she was "five er six years ole when de Wah come on (1860), or maby a lit'le ol'er."

She is a bright old woman, well and spry despite the fact she "wuz conjured onst when I wuz young an' dat lef' me lame an' dis eye plum' out an' de t'other bad."

When asked about the conjuring she said: "No'm, I don't 'zackly know how t'wuz, but enyhow somebody whut knowed how ter 'wu'k roots' got me lame on dis side, an' my eye out, jess kase I wuz a decent, nice lookin' gal, an' went on 'tendin' ter my business an' payin' dem no mind. Dat's de way dey done in dem days, jess jealous of nice colored niggers. Yassum, I wuz sick fer nigh on ter two years an' de doctuhs never knowed what ailed me. Dey done everything dey could, but I wuz conjured an' dey couldn't hep' me. A doctuh-man frum up yander in New Yalk cum down here ter see his folks, an' he tried to kure [HW: cyore] me, but doctuhs kain't [HW: kaan't] kure [HW: cyore] conjured folks, so I had ter lay an' suffer 'til de conjure wore out. Dem whut done dat knowed dey done me wrong, but I kep' trustin' in my Lawd, an' now dey's gone an' I'se er stumblin' roun' yit. No mam, I never knowed jess whut dey done ter me, but hit wuz bad, I kin tell yer dat, hit might nigh kilt me."

Aunt Jane was born on the Gullatt Plantation on the line of Wilkes and Lincoln counties. Her Mother was Liza Gullatt and her father John Mickens who belonged to Mr. Augustus McMekin. "Yassum, my Pa wuz John 'Mickens an' his Marster bought him in Alabamy. All de slaves whut belonged to de McMekins called dey selves 'Mickens. I wuz one of fifteen chillun an' cum er long in betweenst de oldest 'uns an' de youngest sum'ers. I wuz named fer my Mistess Jane Gullatt whut died. Young Marse George Gullatt choosed me out, dough, an' I'd er been his'en ef Freedom hadn't er come. You know dat's de way dey use ter do back in slavery time, de young Mistesses an' Marsters choosed out de little niggers dey wanted fer their'n."

This is another case where the father and mother belonged to different families. The father had a pass to go and come as he pleased, although his family lived a little distance away. Jane said her father's master would have bought her mother if the War hadn't come on and they were set free.

Jane told of the log cabins in the Quarters where all the negroes lived. She said they were all in a row "wid er street in de front, er wide street all set thick wid white mulberry trees fer ter mak' shade fer de chillun ter play in." They never had any punishment only [HW: except] switchings by their Mistess, and that was not often. They played dolls, "us had home-made rag dolls, nice 'uns, an' we'd git dem long grass plumes (Pampas grass) an' mak' dolls out'n dem too. Us played all day long every day. My Mistess' chillun wuz all growed up so jess us little niggers played tergether.

"My Mother spun an' wove de cloth, an' dyed hit, but our Mistess made our clothes. My Grandma, Nancy, wuz de cook an' she fed all de little 'uns in de big ole kitchen whut sot out in de yard. She had a tray she put our victuals on an Uh, Uh, whut good things we had ter eat, an' er plenty of everything! Us et jess whut our white folks had, dey didn't mak' no difference in us when hit cum ter eatin'. My Grandaddy looked atter de meat, he done everything 'bout dat, an' he sho' knowed how ter fix it, too.

"De fust thing I recollects is bein' round in de kitchen when dey wuz makin' ginger cakes an' my Mistess givin' me de pan she made 'em in fer me ter sop hit out. Dey ain't nothin' whut smells good lak' de cookin' in dem days, I kain't smell no victuals lak' dat now. Everything wuz cooked on a big ole open fire place in one end of de kitchen. Dem good ole days done gone now. Folkes done got wiser an' wickeder—dey ain't lak' dey use ter be."

At Christmas Santa Claus found his way to the Quarters on the Gollatt plantation and each little slave had candy, apples, and "sich good things as dat." Aunt Jane gave a glowing description of the preparation for the Christmas season: "Lawdy, how de folks wu'ked gittin' ready fer Chris'mus, fer three er fo' days dey stayed in de kitchen er cookin' an' er bakin'—daye wuz de bes' light bread—great big loaves baked on de fire place, an' cakes an' mo' good ginger cakes. Dey wuz plenty cooked up to las' er long time. An' another thing, dare want no cookin' on Sunday, no mam, no wu'k of no kind. My Mistess had de cook cookin' all day Fridays an' Saddays so when Sunday come dare wuz hot coffee made an' dat wuz all, everything else wuz cooked up an' cold. Everybody went to Church, de grown folks white and black, went to de preachin' an' den all de little niggers wuz called in an de Bible read an' 'splained ter dem.

"Dare wuz preachin' down in de Quarters, but dat wuz at night an' wuz led by de colored preachers. I recollects one night dare wuz a service gwine on in one of de cabins an' all us wuz dare an' ole Uncle Alex Frazier wuz up a linin' off a hymn 'bout

'Broad is de road dat leads ter Death
An' there an' here we travel.'

when in come some mens atter a colored feller whut had stole some sheep an' hogs. Dey kotch 'im, but sho broke up de meetin'. In de hot summer time Uncle George Gullatt use ter preach ter de slaves out under de trees. Uncle George waz a kind of er preacher.

"My Pa didn't 'low his chillun ter go 'roun'. No'm, he kep' us home keerful lak. Young folks in dem days didn't go all over de country lak dey does now, dey stayed at home, an' little chillun wuz kep' back an' dey didn' know no badness lak de chillun do terday. Us never even heared de ole folks talk nothin' whut we oughtn't ter hear. Us jess played an' stayed in a child's place. When we wuz sick de white folks seed dat we wuz 'tended to. Dey use ter mak Jerusalem Oak candy an' give us. Dey took de leaves of dat bush an' boiled 'em an' den use dat water dey wuz boiled in an' put sugar 'nough in hit ter mak candy. An dey used plenty of turpentine on us too—plenty ov hit, an' I believes in dat terday, hit's er good medicine."

When asked about the War, Aunt Jane said she didn't remember much about it. "But dare's one thing 'bout hit I sho' does 'member, an' dat's my young Mistess Beckie's husband, Mr. Frazier, being off fightin' in de Wah, an' she gittin' er letter frum him sayin' he wuz comin' home sich an' sich er day. She wuz so happy she had all de grown slaves wu'kin' gittin' ready fer him. Den dey brung her er letter sayin' he had been kilt, an' she wuz in de yard when she read hit an' if dey hadn't er kotch her she'd ov fell. I 'members de women takin' her in de house an' gittin' her ter bed. She wuz so up sot an' took hit so hard. Dem wuz sho' hard times an' sad 'uns too. 'Course I wuz too small ter know much whut wuz gwine on, but I could tell hit wuz bad frum de way de older folks looked.

"I recollects when dey say Freedom had cum. Dare wuz a speakin' fer de slaves up here in town in Barnett's Grove. Dat mornin' Ole Miss sont all de oldes' niggers to de speakin' an' kep' us little 'uns dat day. She kep' us busy sweepin' de yards an' sich as dat. An' she cooked our dinner an' give hit to us herself. I 'members de grown folks leavin' early dat mornin' in a great big waggin.

"A while after de Wah, Pa took us over to de McMekins place an' we lived dare fer a long time. He died an' lef' us an' den us had ter do de bes' we could. Col. Tolbert hired me fer ter nuss his chillun an' I went over ter his place ter live."

Aunt Jane said she isn't superstitious, but likes to see the new moon clear and bow to it for good luck. She said it is better to show it a piece of money, but as she doesn't always have money handy, she "jess bows to hit nice an' polite". She keeps up with the weather by her rheumatism and the cat: "Ef I has de reumatics I knows hit's gwine ter rain, an' when de cat comes 'round an' sets washin' her face, look fer rain, kase hit's er comin'. I've heared folks say dat hit's bad luck ter stump yo' lef' foot, but I don't know boud dat. But I tell yer, when I meets er cat I allus turns er round 'fore I goes on, dat turns de bad luck er way."

When 19 years of age Jane married Albert Toombs. He belonged to the Toombs family of Wilkes county. Aunt Jane said Albert brought her many gifts while he was courting: "He warnt much on bringin' candy an' nothin' lak dat ter eat, but he brung me shawls an' shoes—sumpin' I could wear." They had four children, but only one is living.

"When I wuz a growin' up", said Aunt Jane, "folks had ter wu'k." She worked on the farm, spun, wove, "done seamster wu'k" and knitted stockings, sox and gloves. She said she carded too, "an' in dem times ef a nigger wanted ter git de kinks out'n dey hair, dey combed hit wid de cards. Now dey puts all kinds ov grease on hit, an' buy straightenin' combs. Sumpin' dat costs money, dat's all dey is, old fashion cards'll straighten hair jess as well as all dis high smellin' stuff dey sells now."

Aunt Jane likes to tell of those days of long ago. Her memory is excellent and she talks well. She says she is living out her Miss Jane's time. "Yassum, my Miss Jane died when she wuz so young, I specks I jess livin' out her days kase I named fer her. But I does miss dem good ole days whut's gone. I'se hungry fer de sight ov a spinnin' wheel—does you know whare's one? Things don't look lak' dey use ter, an' as fer whut we has ter eat, dare ain't no victuals ever smelled an' et as good as dem what dey use ter have on de plantation when I wuz a comin' on. Yassum, folkes has got wiser an' know mo' dan dey did, but dey is wickeder—dey kills now 'stid er conjurin' lak' dey did me."

United States. Work Projects Administration

[HW: Dist. 7
Ex-slave #108]
District 7
Adella S. Dixon

PHIL TOWNS
OLD SLAVE STORY
[Date Stamp: — 8 1937]

[TR: This interview contained many handwritten edits; where text was transposed, meaning was significantly changed, or the edit could not be clearly read, it has been noted.]

PHIL TOWNS

On June 25, 1824, a son was born to Washington and Clara Towns who resided in Richmond, Virginia. This was the fourth child in a family which finally numbered thirteen. Phil, as he was called, does not recall many incidents on this estate as the family moved when he was in his teens. His grandfather and grandmother were brought here from Africa and their description of the cruel treatment they received is his most vivid recollection. His grandmother, Hannah, lived to be 129 years of age.

Mr. George Towns, called "Governor" by all of his slaves as well as his intimate friends, moved to Georgia and settled at Reynolds in Taylor County. Here he purchased a huge tract of land—1350 acres—and built his new home upon this level area on the Flint River. The "big house," a large unpainted structure which housed a family of eighteen, was in the midst of a grove of trees near the highway that formed one of the divisions of the plantation. It was again divided by a local railway nearly a mile from the rear of the house. Eighty-eight slaves were housed in the "quarters" which were on each side of the highway a little below the planter's home.

These "quarters" differed from those found in the surrounding territory as the size of the houses varied with the number in the family. The interiors were nicely furnished and in most instances the families were able to secure any furniture they desired. Feather mattresses, trundle beds and cribs were common and in families where there were many children, large fireplaces—some as many as eight feet wide—were provided so that every one might be [TR: 'able to keep' crossed out] comfortable in winter. A variety of cooking utensils were given and large numbers of waffle irons, etc., then considered luxuries, were found here.

To consider only the general plan of operation, this plantation was no different from the average one in pre-civil war days but there was a phase of the life here which made it a most unusual home. "Governor" was so exceptionally kind to his slaves that they were known as "Gov. Towns' free negroes" to those on the neighboring farms. He never separated families, neither did he strike a slave except on rare occasions. Two things which might provoke his anger to this extent, were: to be told a lie, and to find that a person had allowed some one to take advantage of him. They were never given passes but obtained verbal consent to go where they wished and always remained as long as they chose.

Phil Towns' father worked in the field and his mother did light work in the house, such as assisting in spinning.

Mothers of three or more children were not compelled to work, as the master felt that their children needed care. From early childhood boys and girls were given excellent training. A boy who robbed a bird's nest or a girl who frolicked in a boisterous manner was severely reprimanded. Separate bedrooms for the two sexes were maintained until they married. The girls passed thru two stages—childhood, and at sixteen they became "gals". Three years later they might marry if they chose but the husband had to be older—at least 21. Courtships differed from those of today because there were certain hours for visiting and even though the girl might accompany her sweetheart away from home she had to be back at that hour. They had no clocks but a "time mark" was set by the sun. A young man was not allowed to give his girl any form of gift, and the efforts of some girls to secretly receive gifts which they claimed to have "found", were in vain, for these were taken from them. After the proposal, the procedure was practically the same as is observed today. The consent of the parent and the master was necessary. Marriages were mostly held at night and no pains were spared to make them occasions to be remembered and cherished. Beautiful clothes—her own selections—were given the bride, and friends usually gave gifts for the house. These celebrations, attended by visitors from many plantations, and always by the Towns family, ended in gay "frolics" with cakes, wine, etc., for refreshments.

During the first year of married life the couple remained with the bride's mother who instructed her in the household arts. Disputes between the newlyweds were not tolerated and punishment by the parents was the result of "nagging". At the end of a year, another log cabin was added to the quarters and the couple began housekeeping. The moral code was exceedingly high; the penalty for offenders—married or single, white or colored—was to be banished from the group entirely. Thus illegitimate children were rare enough to be a novelty.

Young Phil was in his teens when he began his first job—coach driver for "Gov." Towns. This was just before they moved to Georgia. He traveled with him wherever he went, and as the Gov. purchased a plantation in Talbot County, (the house still stands), and a home in Macon, (the site of Mt. De Sales Academy), a great deal of his time was spent on the road. Phil never did any other work except to occasionally assist in sweeping the large yard. The other members of this group split rails, did field work, spinning, tailoring and any of the many things that had to be done. Each person might choose the type of work he liked best.

Opportunities to make cash money were plentiful. Some made baskets and did hand work which was sold and the money given the maker. A man or woman who paid Gov. Towns $150.00 might hire himself to the Gov. for a year. When this was done he was paid cash for all the work he did and many were able to clear several hundred dollars in a year. In addition to this opportunity for earning money, every adult had an acre of ground which he might cultivate as he chose. Any money made from the sale of this produce was his own.

Recreation was not considered important so no provision was made in the regular routine. It was, however, possible to obtain "time off" at frequent intervals and these might be termed irregular vacation periods. Evening entertainment at which square dancing was the main attraction, were common. Quill music, from a homemade harmonica, was played when banjoes were not available. These instruments were made by binding with cane five to ten reeds of graduated lengths. A hole was cut in the upper end of each and the music obtained by blowing up and down the scale. Guests came from all neighboring farms and engaged in the "Green Corn" dance which was similar to what is now called Buck dancing. Near the end of such a hilarious evening, the guests were served with persimmon beer and ginger cakes,—then considered delicacies.

"Gov." Towns was interested in assisting any one [HW: wanting to learn]. [TR: Original reads 'desirous of learning.'] The little girls who expressed the desire to become "ladies" were kept in the "big house" and very carefully trained. The tastes of these few were developed to the extent that they excelled the ordinary "quarter" children and were the envy of the group at social affairs.

Sunday was a day of Reverence and all adults were required to attend religious services. The trip was usually made in wagons, oxcarts, etc., although the young women of the big house rode handsome saddle horses. At each church there was placed a stepping block by which they descended from their steeds. White and colored worshipped at the same church, constructed with a partition separating the two parts of the congregation but not extending to the pulpit. Professions of faith were accepted at the same altar while Baptismal services ware held at a local creek and all candidates were baptized on the same day. Regular clothing was worn at this service. Children were not allowed to attend church, and christenings were not common. Small boys, reared entirely apart from strict religious observances, used to slip away and shoot marbles on Sunday.

The health problem was not acute as these people were provided with everything necessary for a contented mind and a robust body. [TR: original line: The health problem was not a very acute one as these people were provided with everything conducive to a contented mind which plays a large part in maintaining a robust body.] However, a Doctor who lived nearby cared for the sick. Two fees were set—the larger one being charged if the patient recovered. Home remedies were used for minor ills—catnip tea for thrash, tea from Samson Snakeroot for cramps, redwood and dogwood bark tea [HW: and horehound candy] for worms, [HW: many] root teas used [HW: medicinally] by this generation. Peach brandy was given to anyone suspected of having pneumonia,—if the patient coughed, it was certain that he was a victim of the disease.

In these days, a mother named her children by a name [TR: unreadable] during pregnancy. [TR: original line: In these days, it was always thought best for the mother to name her children if the proper name for the babe was theoretically revealed to her during pregnancy.] If another name was given the child, the correct one would be so firmly implanted in his subconscious mind that he would never be able to resist the impulse to turn his head when that name was called. The seventh child was always thought to be exceptionally lucky, and [TR: unreadable HW replaces 'the bond of affection between the parents and this child was greater']. This belief persists today in many localities.

Every family was given a weekly supply of food but

this was more for convenience than anything else as they were free to eat anything their appetites called for. They killed chickens, ate vegetables, meats, etc. at any time. The presence of guests at the "quarters" roused Mrs. Towns to activity and she always helped to prepare the menu. One of her favorite items was chicken—prepared four different ways, in pie, in stew, fried, and baked. She gave full directions for the preparation of these delicacies to unskilled cooks. Pound cake was another favorite and she insisted that a pound of butter and a dozen eggs be used in each cake. When the meal was nearly ready, she usually made a trip to the cabin to see if it had been well prepared. The hostess could always tell without any comment whether she had satisfied her mistress, for if she had, a serving was carried back to the big house. Fishing was a form of remunerative recreation enjoyed by all. Everyone usually went on Saturday afternoon, but if only a few made the trip, the catch was shared by all.

Sewing was no easy job as there were few small women among the servants. The cloth made at home, was plentiful, however, and sufficient clothing was made for all. Some persons preferred making their own clothes and this privilege was granted; otherwise they were made in a common sewing room. Ten yards was the average amount of cloth in a dress, homespun and gingham, the usual materials. The men wore suits of osnaburg and jeans. This was dyed to more durable colors through the use of [HW: with] indigo [HW: (blue)] and a dye made from railroad bark (brown).

Phil believes that the screeching of an owl, the bellowing of a cow, and the howling of a dog after dark are signs of death because the [HW: immediate] death of a human being is revealed to animals, which [TR: illegible. 'in turn'?] warn humans. Though we may find some way to rid ourselves of the fear of the warning—the death will occur just the same.

On nearly all plantations there were some slaves who, trying to escape work, hid themselves in the woods. [TR: original line: On nearly all plantations there were some slaves who did not wish to work, consequently, for this, or similar reasons, hid themselves in the woods.] They smuggled food to their hiding place by night, and remained away [HW: lost] in some instances, many months. Their belief in witchcraft caused them to resort to most ridiculous means of avoiding discovery. Phil told the story of a man who visited a conjurer to obtain a "hand" for which he paid fifty dollars in gold. The symbol was a hickory stick which he used whenever he was being chased, and in this manner warded off his pursuers. The one difficulty in this procedure was having to "set up" at a fork or cross roads. Often the fugitive had to run quite a distance to reach such a spot, but when the stick was so placed human beings and even bloodhounds lost his trail. With this assistance, he was able to remain in the woods as long as he liked.

Snakes ware frequent visitor in the cabins of the "quarters". One morning while Betty, a cook, was confined to bed, she sent for Mrs. Towns to tell her that a snake had lain across her chest during the previous night and had tried to get under the cover where her young baby lay asleep. Mrs. Towns was skeptical about the size and activities of the reptile but sent for several men to search the house. They had given up the search when one chanced to glance above the sick woman's bed and there lay the reptile on a shelf. The bed was roped and moved to another part of the room and preparations made to shoot him. Quilts were piled high on the bed so that the noise of the gun would not frighten the baby. When all was ready Mrs. Towns asked the old man with the gun—

"Daddy Luke, can you *kill* the snake?"

"Yessum, mistress," he replied.

"Daddy Luke, can you *kill* the snake?"

"Yessum, mistress."

"Daddy Luke, can you *kill* the snake?"

"Yessum, mistress."

"Shoot!!"

He took careful aim and fired. The huge reptile rolled to the floor.

When the men returned to the yard to work near the woodpile, the mate was discovered by one of the dogs that barked until a log was moved and the second snake killed.

[HW: In those days] small snakes were not feared and for several years it was customary for women to carry a tiny green snake in their bosoms. This fad was discontinued when one of the women was severely injured through a bite on her chest.

Phil remembers when the stars fell in 1833. "They came down like rain," he said. When asked why he failed to keep some, he replied that he was afraid to touch them even after they became black.

[TR: The following paragraphs contain many crossouts replaced by unreadable handwritten edits, and will be indicated by: 'deleted words' replaced by ??.]

Freedom was discussed on the plantation [TR: ??] for many years before the Civil War began. As contented as [TR: 'they' replaced by ??] were [TR: 'there was something to look forward to when they thought of' replaced by ??] being absolutely free. An ex-slave's description of the real cause of the Civil War, deserves a place here. It seems that Lincoln had sent several messages to Davis requesting that he free the slaves. No favorable response was received. Lincoln had a conference with Mr. Davis and to this meeting he carried a Bible and a gun. He tried in vain to convince Davis that he was wrong according to the Bible, so he finally threw the two upon the table and asked Davis to take his choice. He chose the gun. Lincoln grasped the Bible and rushed home. Thus Davis *began* the war but Lincoln had God on his side and so he *ended* it.

One of Gov. Towns' sons went to the army and Phil was sent to care for him while he was there; an aristocratic man never went to the war without his valet. His [HW: Phil's] duty was to cook for him, keep his clothes clean, and to bring the body home if he was killed. Poor soldiers were either buried [HW: where they fell] or left lying on the field for vultures to consume. Food was not so plentiful in the [TR: 'army' replaced by ??] and their diet of flapjacks and canned goods was varied only by coffee and whiskey given when off duty. All cooking was done between two battles or during the lull in a battle. John Towns was soon sent back home as they [HW: the officers] felt he was too [TR: 'valuable a Southerner' crossed out] important to be killed in battle, and his services were needed at home.

Near the close of the war, Sherman made a visit to this vicinity. As was his usual habit, he had [TR: 'obtained' replaced by 'learned'?] the reputation of Gov. Towns before he arrived. He found conditions so ideal [TR: 'that not one thing was touched' replaced by ??]. He talked with [HW: slaves and owners, he] went [TR: 'gaily' deleted] on his way. Phil was so impressed by Sherman that he followed him and camped with the Yankees about where Central City Park is now. He thought that anything a Yankee said was true. [HW: When] One [HW: of them] gave him a knife and told him to go and cut the first man he met, he followed instructions even though he knew the man. [HW: Later] Realizing how foolishly he had acted, he readily apologized and explained why. [HW: The Yankee soldiers robbed beehives barehanded and were never stung, they] seemed to fear nothing but lizards. Never having seen such reptiles they would run in terror at the sight of one. The Confederates never discovered this.

After the close of the war they [HW: federal soldiers] were stationed in the towns to keep order. Union flags were placed everywhere, and a Southerner was accused of not respecting the flag if he even passed under one without bowing. Penalties for this offense were, to be hung up by the thumbs, to carry greasy [HW: greased] poles for a certain time, and numerous other punishments which caused a deal of discomfort to the victims but sent the soldiers and ex-slaves into peals of laughter. The sight of a Yankee soldier sent a Confederate one into hysteria.

[HW: Phil says his fellow] slaves laughed when told

they were free, but Gov. Towns was almost indifferent. His slaves, he said, were always practically free, so a little legal form did not [TR: 'add' replaced by ??] much to them. Nearly every one remained there and worked for wages.

For the past thirty-five years, Phil Towns has been almost totally disabled. Long life seems no novelty to him for he says everyone used to live longer when they honored their elders more. He has eighty-four relatives in Virginia—all older than he, but states that friends who have visited there say he looks more aged than any of them. His great desire is to return to Virginia, as he believes he will be able to find the familiar landmarks in spite of the changes that have taken place.

Mr. Alex Block, of Macon, makes no charges for the old shack in which Phil lives; his food furnished by the Department of Public Welfare is supplemented by interested friends.

PLANTATION LIFE

NEAL UPSON, Age 81
450 4th Street
Athens, Georgia

Written by:
Miss Grace McCune [HW: (White)]
Athens

Edited by:
Mrs. Sarah H. Hall
Athens

and

John N. Booth
District Supervisor
Federal Writers' Project
Residencies 6 & 7
Augusta, Ga.

August 5, 1938

NEAL UPSON

Alternate rain and sunshine had continued for about 10 days and the ditches half filled with water, slippery banks of red clay, and the swollen river necessitating a detour, added to the various difficulties that beset the interviewer as she trudged through East Athens in search of Neal Upson's shabby, three-room, frame house. A magnificent water oak shaded the vine-covered porch where a rocking chair and swing offered a comfortable place to rest.

"Good mornin', Miss," was the smiling greeting of the aged Negro man who answered a knock on the front door. "How is you? Won't you come in? I would ax you to have a cheer on the porch, but I has to stay in de house cause de light hurts my eyes." He had hastily removed a battered old felt hat, several sizes too large for him, and as he shuffled down the hall his hair appeared almost white as it framed his black face. His clean, but faded blue overalls and shirt were patched in several places and heavy brogans completed his costume. The day was hot and humid and he carefully placed two chairs where they would have the advantage of any breeze that might find its way through the open hallway.

"Miss, I'se mighty glad you come today," he began, "cause I does git so lonesome here by myself. My old 'oman wuks up to de court'ouse, cookin' for de folkses in jail, and it's allus late when she gits back home. 'Scuse me for puttin' my old hat back on, but dese old eyes jus' can't stand de light even here in the hall, less I shades 'em."

When asked to tell the story of his life, he chuckled. "Lawsy, Missy," he said. "Does you mean dat you is willin' to set here and listen to old Neal talk? 'Tain't many folkses what wants to hear us old Niggers talk no more. I jus' loves to think back on dem days 'cause dem was happy times, so much better'n times is now. Folkses was better den. Dey was allus ready to help one another, but jus' look how dey is now!

"I was borned on Marster Frank Upson's place down in Oglethorpe County, nigh Lexin'ton, Georgy. Marster had a plantation, but us never lived dar for us stayed at de home place what never had more'n 'bout 80 acres of land 'round it. Us never had to be trottin' to de sto' evvy time us started to cook, 'cause what warn't raised on de home place, Marster had 'em raise out on de big plantation. Evvything us needed t'eat and wear was growed on Marse Frank's land.

"Harold and Jane Upson was my Daddy and Mammy; only folkses jus' called Daddy 'Hal.' Both of 'em was raised right der on de Upson place whar dey played together whilst dey was chillun. Mammy said she had washed and sewed for Daddy ever since she was big enough, and when dey got grown dey jus' up and got married. I was deir only boy and I was de baby chile, but dey had four gals older'n me. Dey was: Cordelia, Anna, Parthene, and Ella. Ella was named for Marse Frank's onliest chile, little Miss Ellen, and our little Miss was sho a good little chile.

"Daddy made de shoes for all de slaves on de plantation and Mammy was called de house 'oman. She done de cookin' up at de big 'ouse, and made de cloth for her own fambly's clothes, and she was so smart us allus had plenty t'eat and wear. I was little and stayed wid Mammy up at de big 'ouse and jus' played all over it and all de folkses up der petted me. Aunt Tama was a old slave too old to wuk. She was all de time cookin' gingerbread and hidin' it in a little trunk what sot by de fireplace in her room. When us chillun was good Aunt Tama give us gingerbread, but if us didn't mind what she said, us didn't git none. Aunt Tama had de rheumatiz and walked wid a stick and I could git in dat trunk jus' 'bout anytime I wanted to. I sho' did git 'bout evvything dem other chillun had, swappin' Aunt Tama's gingerbread. When our white folkses went off, Aunt Tama toted de keys, and she evermore did make dem Niggers stand 'round. Marse Frank jus' laughed when dey made complaints 'bout her.

"In summertime dey cooked peas and other veg'tables for us chillun in a washpot out in de yard in de shade, and us et out of de pot wid our wooden spoons. Dey jus' give us wooden bowls full of bread and milk for supper.

"Marse Frank said he wanted 'em to larn me how to wait on de white folkses' table up at de big 'ouse, and dey started me off wid de job of fannin' de flies away. Mist'ess Serena, Marse Frank's wife, made me a white coat to wear in de dinin' room. Missy, dat little old white coat made me git de onliest whuppin' Marse Frank ever did give me." Here old Neal paused for a hearty laugh. "Us had comp'ny for dinner dat day and I felt so big showin' off 'fore 'em in dat white coat dat I jus' couldn't make dat turkey wing fan do right. Dem turkey wings was fastened on long handles and atter Marster had done warned me a time or two to mind what I was 'bout, the old turkey wing went down in de gravy bowl and when I jerked it out it splattered all over de preacher's best Sunday suit. Marse Frank got up and tuk me right out to de kitchen and when he got through brushin' me off I never did have no more trouble wid dem turkey wings.

"Evvybody cooked on open fireplaces dem days. Dey had swingin' racks what dey called cranes to hang de pots on for bilin'. Dere was ovens for bakin' and de heavy iron skillets had long handles. One of dem old skillets was so big dat Mammy could cook 30 biscuits in it at one time. I allus did love biscuits, and I would go out in de yard and trade Aunt Tama's gingerbread to de other chilluns for deir sheer of biscuits. Den dey would be skeered to eat de gingerbread 'cause I told 'em I'd tell on 'em. Aunt Tama thought dey was sick and told Marse Frank de chilluns warn't eatin' nothin'. He axed 'em what was de matter and dey told him dey had done traded all deir bread to me. Marse Frank den axed me if I warn't gittin' enough t'eat, 'cause he 'lowed dere was enough dar for all. Den Aunt Tama had to go and tell on me. She said I was wuss dan a hog atter biscuits, so our good Marster ordered her to see dat li'l Neal had enough t'eat.

"I ain't never gwine to forgit dat whuppin' my own daddy give me. He had jus' sharpened up a fine new axe for hisself, and I traded it off to a white boy named *Roar* what lived nigh us when I seed him out tryin' to cut wood wid a sorry old dull axe. I sold him my daddy's fine new axe for 5 biscuits. When he found out 'bout dat, he 'lowed he was gwine to give me somepin to make me think 'fore I done any more tradin' of his things. Mist'eas, let me tell you, dat beatin' he give me evermore was a-layin' on of de rod.

"One day Miss Serena put me in de cherry tree to pick cherries for her, and she told me not to eat none 'til I finished; den I could have all I wanted, but I didn't mind her and I et so many cherries I got sick and fell out of de tree. Mist'ess was skeered, but Marse Frank said: 'It's good enough for him, 'cause he didn't mind.'

"Mammy never did give me but one whuppin' neither. Daddy was gwine to de circus and I jus' cut up 'bout it 'cause I wanted to go so bad. Mist'ess give me some cake and I hushed long as I was eatin', but soon as de last cake crumb was swallowed I started bawlin' again. She give me a stick of candy and soon as I et dat I was squallin' wuss dan ever. Mammy told Mist'ess den det she knowed how to quiet me and she retch under de bed for a shoe. When she had done finished layin' dat shoe on me and put it back whar she got it, I was sho willin' to shet my mouth and let 'em all go to de circus widout no more racket from me.

"De fust school I went to was in a little one-room 'ouse in our white folkses' back yard. Us had a white teacher and all he larnt slave chillun was jus' plain readin' and writin'. I had to pass Dr. Willingham's office lots and he was all de time pesterin' me 'bout spellin'. One day he stopped me and axed me if I could spell 'bumble bee widout its tail,' and he said dat when I larnt to spell it, he would gimme some candy. Mr. Sanders, at Lexin'ton, gimme a dime onct. It was de fust money I ever had. I was plumb rich and I never let my Daddy have no peace 'til he fetched me to town to do my tradin'. I was all sot to buy myself a hat, a sto-bought suit of clothes, and some shoes what warn't brogans, but Missy, I wound up wid a gingercake and a nickel's wuth of candy. I used to cry and holler evvy time Miss Serena went off and left me. Whenever I seed 'em gittin' out de carriage to hitch it up, I started beggin' to go. Sometimes she laughed and said; 'All right Neal.' But when she said, 'No Neal,' I snuck out and hid under de high-up carrigge seat and went along jus' de same. Mist'ess allus found me 'fore us got back home, but she jus' laughed and said: 'Well, Neal's my little nigger anyhow.'

"Dem old cord beds was a sight to look at, but dey slept good. Us cyarded lint cotton into bats for mattresses and put 'em in a tick what us tacked so it wouldn't git lumpy. Us never seed no iron springs dem days. Dem cords, criss-crossed from one side of de bed to de other, was our springs and us had keys to tighten 'em wid. If us didn't tighten 'em evvy few days dem beds was apt to fall down wid us. De cheers was homemade too and de easiest-settin' ones had bottoms made out of rye splits. Dem oak-split cheers was all right, and sometimes us used cane to bottom de cheers but evvybody laked to set in dem cheers what had bottoms wove out of rye splits.

"Marster had one of dem old cotton gins what didn't have no engines. It was wuked by mules. Dem old mules was hitched to a long pole what dey pulled 'round and 'round to make de gin do its wuk. Dey had some gins in dem days what had treadmills for de mules to walk in. Dem old treadmills looked sorter lak stairs, but most of 'em was turned by long poles what de mules pulled. You had to feed de cotton by hand to dem old gins and you sho had to be keerful or you was gwine to lose a hand and maybe a arm. You had to jump in dem old cotton presses and tread de cotton down by hand. It tuk most all day long to gin two bales of cotton and if dere was three bales to be ginned us had to wuk most all night to finish up.

"Dey mixed wool wid de lint cotton to spin thread to make cloth for our winter clothes. Mammy wove a lot of dat cloth and de clothes made out of it sho would keep out de cold. Most of our stockin's and socks was knit at home, but now and den somebody would git hold of a sto-bought pair for Sunday-go-to-meetin' wear.

"Colored folkses went to church wid deir own white folkses and sot in de gallery. One Sunday us was all settin' in dat church listenin' to de white preacher, Mr. Hansford, tellin' how de old debbil was gwine to git dem what didn't do right." Here Neal burst into uncontrollable laughter. His sides shook and tears ran down his face. Finally he began his story again: "Missy, I jus' got to tell you 'bout dat day in de meetin' 'ouse. A Nigger had done run off from his marster and was hidin' out from one place to another. At night he would go steal his somepin t'eat. He had done stole some chickens and had 'em wid him up in de church steeple whar he was hidin' dat day. When daytime come he went off to sleep lak Niggers will do when dey ain't got to hustle, and when he woke up Preacher Hansford was tellin' 'em 'bout de debbil was gwine to git de sinners. Right den a old rooster what he had stole up and crowed so loud it seemed lak Gabriel's trumpet on Judment Day. Dat runaway Nigger was skeered 'cause he knowed dey was gwine to find him sho, but he warn't skeered nuffin' compared to dem Niggers settin' in de gallery. Dey jus' knowed dat was de voice of de debbil what had done come atter 'em. Dem Niggers never stopped prayin' and testifyin' to de Lord, 'til de white folkses had done got dat runaway slave and de rooster out of de steeple. His marster was der and tuk him home and give him a good, sound thrashin'.

"Slaves was 'lowed to have prayermeetin' on Chuesday (Tuesday) and Friday 'round at de diffunt plantations whar deir marsters didn't keer, and dere warn't many what objected. De good marsters all give deir slaves prayermeetin' passes on dem nights so de patterollers wouldn't git 'em and beat 'em up for bein' off deir marster's lands. Dey 'most nigh kilt some slaves what dey cotch out when dey didn't have no pass. White preachers done de talkin' at de meetin'houses, but at dem Chuesday and Friday night prayermeetin's, it was all done by Niggers. I was too little to 'member much 'bout dem meetin's, but my older sisters used to talk lots 'bout 'em long atter de war had brung our freedom. Dere warn't many slaves what could read, so dey jus' talked 'bout what dey had done heared de white preachers say on Sunday. One of de fav'rite texties was de third chapter of John, and most of 'em jus' 'membered a line or two from dat. Missy, from what folkses said 'bout dem meetin's, dere was sho a lot of good prayin' and testifyin', 'cause so many sinners repented and was saved. Sometimes at dem Sunday meetin's at de white folkses' church dey would have two or three preachers de same dey. De fust one would give de text and preach for at least a hour, den another one would give a text and do his preachin', and 'bout dat time another one would rise up and say dat dem fust two brudders had done preached enough to save 3,000 souls, but dat he was gwine to try to double dat number. Den he would do his preachin' and atter dat one of dem others would git up and say: 'Brudders and Sisters, us is all here for de same and only purpose—dat of savin' souls. Dese other good brudders is done preached, talked, and prayed, and let the gap down; now I'm gwine to raise it. Us is gwine to git 'ligion enough to take us straight through dem pearly gates. Now, let us sing whilst us gives de new brudders and sisters de right hand of fellowship. One of dem old songs went sort of lak dis:

> 'Must I be born to die
> And lay dis body down?'

"When dey had done finished all de verses and choruses of dat dey started:

> 'Amazin' Grace, How sweet de sound
> Dat saved a wretch lak me.'

"'Fore dey stopped dey usually got 'round to singin':

> 'On Jordan's stormy banks I stand,
> And cast a wishful eye,
> To Canaan's fair and happy land

Whar my possessions lie.'

"Dey could keep dat up for hours and it was sho' good singin', for dat's one thing Niggers was born to do—to sing when dey gits 'ligion.

"When old Aunt Flora come up and wanted to jine de church she told 'bout how she had done seed de Hebenly light and changed her way of livin'. Folkses testified den 'bout de goodness of de Lord and His many blessin's what He give to saints and sinners, but dey is done stopped givin' Him much thanks any more. Dem days, dey 'zamined folkses 'fore dey let 'em jine up wid de church. When dey started 'zaminin' Aunt Flora, de preacher axed her: 'Is you done been borned again and does you believe dat Jesus Christ done died to save sinners?' Aunt Flora she started to cry; and she said: 'Lordy, Is He daid? Us didn't know dat. If my old man had done 'scribed for de paper lak I told him to, us would have knowed when Jesus died?'" Neal giggled. "Missy," he said, "ain't dat jus' lak one of dem old-time Niggers? Dey jus' tuk dat for ign'ance and let her come on into de church.

"Dem days it was de custom for marsters to hire out what slaves dey had dat warn't needed to wuk on deir own land, so our marster hired out two of my sisters. Sis' Anna hired to a fambly 'bout 16 miles from our place. She didn't lak it dar so she run away and I found her hid out in our 'tater 'ouse. One day when us was playin' she called to me right low and soft lak and told me she was hongry and for me to git her somepin t'eat but not to tell nobody she was dar. She said she had been dar widout nothin' t'eat for several days. She was skeered Marster might whup her. She looked so thin and bad I thought she was gwine to die, so I told Mammy. Her and Marster went and brung

Anna to de 'ouse and fed her. Dat pore chile was starved most to death. Marster kept her at home for 3 weeks and fed her up good, den he carried her back and told dem folkses what had hired her dat dey had better treat Anna good and see dat she had plenty t'eat. Marster was drivin' a fast hoss dat day, but bless your heart, Anna beat him back home dat day. She cried and tuk on so, beggin' him not to take her back dar no more dat he told her she could stay home. My other sister stayed on whar she was hired out 'til de war was over and dey give us our freedom.

"Daddy had done hid all Old Marster's hosses when de yankees got to our plantation. Two of de ridin' hosses was in de smokehouse and another good trotter was in de hen 'ouse. Old Jake was a slave what warn't right bright. He slep' in de kitchen, and he knowed whar Daddy had hid dem hosses, but dat was all he knowed. Marster had give Daddy his money to hide too, and he tuk some of de plasterin' off de wall in Marster's room and put de box of money inside de wall. Den he fixed dat plasterin' back so nice you couldn't tell it had ever been tore off. De night dem yankees come, Daddy had gone out to de wuk 'ouse to git some pegs to fix somepin (us didn't have no nails dem days). When de yankees rid up to de kitchen door and found Old Jake right by hisself, dat pore old fool was skeered so bad he jus' started right off babblin' 'bout two hosses in de smoke'ouse and one in de hen 'ouse, but he was tremblin' so he couldn't talk plain. Old Marster heared de fuss dey made and he come down to de kitchen to see what was de matter. De yankees den ordered Marster to git 'em his hosses. Marster called Daddy and told him to git de hosses, but Daddy, he played foolish lak and stalled 'round lak he didn't have good sense. Dem sojers raved and fussed all night long 'bout dem hosses, but dey never thought 'bout lookin' in de smoke'ouse and hen 'ouse for 'em and 'bout daybreak dey left widout takin' nothin'. Marster said he was sho proud of my Daddy for savin' dem good hosses for him.

[TR: 'Horses saved' written in margin.]

"Marster had a long pocketbook what fastened at one end wid a ring. One day when he went to git out some money he dropped a roll of bills dat he never seed, but Daddy picked it up and handed it back to him right away. Now my Daddy could have kept dat money jus' as easy, but he was a 'ceptional man and believed evvbody ought to do right.

"Aunt Tama's old man, Uncle Griff, come to live wid her on our place atter de war was over. 'Fore den he had belonged to a man named Colquitt.[HW: !!] Marster pervided a home for him and Aunt Tama 'til dey was both daid. When dey was buildin' de fust colored Methodist church in dat section Uncle Griff give a whole hundred dollars to de buildin' fund. Now it tuk a heap of scrimpin' for him to save dat much money 'cause he never had made over $10 a month. Aunt Tama had done gone to Glory a long time when Uncle Griff died. Atter dey buried him dey come back and was 'rangin' de things in his little cabin. When dey moved dat little trunk what Aunt Tama used to keep gingerbread in, dey found jus' lots of money in it. Marster tuk keer of dat money 'til he found Uncle Griff's own sister and den he give it all to her.

"One time Marster missed some of his money and he didn't want to 'cuse nobody, so he 'cided he would find out who had done de debbilment. He put a big rooster in a coop wid his haid stickin' out. Den he called all de

Niggers up to de yard and told 'em somebody had been stealin' his money, and dat evvybody must git in line and march 'round dat coop and tetch it. He said dat when de guilty ones tetched it de old rooster would crow. Evvybody tetched it 'cept one old man and his wife; dey jus' wouldn't come nigh dat coop whar dat rooster was a-lookin' at evvybody out of his little red eyes. Marster had dat old man and 'oman sarched and found all de money what had been stole.

"Mammy died about a year atter de war, and I never will forgit how Mist'ess cried and said: 'Neal, your mammy is done gone, and I don't know what I'll do widout her.' Not long atter dat, Daddy bid for de contract to carry de mail and he got de place, but it made de white folkses mighty mad, 'cause some white folkses had put in bids for dat contract. Dey 'lowed dat Daddy better not never start out wid dat mail, 'cause if he did he was gwine to be sorry. Marster begged Daddy not to risk it and told him if he would stay dar wid him he would let him have a plantation for as long as he lived, and so us stayed on dar 'til Daddy died, and a long time atter dat us kept on wukin' for Old Marster.

"White folkses owned us back in de days 'fore de war but our own white folkses was mighty good to deir slaves. Dey had to larn us 'bedience fust, how to live right, and how to treat evvybody else right; but de best thing dey larned us was how to do useful wuk. De onliest time I 'member stealin' anything 'cept Aunt Tama's gingerbread was one time when I went to town wid Daddy in de buggy. When us started back home a man got in de seat wid Daddy and I had to ride down in de back of de buggy whar Daddy had hid a jug of liquor. I could hear it slushin' 'round and so I got to wantin' to know how it tasted. I pulled out de corncob stopper and tuk one taste. It was so good I jus' kep' on tastin' 'til I passed out, and didn't know when us got home or nuffin else 'til I waked up in my own bed next day. Daddy give me a tannin' what I didn't forgit for a long time, but dat was de wussest drunk I ever was. Lord, but I did love to follow my Daddy.

"Folkses warn't sick much in dem days lak dey is now, but now us don't eat strong victuals no more. Us raked out hot ashes den and cooked good old ashcakes what was a heap better for us dan dis bread us buys from de stores now. Marster fed us plenty ashcake, fresh meat, and ash roasted 'taters, and dere warn't nobody what could out wuk us.

"A death was somepin what didn't happen often on our plantation, but when somebody did die folkses would go from miles and miles around to set up and pray all night to comfort de fambly of de daid. Dey never made up de coffins 'til atter somebody died. Den dey measured de corpse and made de coffin to fit de body. Dem coffins was lined wid black calico and painted wid lampblack on de outside. Sometimes dey kivvered de outside wid black calico lak de linin'. Coffins for white folkses was jus' lak what dey had made up for deir slaves, and dey was all buried in de same graveyard on deir own plantations.

"When de war was over dey closed de little one-room school what our good Marster had kept in his back yard for his slaves, but out young Miss Ellen larnt my sister right on 'til she got whar she could teach school. Daddy fixed up a room onto our house for her school and she soon had it full of chillun. Dey made me study too, and I sho did hate to have to go to school to my own aister for she evermore did take evvy chance to lay dat stick on me, but I s'pects she had a right tough time wid me. When time come 'round to celebrate school commencement, I was one proud little Nigger 'cause I never had been so dressed up in my life before. I had on a red waist, white pants, and a good pair of shoes; but de grandest thing of all 'bout dat outfit was dat Daddy let me wear his watch. Evvybody come for dat celebration. Dere was over 300 folks at dat big dinner, and us had lots of barbecue and all sorts of good things t'eat. Old Marster was dar, and when I stood up 'fore all dem folks and said my little speech widout missin' a word, Marster sho did laugh and clap his hands. He called me over to whar he was settin' and said: 'I knowed you could larn if you wanted to.' *Best of all, he give me a whole dollar.* [TR: 'for reciting a speech' written in margin.] I was rich den, plumb rich. One of my sisters couldn't larn nothin'. De only letters she could ever say was 'G-O-D.' No matter what you axed her to spell she allus said 'G-O-D.' She was a good field hand though and a good 'oman and she lived to be more dan 90 years old.

"Now, talkin' 'bout frolickin', us really used to dance. What I means, is sho 'nough old-time break-downs. Sometimes us didn't have no music 'cept jus' beatin' time on tin pans and buckets but most times Old Elice Hudson played his fiddle for us, and it had to be tuned again atter evvy set us danced. He never knowed but one tune and he played dat over and over. Sometimes dere was 10 or 15 couples on de floor at de same time and us didn't think nothin' of dancin' all night long. Us had plenty of old corn juice for refreshment, and atter Elice had two or three cups of dat juice, he could git 'Turkey in de Straw' out of dat fiddle lak nobody's business.

"One time a houseboy from another plantation wanted to come to one of our Saddy night dances, so his marster told him to shine his boots for Sunday and fix his hoss for de night and den he could git off for de frolic. Abraham shined his marster's boots 'till he could see hisself in 'em, and dey looked so grand he was tempted to try 'em on. Dey was a little tight but he thought he could wear 'em, and he wanted to show hisself off in 'em at de dance. Dey warn't so easy to walk in and he was 'fraid he might git 'em scratched up walkin' through de fields, so he snuck his Marster's hoss out and rode to de dance. When Abraham rid up dar in dem shiny boots, he got all de gals' 'tention. None of 'em wanted to dance wid de other Niggers. Dat Abraham was sho sruttin' 'til somebody run in and told him his hoss had done broke its neck. He had tied it to a limb and sho 'nough, some way, dat hoss had done got tangled up and hung its own self. Abraham begged de other Nigger boys to help him take de deid hoss home, but he had done tuk deir gals and he didn't git no help. He had to walk 12 long miles home in dem tight shoes. De sun had done riz up when he got dar and it warn't long 'fore his Marster was callin': 'Abraham, bring me my boots.' Dat Nigger would holler out: 'Yas sah! I'se a-comin'. But dem boots wouldn't come off 'cause his foots had done swelled up in 'em. His marster kept on callin' and when Abraham seed he couldn't put it off no longer, he jus' cut dem boots off his foots and went in and told what he had done. His marster was awful mad and said he was a good mind to take de hide off Abraham's back. 'Go git my hoss quick, Nigger, 'fore I most kills you,' he yelled. Den Abraham told him: 'Marster I knows you is gwine to kill me now, but your hoss is done daid.' Den pore Abraham had to out and tell de whole story and his marster got to laughin' so 'bout how he tuk all de gals away from de other boys and how dem boots hurt him dat it looked lak he never would stop. When he finally did stop laughin' and shakin' his sides he said: 'Dat's all right Abraham. Don't never let nobody beat your time wid de gals.' And dat's all he ever said to Abraham 'bout it.

"When my sister got married, us sho did have a grand time. Us cooked a pig whole wid a shiny red apple in its mouth and set it right in de middle of de long table what us had built out in de yard. Us had evvything good to go wid dat pig, and atter dat supper, us danced all night long. My sister never had seed dat man but one time 'fore she married him.

"My Daddy and his cousin Jim swore wid one another dat if one died 'fore de other dat de one what was left would look atter de daid one's fambly and see dat none of de chillun was bound out to wuk for nobody. It warn't long atter dis dat Daddy died. I was jus' fourteen, and was wukin' for a brick mason larnin' dat trade. Daddy had done been sick a while, and one night de fambly woke me up and said he was dyin'. I run fast as I could for a doctor but Daddy was done daid when I got back. Us buried him right side of Mammy in de old graveyard. It was most a year atter dat 'fore us had de funeral sermon preached. Dat was de way folkses done den. Now Mammy and Daddy was both gone, but old Marster said us chillun could live dar long as us wanted to. I went on back to wuk, 'cause I was crazy to be as good a mason as my Daddy was. In Lexin'ton dere is a rock wall still standin' 'round a whole square what Daddy built in slavery time. Long as he lived he blowed his bugle evvy mornin' to wake up all de folkses on Marse Frank's plantation. He never failed to blow dat bugle at break of day 'cep on Sundays, and evvybody on dat place 'pended on him to wake 'em up.

"I was jus' a-wukin' away one day when Cousin Jim sent for me to go to town wid him. Missy, dat man brung ne right here to Athens to de old courthouse and bound me out to a white man. He done dat very thing atter swearin' to my Daddy he wouldn't never let dat happen. I didn't want to wuk dat way, so I run away and went back home to wuk. De sheriff come and got me and said I had to go back whar I was bound out or go to jail. Pretty soon I runned away again and went to Atlanta, and dey never bothered me 'bout dat no more.

"De onliest time I ever got 'rested was once when I come to town to see 'bout gittin' somebody to pick cotton for me and jus' as I got to a certain Nigger's house de police come in and caught 'em in a crap game. Mr. McCune, de policeman, said I would have to go 'long wid de others to jail, but he would help me atter us got der and he did. He 'ranged it so I could hurry back home.

"'Bout de best times us had in de plantation days was de corn shuckin's, log rollin's and syrup cookin's. Us allus finished up dem syrup cookin's wid a candy pullin'.

"Atter he had all his corn gathered and put in big long piles, Marster 'vited de folkses from all 'round dem parts. Dat was de way it was done; evvybody helped de others git de corn shucked. Nobody thought of hirin' folkses and payin' out cash money for extra wuk lak dat. Dey 'lected a gen'ral to lead off de singin' and atter he got 'em to keepin' time wid de singin' de little brown jug was passed 'round. When it had gone de rounds a time or two, it was a sight to see how fast dem Niggers could keep time to dat singin'. Dey could do all sorts of double time den when dey had swigged enough liquor. When de corn was all shucked dey feasted and den drunk more liquor and danced as long as dey could stand up. De log-rollin's and candy pullin's ended de same way. Dey was sho grand good times.

"I farmed wid de white folkses for 32 years and never had no trouble wid nobody. Us allus settled up fair and square and in crop time dey never bothered to come 'round to see what Neal was doin', 'cause dey knowed dis Nigger was wukin' all right. Dey was all mighty good to me. Atter I got so old I couldn't run a farm no more I wuked in de white folkses' gyardens and tended deir flowers. I had done been wukin' out Mrs. Steve Upson's flowers and when she 'come to pay, she axed what my name was. When I told her it was Neal Upson she wanted to know how I got de Upson name. I told her Mr. Frank Upson had done give it to me when I was his slave. She called to Mr. Steve and dey lak to have talked me to death, for my Marse Frank and Mr. Steve's daddy was close kinfolkses.

"Atter dat I wuked deir flowers long as I was able to walk way off up to deir place, but old Neal can't wuk no more. Mr. Steve and his folkses comes to see me sometimes and I'se allus powerful glad to see 'em.

"I used to wuk some for Miss Mary Bacon. She is a mighty good 'oman and she knowed my Daddy and our good Old Marster. Miss Mary would talk to me 'bout dem old days and she allus said: 'Neal, let's pray,' 'fore I left. Miss Mary never did git married. She's one of dem solitary ladies.

"Now, Missy, how come you wants to know 'bout my weddin'? I done been married two times, but it was de fust time dat was de sho 'nough 'citin' one. I courted dat gal for a long, long time while I was too skeered to ax her Daddy for her. I went to see her evvy Sunday jus' 'termined to ax him for her 'fore I left, and I would stay late atter supper, but jus' couldn't git up nerve enough to do it. One Sunday I promised myself I would ax him if it kilt me, so I went over to his house early dat mornin' and told Lida, dat was my sweetheart's name—I says to her: 'I sho is gwine to ax him today.' Well, dinnertime come, suppertime come, and I was gittin' shaky in my jints when her Daddy went to feed his hogs and I went along wid him. Missy, dis is de way I finally did ax him for his gal. He said he was goin' to have some fine meat come winter. I axed him if it would be enough for all of his fambly, and he said: 'How come you ax dat, boy?' Den I jus' got a tight hold on dat old hog pen and said: 'Well, Sir, I jus' thought if you didn't have enough for all of 'em, I could take Lida.' I felt myself goin' down. He started laughin' fit to kill. 'Boy,' he says, 'Is you tryin' to ax for Lida? If so, I don't keer 'cause she's got to git married sometime.' I was so happy I left him right den and run back to tell Lida dat he said it was all right.

"Us didn't have no big weddin'. Lida had on a new calico dress and I wore new jeans pants. Marster heared us was gittin' married dat day and he sont his new buggy wid a message for us to come right dar to him. I told Lida us better go, so us got in dat buggy and driv off, and de rest of de folkses followed in de wagon. Marster met us in front of old Salem Church. He had de church open and Preacher John Gibson waitin' der to marry us. Us warn't 'spectin' no church weddin', but Marster said dat Neal had to git married right. He never did forgit his Niggers. Lida she's done been daid a long time, and I'se married again, but dat warn't lak de fust time."

By now, Neal was evidently tired out but as the interviewer prepared to leave, Neal said: "Missy, I'se sho got somepin to tell my old 'oman when she gits home. She don't lak to leave me here by myself. I wish dere was somebody for me to talk to evvyday, for I'se had sich a good time today. I don't s'pect it's gwine to be long 'fore old Neal goes to be wid dem I done been tellin' you 'bout, so don't wait too long to come back to see me again."

United States. Work Projects Administration

[HW: Georgia]
PLANTATION LIFE AS VIEWED BY AN EX-SLAVE

JOHN F. VAN HOOK, Age 76
Newton Bridge Road
Athens, Georgia

Written by:
Mrs. Sadie B. Hornsby
Area 6
Athens

Edited by:
Mrs. Sarah H. Hall
Athens

and

John N. Booth
Area Supervisor of
Federal Writers'
Project—Areas 6 & 7,
Augusta, Ga.

Dec. 1, 1938

JOHN F. VAN HOOK

John F. Van Hook was a short, stout man with a shining bald pate, a fringe of kinky gray hair, kindly eyes, and a white mustache of the Lord Chamberlain variety. His shabby work clothes were clean and carefully mended, and he leaned on a cane for support.

John was looking for the "Farm Bureau Office," but he agreed to return for an interview after he had transacted his business. When he reappeared a short time later and settled down in a comfortable chair he gave the story of his early life with apparent enjoyment.

In language remarkably free of dialect, John began by telling his full name and added that he was well known in Georgia and the whole country. "Until I retired," he remarked, "I taught school in North Carolina, and in Hall, Jackson, and Rabun Counties, in Georgia. I am farming now about five miles from Athens in the Sandy Creek district. I was born in 1862 in Macon County, North Carolina, on the George Seller's plantation, which borders the Little Tennessee River.

"I don't know anything much, first hand, about the war period, as I was quite a child when that ended, but I can tell you all about the days of Reconstruction. What I know about the things that took place during the war was told me by my mother and other old people.

"My father was Bas Van Hook and he married Mary Angel, my mother. Mother was born on Marse Dillard Love's plantation, and when his daughter, Miss Jenny, married Marse Thomas Angel's son, Marse Dillard gave Mother to Miss Jenny and when Little Miss Jenny Angel was born, Mother was her nurse. Marse Thomas and Miss Jenny Angel died, and Mother stayed right there keeping house for Little Miss Jenny and looking after her. Mother had more sense than all the rest of the slaves put together, and she even did Little Miss Jenny's shopping.

"My father was the only darkey Old Man Isaac Van Hook owned, and he did anything that came to hand: he was a good carpenter and mechanic and helped the Van Hooks to build mills, and he made the shoes for that settlement. Thomas Aaron, George, James, Claude, and

Washington were my five brothers, and my sisters were Zelia, Elizabeth, and Candace. Why, Miss, the only thing I can remember right off hand that we children done was fight and frolic like youngsters will do when they get together. With time to put my mind on it, I would probably recollect our games and songs, if we had any.

"Our quarters was on a large farm on Sugar Fork River. The houses were what you would call log huts and they were scattered about promiscuously, no regular lay-out, just built wherever they happened to find a good spring convenient. There was never but one room to a hut, and they wern't particular about how many darkies they put in a room.

"White folks had fine four-poster beds with a frame built around the top of the bed, and over the frame hung pretty, ruffled white curtains and a similar ruffled curtain was around the bottom of the bed; the curtains made pretty ornaments. Slaves had beds of this general kind, but they warn't quite as pretty and fine. Corded springs were the go then. The beds used by most of the slaves in that day and time were called 'Georgia beds,' and these were made by boring two holes in the cabin wall, and two in the floor, and side pieces were run from the holes in the wall to the posts and fastened; then planks were nailed around the sides and foot, box-fashion, to hold in the straw that we used for mattresses; over this pretty white sheets and plenty of quilts was spreaded. Yes, mam, there was always plenty of good warm cover in those days. Of course, it was home-made, all of it.

"My grandfather was a blacksmith and farmhand owned by Old Man Dillard Love. According to my earliest recollection my grandmother Van Hook was dead and

I have no memories about her. My great, great grandmother, Sarah Angel, looked after slave children while their mothers were at work. She was a free woman, but she had belonged to Marse Tommy Angel and Miss Jenny Angel; they were brother and sister. The way Granny Sarah happened to be free was; one of the women in the Angel family died and left a little baby soon after one of Granny's babies was born, and so she was loaned to that family as wet nurse for the little orphan baby. They gave her her freedom and took her into their home, because they did not want her sleeping in slave quarters while she was nursing the white child. In that settlement, it was considered a disgrace for a white child to feed at the breast of a slave woman, but it was all right if the darkey was a free woman. After she got too old to do regular work, Granny Sarah used to glean after the reapers in the field to get wheat for her bread. She had been a favored slave and allowed to do pretty much as she pleased, and after she was a free woman the white folks continued to look after her every need, but she loved to do for herself as long as she was able to be up and about.

"What did we have to eat then? Why, most everything; ash cakes was a mighty go then. Cornbread dough was made into little pones and placed on the hot rocks close to the fire to dry out a little, then hot ashes were raked out to the front of the fireplace and piled over the ash cakes. When thoroughly done they were taken out and the ashes washed off; they were just like cake to us children then. We ate lots of home-made lye hominy, beans, peas, and all kinds of greens, cooked with fat meat. The biggest, and maybe the best thing in the way of vegetables that we had then was the white-head cabbage; they grew large up there in Carolina where I lived. There was just one big garden to feed all the folks on that farm.

"Marse George had a good 'possum dog that he let his slaves use at night. They would start off hunting about 10 o'clock. Darkies knew that the best place to hunt for 'possums was in a persimmon tree. If they couldn't shake him out, they would cut the tree down, but the most fun was when we found the 'possum in a hollow log. Some of the hunters would get at one end of the log, and the others would guard the other end, and they would build a fire to smoke the 'possum out. Sometimes when they had to pull him out, they would find the 'possum in such a tight place that most of his hair would be rubbed off before they could get him out. Darkies hunted rabbits, squirrels, coons, all kinds of birds, and 'specially they was fond of going after wild turkeys. Another great sport was hunting deer in the nearby mountains. I managed to get a shot at one once. Marse George was right good about letting his darkies hunt and fish at night to get meat for themselves. Oh! Sure, there were lots of fish and they caught plenty of 'em in the Little Tennessee and Sugar Fork Rivers and in the numerous creeks that were close by. Red horse, suckers, and salmon are the kinds of fish I remember best. They were cooked in various ways in skillets, spiders, and ovens on the big open fireplace.

"Now, about the clothes we wore in the days of the war, I couldn't rightly say, but my Mother said we had good comfortable garments. In the summer weather, boys and men wore plain cotton shirts and jeans pants. The home-made linsey-woolsy shirts that we wore over our cotton shirts, and the wool pants that we wore in winter, were good and warm; they had brogan shoes in winter too. Folks wore the same clothes on Sundays as through the week, but they had to be sure that they were nice and clean on Sundays. Dresses for the women folks were made out of cotton checks, and they had sunbonnets too.

"Marse George Sellars, him that married Miss Ca'line Angel, was my real master. They had four children, Bud, Mount, Elizabeth, and, and er; I just can't bring to recollect the name of their other girl. They lived in a two-story frame house that was surrounded by an oak grove on the road leading from Franklin, North Carolina, to Clayton, Georgia. Hard Sellars was the carriage driver, and while I am sure Marse George must have had an overseer, I don't remember ever hearing anybody say his name.

"Really, Miss, I couldn't say just how big that plantation was, but I am sure there must have been at least four or five hundred acres in it. One mighty peculiar thing about his slaves was that Marse George never had more than 99 slaves at one time; every time he bought one to try to make it an even hundred, a slave died. This happened so often, I was told, that he stopped trying to keep a hundred or more, and held on to his 99 slaves, and long as he did that, there warn't any more deaths than births among his slaves. His slaves had to be in the fields when the sun rose, and there they had to work steady until the sun went down. Oh! Yes, mam, Marse Tommy Angel was mighty mean to his slaves, but Miss Jenny, his sister, was good as could be; that is the reason she gave my mother to her sister, Miss Ca'line Sellars; because she thought Marse Tommy was too hard on her.

"I heard some talk as to how after the slaves had worked hard in the field all day and come to the house at night, they were whipped for mighty small offenses. Marse George would have them tied hand and foot over a barrel and would beat them with a cowhide, or cat-o'-nine tails lash. They had a jail in Franklin as far back as I can recollect. Old Big Andy Angel's white folks had him put in jail a heap of times, because he was a rogue and stole everything he could get his hands on. Nearly everybody was afraid of him; he was a great big double jointed man, and was black as the ace of spades. No, mam, I never saw any slaves sold, but my father's mother and his sister were sold on the block. The white folks that bought 'em took them away. After the war was over my father tried to locate 'em, but never once did he get on the right track of 'em.

"Oh! Why, my white folks took a great deal of pains teaching their slaves how to read and write. My father could read, but he never learned to write, and it was from our white folks that I learned to read and write. Slaves read the Bible more than anything else. There were no churches for slaves on Marse George's plantation, so we all went to the white folks' church, about two miles away; it was called Clarke's Chapel. Sometimes we went to church at Cross Roads; that was about the same distance across Sugar Fork River. My mother was baptized in that Sugar Fork River by a white preacher, but that is the reason I joined the Baptist church, because my mother was a Baptist, and I was so crazy about her, and am 'til yet.

"There were no funeral parlors in those days. They just funeralized the dead in their own homes, took them to the graveyard in a painted home-made coffin that was lined with thin bleaching made in the loom on the plantation, and buried them in a grave that didn't have any bricks or cement about it. That brings to my memory those songs they sung at funerals. One of them started off something like this, *I Don't Want You to Grieve After Me*. My mother used to tell me that when she was baptized they sung, *You Shall Wear a Lily-White Robe*. Whenever I get to studying about her it seems to me I can hear my mother singing that song again. She did love it so much.

"No, mam, there didn't none of the darkies on Marse George Sellar's place run away to the North, but some on Marse Tommy Angel's place ran to the West. They told me that when Little Charles Angel started out to run away a bird flew in front of him and led him all the way to the West. Understand me, I am not saying that is strictly so, but that is what I heard old folks say, when I was young. When darkies wanted to get news to their girls or wives on other plantations and didn't want Marse George to know about it, they would wait for a dark night and would tie rags on their feet to keep from making any noise that the paterollers might hear, for if they were caught out without a pass, that was something else. Paterollers would go out in squads at night and whip any darkies they caught out that could not show passes. Adam Angel was a great big man, weighing about 200 pounds, and he slipped out one night without a pass. When the paterollers found him, he was at his girl's place where they were out in the front yard stewing lard for the white folks. They knew he didn't belong on that plantation, so they asked him to show his pass. Adam didn't have one with him, and he told them so. They made a dive for him, and then, quick as a flash, he turned over that pot of boiling lard, and while they were getting the hot grease off of them he got away and came back to his cabin. If they had caught Adam, he would have needed some of that spilt grease on him after the beating they would have give him. Darkies used to stretch ropes and grapevines across the road where they knew paterollers would be riding; then they would run down the road in front of them, and when they got to the rope or vine they would jump over it and watch the horses stumble and throw the paterollers to the ground. That was a favorite sport of slaves.

"After the darkies got in from the field at night, ate their supper, and finished up the chores for the day, on nights when the moon shone bright the men would work in their own cotton patches that Marse George allowed them; the women used their own time to wash, iron, patch, and get ready for the next day, and if they had time they helped the men in their cotton patches. They worked straight on through Saturdays, same as any other day, but the young folks would get together on Saturday nights and have little parties.

"How did they spend Sundays? Why, they went to church on Sunday and visited around, holding prayer-meetings at one another's cabins. Now, Christmas morning! Yes, mam, that was a powerful time with the darkies, if they didn't have nothing but a little sweet cake, which was nothing more than gingerbread. However, Marse George did have plenty of good things to eat at that time, such as fresh pork and wild turkeys, and we were allowed to have a biscuit on that day. How we did frolic and cut up at Christmas! Marse George didn't make much special to do on New Year's Day as far as holiday was concerned; work was the primary object, especially in connection with slaves.

"Oh-oo-h! Everybody had cornshuckings. The man designated to act as the general would stick a peacock tail feather in his hat and call all the men together and give his orders. He would stand in the center of the corn pile, start the singing, and keep things lively for them. Now and then he would pass around the jug. They sang a great deal during cornshuckings, but I have forgotten the words to those songs. Great excitement was expressed whenever a man found a red ear of corn, for that counted 20 points, a speckled ear was 10 points and a blue ear 5 points, toward a special extra big swig of liquor whenever a person had as many as 100 points. After the work was finished they had a big feast spread on long tables in the yard, and dram flowed plentiful, then they played ball, tussled, ran races, and did anything they knew how to amuse themselves.

"Now, Ladies," John said, "please excuse me. I left my wife at home real sick, and I just must hurry to the drug store and get some flaxseed so I can make a poultice for her." As he made a hasty departure, he agreed to complete the story later at his home, and gave careful directions for finding the place.

A month later, two visitors called on John at his small, unpainted house in the center of a hillside cotton patch.

A tall, thin Negress appeared in the doorway. "Yes, mam, John Van Hook lives here. He's down in the field with his hoe, digging 'taters." She leaned from the porch and called, "Daddy, Daddy! Somebody wants to see you." Asked if John was her father, she answered "No, mam, he is my husband. I started calling him Daddy when our child was little, so I've been calling him that ever since. My name is Laney."

The walls of the room into which John invited his

callers were crudely plestered with newspapers and the small space was crowded with furniture of various kinds and periods. The ladder-back chairs he designated for his guests were beautiful. "They are plantation-made," he explained, "and we've had 'em a mighty long time." On a reading table a pencil and tablet with a half-written page lay beside a large glass lamp. Newspapers and books covered several other tables. A freshly whitewashed hearth and mantel were crowned by an old-fashioned clock, and at the end of the room a short flight of steps led to the dining room, built on a higher floor level.

"Now, let's see! Where was I?," John began. "Oh, yes, we were talking about cornshuckings, when I had to leave your office. Well, I haven't had much time to study about those cornshucking songs to get all the words down right, but the name of one was *General Religh Hoe*, and there was another one that was called, *Have a Jolly Crowd, and a Little Jolly Johnny*.

"Now you needn't to expect me to know much about cotton pickings, for you know I have already told you I was raised in North Carolina, and we were too far up in the mountains for cotton growing, but I have lived in a cotton growing country for forty-odd years.

"As to parties and frolics, I guess I could have kept those things in mind, but when I realized that being on the go every night I could get off, week in and week out, was turning my mind and heart away from useful living, I tried to put those things out of my life and to train myself to be content with right living and the more serious things of life, and that's why I can't remember more of the things about our frolics that took place as I was growing up. About all I remember about the dances was when we danced the cotillion at regular old country break-downs. Folks valued their dances very highly then, and to be able to perform them well was a great accomplishment. *Turkey in the Straw* is about the oldest dance tune I can remember. Next to that is *Taint Gonna Rain No More*, but the tune as well as words to that were far different from the modern song by that name. *Rabbit Hair* was another favorite song, and there were dozens of others that I just never tried to remember until you asked me about them.

"My father lived in Caswell County and he used to tell us how hard it was for him to get up in the morning after being out most of the night frolicking. He said their overseer couldn't talk plain, and would call them long before crack of dawn, and it sounded like he was saying, 'Ike and a bike, Ike and a bike.' What he meant was, 'Out and about! Out and about!'

"Marriage in those days was looked upon as something very solemn, and it was mighty seldom that anybody ever heard of a married couple trying to get separated. Now it's different. When a preacher married a couple, you didn't see any hard liquor around, but just a little light wine to liven up the wedding feast. If they were married by a justice of the peace, look out, there was plenty of wine and," here his voice was almost awe-stricken, "even whiskey too."

Laney interrupted at this stage of the story with, "My mother said they used to make up a new broom and when the couple jumped over it, they was married. Then they gave the broom to the couple to use keeping house." John was evidently embarrassed. "Laney," he said, "that was never confirmed. It was just hearsay, as far as you know, and I wouldn't tell things like that.

"The first colored man I ever heard preach was old man Johnny McDowell. He married Angeline Pennon and William Scruggs, uncle to Ollie Scruggs, who lives in Athens now. After the wedding they were all dancing around the yard having a big time and enjoying the wine and feast, and old man McDowell, sitting there watching them, looked real thoughtful and sad; suddenly he said: 'They don't behave like they knew what's been done here today. Two people have been joined together for life. No matter what comes, or what happens, these two people must stand by each other, through everything, as long as they both shall live.' Never before had I had such thoughts at a wedding. They had always just been times for big eats, dancing, frolicking, and lots of jokes, and some of them pretty rough jokes, perhaps. What he said got me to thinking, and I have never been careless minded at a wedding since that day. Brother McDowell preached at Clarke's Chapel, about five miles south of Franklin, North Ca'lina, on the road leading from England to Georgia; that road ran right through the Van Hook place."

Again Laney interrupted her husband. "My mother said they even had infare dinners the next day after the wedding. The infare dinners were just for the families of the bride and groom, and the bride had a special dress for that occasion that she called her infare dress. The friends of both parties were there at the big feast on the wedding day, but not at the infare dinner."

"And there was no such a thing as child marriages heard of in those days," John was speaking again. "At least none of the brides were under 15 or 16 years old.

Now you can read about child brides not more than 10 years old, 'most ever' time you pick up a paper.

"I don't remember much, about what I played until I got to be about 10 years old. I was a terrible little fellow to imitate things. Old man Tommy Angel built mills, and I built myself a little toy mill down on the branch that led to Sugar Fork River. There was plenty of nice soapstone there that was so soft you could cut it with a pocket knife and could dress it off with a plane for a nice smooth finish. I shaped two pieces of soapstone to look like round millstones and set me up a little mill that worked just fine.

"We run pretty white sand through it and called that our meal and flour. My white folks would come down to the branch and watch me run the little toy mill. I used to make toy rifles and pistols and all sorts of nice playthings out of that soapstone. I wish I had a piece of that good old soapstone from around Franklin, so I could carve some toys like I used to play with for my boy."

"We caught real salmon in the mountain streams," John remarked. "They weighed from 3 to 25 pounds, and kind of favored a jack fish, only jack fishes have duck bills, and these salmon had saw teeth. They were powerful jumpers and when you hooked one you had a fight on your hands to get it to the bank no matter whether it weighed 3 or 25 pounds. The gamest of all the fish in those mountain streams were red horses. When I was about 9 or 10 years old I took my brother's fish gig and went off down to the river. I saw what looked like the shadow of a stick in the clear water and when I thrust the gig at it I found mighty quick I had gigged a red horse. I did my best to land it but it was too strong for me and pulled loose from my gig and darted out into deep water. I ran fast as I could up the river bank to the horseshoe bend where a flat bottom boat belonging to our family was tied. I got in that boat and chased that fish 'til I got him. It weighed 6 pounds and was 2 feet and 6 inches long. There was plenty of excitement created around that plantation when the news got around that a boy, as little as I was then, had landed such a big old fighting fish."

"Suckers were plentiful and easy to catch but they did not give you the battle that a salmon or a red horse could put up and that was what it took to make fishing fun. We had canoes, but we used a plain old flat boat, a good deal like a small ferry boat, most of the time. There was about the same difference in a canoe and a flat boat that there is in a nice passenger automobile and a truck."

When asked if he remembered any of the tunes and words of the songs he sang as a child, John was silent for a few moments and then began to sing:

"A frog went courtin'
And he did ride
Uh hunh
With a sword and pistol
By his side
Uh hunh.

"Old uncle Rat laughed,
Shook his old fat side;
He thought his niece
Was going to be the bride.
Uh hunh, uh hunh

"Where shall the wedding be?

Uh hunh
Where shall the wedding be?
Uh hunh

"Way down yonder
In a hollow gum tree.
Uh hunh, un hunh, uh hunh.
"Who shall the waiters be?
Uh hunh

Granddaddy Louse and a
Black-eyed flea.
Uh hunh, uh hunh, uh hunh."

 Laney reminded him of a song he used to sing when their child was a baby. "It is hard for me to formulate its words in my mind. I just cannot seem to get them," he answered, "but I thought of this one the other night and promised myself I would sing it for you sometime. It's *Old Granny Mistletoe*.

"Old Granny Mistletoe,
Lyin' in the bed,
Out the window
She poked her head.

"She says, 'Old Man,
The gray goose's gone,
And I think I heard her holler,
King-cant-you-O, King-cant-you-O!'

"The old fox stepped around,
A mighty fast step.
He hung the old gray goose

Up by the neck.

"Her wings went flip-flop
Over her back,
And her legs hung down.
Ding-downy-O, ding-downy-O.

"The old fox marched
On to his den.
Out come his young ones,
Some nine or ten.

"Now we will have
Some-supper-O, some-summer-O.
Now we will have
Some-supper-O, some-supper-O."

"The only riddle I remember is the one about: 'What goes around the house, and just makes one track?' I believe they said it was a wheelbarrow. Mighty few people in that settlement believed in such things as charms. They were too intelligent for that sort of thing.

"Old man Dillard Love didn't know half of his slaves. They were called 'Love's free niggers.' Some of the white folks in that settlement would get after their niggers and say 'who do you think you are, you must think you are one of Dillard Love's free niggers the way you act.' Then the slave was led to the whipping post and brushed down, and his marster would tell him, 'now you see who is boss.'

"Marse Dillard often met a darkey in the road, he would stop and inquire of him, 'Who's nigger is you?'

The darkey would say 'Boss I'se your nigger.' If Marse Dillard was feeling good he would give the darkey a present. Heaps of times he gave them as much as five dollars, 'cording to how good he was feeling. He treated his darkies mighty good.

"My grandfather belonged to Marse Dillard Love, and when the war was declared he was too old to go. Marse George Sellars went and was wounded. You know all about the blanket rolls they carried over their shoulders. Well, that bullet that hit him had to go all the way through that roll that had I don't know how many folds, and its force was just about spent by the time it got to his shoulder; that was why it didn't kill him, otherwise it would have gone through him. The bullet was extracted, but it left him with a lame shoulder.

"Our Mr. Tommy Angel went to the war, and he got so much experience shooting at the Yankees that he could shoot at a target all day long, and then cover all the bullet holes he made with the palm of one hand. Mr. Tommy was at home when the Yankees come though.

"Folks around our settlement put their darkies on all their good mules and horses, and loaded them down with food and valuables, then sent them to the nearby mountains and caves to hide until the soldiers were gone. Mr. Angel himself told me later that lots of the folks who came around pilfering after the war, warn't northerners at all, but men from just anywhere, who had fought in the war and came back home to find all they had was gone, and they had to live some way.

"One day my father and another servant were laughing fit to kill at a greedy little calf that had caught his head in the feed basket. They thought it was just too funny. About that time a Yankee, in his blue uniform coming down the road, took the notion the men were laughing at him. 'What are you laughing at?' he said, and at that they lit out to run. The man called my father and made him come back, 'cause he was the one laughing so hard. Father thought the Yankee vas going to shoot him before he could make him understand they were just laughing at the calf.

"When the war was over, Mr. Love called his slaves together and told them they had been set free. He explained everything to them very carefully, and told them he would make farming arrangements for all that wanted to stay on there with him. Lots of the darkies left after they heard about folks getting rich working on the railroads in Tennessee and about the high wages that were being paid on those big plantations in Mississippi. Some of those labor agents were powerful smart about stretching the truth, but those folks that believed them and left home found out that it's pretty much the same the world over, as far as folks and human nature is concerned. Those that had even average common sense got along comfortable and all right in Tennessee and Mississippi, and those that suffered out there were the sort that are so stupid they would starve in the middle of a good apple pie. My brother that went with the others to Tennessee never came back, and we never saw him again.

"My father did not want me to leave our home at Franklin, North Carolina, and come to Georgia, for he had been told Georgia people were awful mean. There was a tale told us about the Mr. Oglethorpe, who settled Georgia, bringing over folks from the jails of England to settle in Georgia and it was said they became the ruling class of the State. Anyway, I came on just the same, and pretty soon I married a Georgia girl, and have found the people who live here are all right."

Laney eagerly took advantage of the pause that followed to tell of her mother's owner. "Mother said that he was an old, old man and would set in his big armchair 'most all day. When he heard good news from the soldiers he would drum his fingers on his chair and pat his feet, whilst he tried to sing, 'Te Deum, Te Deum. Good news today! We won today!' Whenever he heard the southern armies were losing, he would lie around moaning and crying out loud. Nobody could comfort him then."

John was delighted to talk about religion. "Yes, mam, after the war, darkies used to meet at each others' houses for religious services until they got churches of their own. Those meetings were little more than just prayer-meetings. Our white folks were powerful careful to teach their slaves how to do the right thing, and long after we were free Mr. Tommy would give long talks at our meetings. We loved to listen to him and have him interested in us, for we had never been treated mean like heaps of the slaves in that neighborhood had.

"One white man in our county needed the help of the Lord. His name was Boney Ridley and he just couldn't keep away from liquor. He was an uncle of that famous preacher and poet, Mr. Caleb Ridley. One day when Mr. Boney had been drinking hard and kind of out of his head, he was stretched out on the ground in a sort of stupor. He opened his eyes and looked at the buzzards circling low over him and said, sort of sick and fretful-like, 'Git on off, buzzards; I ain't dead yet.'"

"The Reverend Doctor George Truett was a fine boy and he has grown into a splendid man. He is one of God's chosen ones. I well remember the first time I heard him speak. I was a janitor at the State Normal School when he was a pupil there in 1887. I still think he is about the greatest orator I ever listened to. In those days, back in 1887, I always made it convenient to be doing something around the school room when time came for him to recite or to be on a debate. After he left that school he went on to the Seminary at Louisville and he has become known throughout this country as a great Christian.

"I started teaching in old field schools with no education but just what our white folks had taught me. They taught me to read and write, and I must say I really was a mighty apt person, and took advantage of every opportunity that came my way to learn. You know, teaching is a mighty good way to learn. After I had been teaching for some time I went back to school, but most of my knowledge was gotten by studying what books and papers I could get hold of and by watching folks who were really educated; by listening carefully to them, I found I could often learn a good deal that way."

Laney could be quiet no longer. "My husband," she said, "is a self-made man. His educated brother, Claude, that graduated from Maryville School in Tennessee, says that he cannot cope with my husband."

John smiled indulgently and continued: "We were in sad and woeful want after the war. Once I asked my father why he let us go so hungry and ragged, and he answered: 'How can we help it? Why, even the white folks don't have enough to eat and wear now.'

"Eleven years ago I rented a little farm from. Mr. Jasper Thompson, in Jackson County. After the boll-weevil got bad I came to the other side of the river yonder, where I stayed 7 years. By this time most of the children by my first two wives had grown up and gone off up north. My first wife's children were Robert, Ella, the twins, Julius and Julia Anne, (who died soon after they were grown-up), and Charlie, and Dan. Robert is in Philadelphia, Ella in Cincinnati, and Dan is dead.

"Fred, George, and Johnny, my second wife's children are all living, but are scattered in far-off places.

"Everybody was powerful sorry to hear about Lincoln's assassination. At that time Jefferson Davis was considered the greatest man that ever lived, but the effect of Lincoln's life and deeds will live on forever. His life grows greater in reputation with the years and his wisdom more apparent.

"As long as we were their property our masters were mighty careful to have us doctored up right when there was the least sign of sickness. There was always some old woman too old for field work that nursed the sick on the big plantations, but the marsters sent for regular doctors mighty quick if the patient seemed much sick.

"After the war we were slower to call in doctors because we had no money, and that's how I lost my good right eye. If I had gone to the doctor when it first got hurt it would have been all right now. When we didn't have money we used to pay the doctor with corn, fodder, wheat, chickens, pork, or anything we had that he wanted.

"We learned to use lots of herbs and other homemade remedies during the war when medicine was scarce at the stores, and some old folks still use these simple teas and poultices. Comfrey was a herb used much for poultices on risings, boils, and the like, and tea made from it is said to be soothing to the nerves. Garlic tea was much used for worms, but it was also counted a good pneumonia remedy, and garlic poultices helped folks to breathe when they had grippe or pneumonia. Boneset tea was for colds. Goldenrod was used leaf, stem, blossom, and all in various ways, chiefly for fever and coughs. Black snake root was a good cure for childbed fever, and it saved the life of my second wife after her last child was born. Slippery ellum was used for poultices to heal burns, bruises, and any abrasions, and we gargled slippery ellum tea to heal sore throats, but red oak bark tea was our best sore throat remedy. For indigestion and shortness of the breath we chewed calamus root or drank tea made from it. In fact, we still think it is mighty useful for those purposes. It was a long time after the war before there were any darkies with enough medical education to practice as doctors. Dr. Doyle in Gainesville was the first colored physician that I ever saw.

"The world seems to be gradually drifting the wrong way, and it won't get any better 'til all people put their belief—and I mean by that—simple faith, in the Bible. What they like of it they are in the habit of quoting, but they distort it and try to make it appear to mean whatever will suit their wicked convenience. They have got to take the whole Bible and live by it, and they must remember they cannot leave out those wise old laws of the Old Testament that God gave for men everywhere to live by."

Laney had quietly left the room, but as the visitors were taking their departure she returned with a small package. "This," she explained, "is some calamus root that I raised and dried myself, and I hope it comes in handy whenever you ladies need something for the indigestion."

"Next time you come, I hope to have more songs remembered and written down for you," promised John.

PLANTATION LIFE AS VIEWED BY AN EX-SLAVE

ADDIE VINSON, Age 86
653 Dearing Street
Athens, Georgia

Written By:
Mrs. Sadie B. Hornsby
Athens, Georgia

Edited By:
Mrs. Sarah H. Hall
Athens, Georgia

and

John N. Booth
WPA Residency No. 6 & 7

August 23, 1938

ADDIE VINSON

Perched on an embankment high above the street level is the four-room frame cottage where Addie Vinson lives with her daughter. The visitor scrambled up the steep incline to the vine covered porch, and a rap on the front door brought prompt response. "Who dat?" asked a very black woman, who suddenly appeared in the hall. "What you want?... Yassum, dis here's Addie, but dey calls me Mammy, 'cause I'se so old. I s'pects I'se most nigh a hunnert and eight years old."

The old Negress is very short and stout. Her dark blue calico dress was striped with lines of tiny polka dots, and had been lengthened by a band of light blue outing flannel with a darker blue stripe, let in just below the waist line. Her high-topped black shoes were worn over grey cotton hose, and the stocking cap that partially concealed her white hair was crowned by a panama hat that flopped down on all sides except where the brim was fastened up across the front with two conspicuous "safety-first" pins. Addie's eyesight is poor, and she claims it was "plum ruint by de St. Vitus's dance," from which she has suffered for many years. She readily agreed to tell of her early life, and her eyes brightened as she began: "Lawsy, Missy! Is dat what you come 'ere for? Oh, dem good old days! I was thinkin' 'bout Old Miss jus' t'other day.

"I was borned down in Oconee County on Marse Ike Vinson's place. Old Miss was Marse Ike's mother. My Mammy and Pappy was Peter and 'Nerva Vinson and dey was both field hands. Marse Ike buyed my Pappy from Marse Sam Brightwell. Me and Bill, Willis, Maze, Harrison, Easter, and Sue was all de chillun my Mammy and Pappy had. Dere warn't but four of us big enough to wuk when Marse Ike married Miss Ann Hayes and dey tuk Mammy wid 'em to dey new home in town. I stayed dar on de plantation and done lots of little jobs lak waitin' on table; totin' Old Miss' breakfast to her in her room evvy mornin', and I helped 'tend to de grainery. Dey says now dat folkses is livin' in dat old grainery house.

"Dat was a be-yootiful place, wid woods, cricks, and fields spread out most as fur as you could see. De slave quarters would'a reached from here to Milledge Avenue. Us lived in a one-room log cabin what had a chimbly made out of sticks and mud. Dem homemade beds what us slep' on had big old high posties wid a great big knob on de top of each post. Our matt'esses was coarse homewove cloth stuffed wid field straw. You know I laked dem matt'esses 'cause when de chinches got too bad you could shake out dat straw and burn it, den scald de tick and fill it wid fresh straw, and rest in peace again. You can't never git de chinches out of dese cotton matt'esses us has to sleep on now days. Pillows? What you talkin' 'bout? You know Niggers never had no pillows dem days, leaseways us never had none. Us did have plenty of kivver dough. Folkses was all time a-piecin' quilts and having quiltin's. All dat sort of wuk was done at night.

"Pappy's Ma and Pa was Grandma Nancy and Grandpa Jacob. Day was field hands, and dey b'longed to Marse Obe Jackson. Grandma Lucy and Grandpa Toney Murrah was owned by Marse Billy Murrah. Marse Billy was a preacher what sho could come down wid de gospel at church. Grandma Lucy was his cook. Miss Sadie LeSeur got Grandma Lucy and tuk her to Columbus, Georgy, and us never seed our grandma no more. Miss Sadie had been one of de Vinson gals. She tuk our Aunt Haley 'long too to wait on her when she started out for Europe, and 'fore dey got crost de water, Aunt Haley, she died on de boat. Miss Sarah, she had a time keepin' dem boatsmens from th'owing Aunt Haley to de sharks. She is buried in de old country somewhar.

"Now Missy, how was Nigger chillun gwine to git holt of money in slavery time? Old Marse, he give us plenty of somepin t'eat and all de clothes us needed, but he sho kep' his money for his own self.

"Now 'bout dat somepin t'eat. Sho dat! Us had plenty of dem good old collards, turnips, and dem sort of oatments, and dar was allus a good chunk of meat to bile wid 'em. Marse Ike, he kep' plenty of evvy sort of meat folkses knowed about dem days. He had his own beef cattle, lots of sheep, and he killed more'n a hunnert hogs evvy year. Dey tells me dat old bench dey used to lay de meat out on to cut it up is standin' dar yet.

"'Possums? Lawd, dey was plentiful, and dat ain't all dere was on dat plantation. One time a slave man was 'possum huntin' and, as he was runnin' 'round in de bresh, he looked up and dar was a b'ar standin' right up on his hind laigs grinnin' and ready to eat dat Nigger up. Oh, good gracious, how dat Nigger did run! Dey fetched in 'possums in piles, and dere was lots of rabbits, fixes, and coons. Dem coon, fox and 'possum hounds sho knowed deir business. Lawsy, I kin jus' smell one of dem good old 'possums roastin' right now, atter all dese years. You parbiled de 'possum fust, and den roasted him in a heavy iron skillet what had a big old thick lid. Jus' 'fore de 'possum got done, you peeled ash-roasted 'taters and put 'em all 'round da 'possum so as day would soak up some of dat good old gravy, and would git good and brown. Is you ever et any good old ashcake? You wropped de raw hoecake in cabbage or collard leafs and roasted 'em in de ashes. When dey got done, you had somepin fit for a king to eat.

"De kitchen was sot off a piece from de big house, and our white folkses wouldn't eat deir supper 'fore time to light de lamps to save your life; den I had to stan' 'hind Old Miss' cheer and fan her wid a turkey-feather fan to keep de flies off. No matter how rich folkses was dem days dere warn't no screens in de houses.

"I never will forgit pore old Aunt Mary; she was our cook, and she had to be tapped evvy now and den 'cause she had de drapsy so bad. Aunt Mary's old man was Uncle Harris, and I 'members how he used to go fishin' at night. De udder slaves went fishin' too. Many's de time I'se seed my Mammy come back from Barber's Crick wid a string of fish draggin' from her shoulders down to de ground. Me, I laked milk more'n anything else. You jus' oughta seed dat place at milkin' time. Dere was a heap of cows a fightin', chillun hollerin', and sich a bedlam as you can't think up. Dat old plantation was a grand place for chillun, in summertime 'specially, 'cause dere was so many branches and cricks close by what us chillun could hop in and cool off.

"Chillun didn't wear nothin' but cotton slips in summer, but de winter clothes was good and warm. Under our heavy winter dresses us wore quilted underskirts dat was sho nice and warm. Sunday clothes? Yes Mar'm, us allus had nice clothes for Sunday. Dey made up our summertime Sunday dresses out of a thin cloth called Sunday-parade. Dey was made spenser fashion, wid ruffles 'round de neck and waist. Our ruffled petticoats was all starched and ironed stiff and slick, and us jus' knowed our long pantalettes, wid deir scalloped ruffles, was mighty fine. Some of de 'omans would wuk fancy eyelets what dey punched in de scallops wid locust thorns. Dem pantalettes was buttoned on to our drawers. Our Sunday dresses for winter was made out of linsey-woolsey cloth. White ladies wore hoopskirts wid deir dresses, and dey looked lak fairy queens. Boys wore plain shirts in summer, but in winter dey had warmer shirts and quilted pants. Dey would put two pair of britches togedder and quilt 'em up so you couldn't tell what sort of cloth dey was made out of. Dem pants was called suggins.

"All de Niggers went barfoots in summer, but in winter us all wore brogans. Old Miss had a shoe shop in de cellar under de big house, and when dem two white 'omans dat she hired to make our shoes come, us knowed wintertime was nigh. Dem 'omans would stay 'til day had made up shoes enough to last us all winter long, den dey would go on to de next place what dey s'pected to make shoes.

"Marse Ike Vinson was sho good to his Niggers. He was de hanger, 'cept he never hung nobody. Him and Miss Ann had six chillun. Dey was Miss Lucy, Miss Myrt, Miss Sarah, Miss Nettie, Marse Charlie, and Marse Tom. Marse Ike's ma, Old Miss, wouldn't move to town wid him and Miss Ann; she stayed on in de big house on de plantation. To tell de truf I done forgot Old Miss' name. De overseer and his wife was Mr. Edmond and Miss Betsey, and dey moved up to de big house wid old Miss atter Marse Ike and Miss Ann moved to town. Stiles Vinson was de carriage driver, and he fotched Marse Ike out to de plantation evvy day. Lord! Gracious alive! It would take a week to walk all over dat plantation. Dere was more'n a thousand acres in it and, countin' all de chillun, dere was mighty nigh a hunnert slaves.

"Long 'fore day, dat overseer blowed a bugle to wake up de Niggers. You could hear it far as High Shoals, and us lived dis side of Watkinsville. Heaps of folkses all over dat part of de country got up by dat old bugle. I will never forgit one time when de overseer said to us chillun, 'You fellows go to de field and fetch some corn tops.' Mandy said: 'He ain't talkin' to us 'cause us ain't fellows and I ain't gwine.' Bless your sweet life, I runned and got dem corn tops, 'cause I didn't want no beatin'. Dem udder 'chillun got deir footses most cut off wid dem switches whan dat overseer got to wuk to sho 'em dey had to obey him. Dat overseer sho did wuk de Niggers hard; he driv' 'em all de time. Dey had to go to de field long 'fore sun-up, and it was way atter sundown 'fore dey could stop dat field wuk. Den dey had to hustle to finish deir night wuk in time for supper, or go to bed widout it.

[HW sidenote: Beating]

"You know dey whupped Niggers den. Atter dey had done wukked hard in de fields all day long, de beatin' started up, and he allus had somepin in mind to beat 'em about. When dey beat my Aunt Sallie she would fight back, and once when Uncle Randall said somepin he hadn't oughta, dat overseer beat him so bad he couldn't wuk for a week. He had to be grez all over evvy day wid hoalin' ointment for a long time 'fore dem gashes got well.

"Rita and Retta was de Nigger 'omans what put pizen in some collards what dey give Aunt Vira and her baby to eat. She had been laughin' at a man 'cause his coat-tail was a-flappin' so funny whilst he was dancin', and dem two Jezebels thought she was makin' fun of dem. At de graveyard, 'fore dey buried her, dey cut her open and found her heart was all decayed. De overseer driv dem 'omans clear off de plantation, and Marster, he was mighty mad. He said he had done lost 'bout $2,000. If he had kotched dem 'omans he woulda hung 'em, cause he was de hanger. In 'bout two weeks dat overseer left dar, and Old Marse had to git him anudder man to take his place.

"Sho! Dere was a jail for slaves and a hangin' place right in front of de jail, but none of Old Marster's Niggers warn't never put in no jailhouse. Oh God! Yes, dey sold slaves. My own granddaddy was made to git up on dat block, and dey sold him. One time I seed Old Marse buy four boys." At this point the narrative ceased when Addie suddenly remembered that she must stop to get supper for the daughter, who would soon be returning from work.

The visitor called early in the morning of the following day, and found Addie bent over her washtubs in the back yard. "Have dat cheer," was the greeting as the old Negress lifted a dripping hand to point out a chair under the spreading branches of a huge oak tree, "You knows you don't want to hear no more 'bout dat old stuff," she said, "and anyhow, is you gittin' paid for doin' dis?" When the visitor admitted that these interviews were part of her salaried work, Addie quickly asked: "What is you gwine to give me?"

When the last piece of wash had been hung on the line and Addie had turned a large lard can upside down for a stool, she settled down and began to talk freely.

"No Ma'm, dey didn't low Niggers to larn how to read and write. I had to go wid de white chillun to deir school on Hog Mountain road evvy day to wait on 'em. I toted water for 'em kep' de fire goin', and done all sorts of little jobs lak dat. Miss Martha, de overseer's daughter, tried to larn me to read and write, but I wouldn't take it in.

"No Ma'm dere warn't no churches for Niggers in slavery time, so slaves had to go to deir white folkses churches. Us went to church at Betty Berry (Bethabara) and Mars Hill. When time come for de sermon to de Niggers, sometimes de white folkses would leave and den again dey would stay, but dat overseer, he was dar all de time. Old man Isaac Vandiver, a Nigger preacher what couldn't read a word in de Bible, would git up in dat pulpit and talk from his heart. You know dere's heaps of folkses what's got dat sort of 'ligion—it's deep in deir hearts. De Reverend Freeman was de white folkses' preacher. I laked him best, for what he said allus sounded good to me.

"At funerals us used to sing *Hark From De Tomb A Doleful Sound.* I never went to no funerals, but Old Marster's and Aunt Nira's, 'fore de end of de war.

"When Old Marster went off to de war, he had all his slaves go to de musterin' ground to see him leave. He was captain of his company from Oconee County, and 'fore he left he had de mens in dat company bury deir silver and gold, deir watches, rings, and jus' anything dey wanted to keep, on Hog Mountain. Ha lef' a guard to watch de hidin' place so as dey would have somepin when dey come back home, den dey marched back to de musterin' ground dat was twixt de Hopkins' plantation and Old Marster's place. Uncle Solomon went along to de war to tote Marster's gun, cook for him, and sich lak. It warn't long 'fore old Marse was kilt in dat war, and Uncle Solomon fetches him back in a coffin. All de slaves dat went to de buryin' jus' trembled when guns was fired over Old Marster's grave. Dat was done to show dat Old Marster had been a powerful high-up man in de army.

"Good Gracious! Dere didn't nary a Nigger go off from our place to de North, 'cause us was skeered of dem Yankees. Dere was a white slave-trader named McRaleigh what used to come to Old Marster's plantation to buy up Niggers to take 'em to de Mississippi bottoms. When us seed him comin' us lit out for de woods. He got Aunt Rachel; you could hear her hollerin' a mile down de road.

"Oh! Good Lord! Dem patterollers was awful. Folkses what dey cotched widout no paper, dey jus' plum wore out. Old man John was de fiddler on our place, and when de patterollers cotched him dey beat him up de wust of all, 'cause him and his fiddle was all de time drawin' Niggers out to do dances.

"If Old Marster wanted to send a massage he sont Uncle Randall on a mule named Jim. Sometimes dat old mule tuk a notion he didn't want to go; den he wouldn't budge. I ricollects one time dey tuk a bundle of fodder and tied it to Old Jim's tail, but still he wouldn't move. Old Marster kep' a special man to fetch and carry mail for de plantation in a road cyart, and nobody warn't 'lowed to go nigh dat cyart.

"When slaves got in from de fields at night dey cooked and et deir supper and went to bed. Dey had done been wukin' since sunup. When dere warn't so much to do in de fields, sometimes Old Marster let his Niggers lay off from wuk atter dinner on Saddays. If de chinches was most eatin' de Niggers up, now and den de 'omans was 'lowed to stay to de house to scald evvything and clear 'em out, but de menfolkses had to go on to de field. On Sadday nights de 'omans patched, washed, and cut off peaches and apples to dry in fruit season. In de daytime dey had to cut off and dry fruit for Old Miss. When slaves got smart wid deir white folkses, deir Marsters would have 'em beat, and dat was de end of de matter. Dat was a heap better'n dey does now days, 'cause if a Nigger gits out of place dey puts him on de chaingang. [TR: 'Whipping' written in margin.]

"Sunday was a day off for all de slaves on our plantation. Cause, de mens had to look atter de stock in de lot right back of de cabins. De 'omans cooked all day for de next week. If dey tuk a notion to go to church, mules was hitched to wagons made lak dippers, and dey jigged off down de road. Us had four days holiday for Christmas. Old Miss give us lots of good things to eat dem four days; dere was cake, fresh meat, and all kinds of dried fruit what had been done stored away. All de Niggers tuk dat time to rest but my Mammy. She tuk me and went 'round to de white folkses' houses to wash and weave. Dey said I was a right smart, peart little gal, and white folkses used to try to hire me from Old Miss. When dey axed her for me, Old Miss allus told 'em: 'You don't want to hire dat gal; she ain't no 'count.' She wouldn't let nobody hire her Niggers, 'cept Mammy, 'cause she knowed Mammy warn't gwine to leave her nohow. On New Year's Day, if dere warn't too much snow on de ground, de Niggers burnt brush and cleared new ground.

"When Aunt Patience led de singin' at cornshuckin's, de shucks sho'ly did fly. Atter de corn was shucked, dey fed us lots of good things and give us plenty of liquor. De way cotton pickin' was managed was dis: evvybody dat picked a thousand pounds of cotton in a week's time was 'lowed a day off. Mammy picked her thousand pounds evvy week.

"Dances? Now you's talkin' 'bout somepin' sho' 'nough. Old John, de fiddler man, was right dere on our plantation. Niggers dat had done danced half de night would be so sleepy when de bugle sounded dey wouldn't have time to cook breakfast. Den 'bout de middle of de mawnin' dey would complain 'bout bein' so weak and hongry dat de overseer would fetch 'em in and have 'em fed. He let 'em rest 'bout a hour and a half; den he marched 'em back to de field and wuked 'em 'til slap black dark. Aunt Sook was called de lead wench. If de moon warn't out, she put a white cloth 'round her shoulders and led 'em on.

"Didn't none of Old Marsters chillun marry in slavery time, but Old Miss, she let us see a Nigger gal named Frances Hester git married. When I sot down to dat weddin' supper I flung de chicken bones over my shoulder, 'cause I didn't know no better. I don't 'member what gals played when I was little, but boys played ball all day long if dey was 'lowed to. One boy, named Sam, played and run so hard he tuk his bed Monday and never got up no more.

"I heared tell of Raw Haid and Bloody Bones. Old folkses would skeer us most nigh to death tellin' us he was comin'. Mankind! Us made for de house den. Missy, please mam, don't ax me 'bout dem ha'nts. I sees 'em all de time. Atter she had done died out, Old Miss used to come back all de time. She didn't lak it 'cause day wropped her in a windin' sheet and buried her by de doorsteps, but I reckon dey done fixed her by now, 'cause she don't come back no more. Dere's a house in Athens, called de Bell House, dat nobody kin live in, 'cause a man run his wife from home and atter she died, she come back and ha'nted dat house.

"Lawd have mercy! Look here, don't talk lak dat. I ain't told you before but part o' dis here yard is conjured. A man comes here early evvy mornin' and dresses dis yard down wid conjuration. Soon as I sot down here to talk to you, a pain started in my laigs, and it is done gone all over me now. I started to leave you and go in de house. Come on. Let's leave dis yard right now. Hurry!" On reaching the kitchen Addie hastily grasped the pepper box and shook its contents over each shoulder and on her head, saying: "Anything hot lak dis will sho drive dis spell away. De reason I shakes lak I does, one day I was in de yard and somepin cotch me. It helt fast to my footses, den I started to shake all over, and I been shakin' ever since. A white 'oman gimme some white soap, and evvy mornin' I washes myself good wid dat soap 'fore I puts on my clothes."

Leaving the kitchen, Addie entered the front room which serves as a bedroom. "Lawdy, Missy!" she exclaimed, "Does you smell dat funny scent? Oh, Good Lawd! Jus' look at dem white powders on my doorstep! Let me git some hot water and wash 'em out quick! Now Missy, see how dese Niggers 'round here is allus up to deir meanness? Dere's a man in de udder room bilin' his pizen right now. I has to keep a eye on him all de time or dis here old Nigger would be in her grave. I has to keep somepin hot all de time to keep off dem conjure spells. I got three pids of pepper most ready to pick, and I'se gwine to tie 'em 'round my neck, den dese here spells folkses is all de time tryin' to put on me won't do me no harm."

Addie now lowered her voice to a stage whisper. "I found a folded up piece of white paper under our back doorstep dis very mornin'. Bless your life, I got a stick from de kitchen quick and poked it in a crack in de steps and got it out 'fore I put my foots down on dem steps. I sho did."

Here Addie reverted to her story of the plantation. "Old Marster was mighty good to his Niggers," she said.

When any of 'em got sick Old Miss sont to town for him, and he allus come right out and fetched a doctor. Old Miss done her very best for Pappy when he was tuk sick, but he died out jus' de same. Pappy used to drive a oxcart and, when he was bad off sick and out of his haid, he hollered out: 'Scotch dat wheel! Scotch dat wheel!' In his mind, he was deep in de bad place den, and didn't know how to pray. Old Miss, she would say: 'Pray, Pete, Pray.' Old Miss made a heap of teas from diff'unt things lak pennyroyal, algaroba wood, sassafras, flat tobacco, and mullein. Us wore rabbits foots, little bags of asfiddy (asafetida), and garlic tabs 'round our necks to keep off mis'ries. I wishes I had a garlic tab to wear 'round my neck now.

"One day Old Miss called us togedder and told us dat us was free as jay birds. De Niggers started hollerin': 'Thank de Lawd, us is free as de jay birds.' 'Bout dat time a white man come along and told dem Niggers if he heared 'em say dat again he would kill de last one of 'em. Old Miss axed us to stay on wid her and dar us stayed for 'bout three years. It paid us to stay dere 'stead of runnin' off lak some udder Niggars dat played de fool done. T'warn't long 'fore dem Yankees come 'long, and us hustled off to town to see what dey looked lak. I never seed so many mens at one time in my life before. When us got back to de plantation de overseer told us not to drink no water out of de well, 'cause somebody had done put a peck of pizen in dar. He flung a whole bushel of salt in de well to help git rid of de pizen.

"Atter de end of de war, I went to wuk as a plow-hand. I sho did keep out of de way of dem Ku Kluxers. Folkses would see 'em comin' and holler out: 'De Ku Kluxers is ridin' tonight. Keep out of deir way, or dey will sho kill you.' Dem what was skeered of bein' cotched and beat up, done deir best to stay out of sight.

"It was a long time atter de war was done over 'fore schools for Niggers was sot up, and den when Nigger chillun did git to go to school dey warn't 'lowed to use de old blue-back spellin' book 'cause white folkses said it larn't 'em too much.

"It was two or three years atter de war 'fore any of de Niggers could save up enough money to start buyin' land, and den, if dey didn't watch dey steps mighty keerful, de white folkses would find a way to git dat land back from de Niggers.

"What! Is I got to tell you 'bout dat old Nigger I got married up wid? I don't want to talk 'bout dat low down, no 'count devil. Anyhow, I married Ed Griffeth and, sho dat, I had a weddin'. My weddin' dress was jus' de purtiest thing; it was made out of parade cloth, and it had a full skirt wid ruffles from de knees to de hem. De waist fitted tight and it was cut lowneck wid three ruffles 'round de shoulder. Dem puff sleeves was full from de elbow to de hand. All dem ruffles was aidged wid lace and, 'round my waist I wore a wide pink sash. De underskirt was trimmed wid lace, and dere was lace on de bottom of de drawers laigs. Dat was sho one purty outfit dat I wore to marry dat no 'count man in. I had bought dat dress from my young Mist'ess.

"Us had seven chillun and ten grandchillun. Most of 'em is livin' off up in Detroit. If Ed ain't daid by now he ought to be; he was a good match for de devil.

"I reckon Mr. Lincoln and Mr. Jeff Davis done right as

fur as dey knowed how and could. If dem northern folkses hadn't fotched us here, us sho wouldn't never have been here in de fust place. Den dey hauled off and said de South was mean to us Niggers and sot us free, but I don't know no diffunce. De North sho let us be atter dat war, and some of de old Niggers is still mad 'cause dey is free and ain't got no Marster to feed 'em and give 'em good warm clothes no more.

"Oh! You gits happy when you jines up wid de church. I sho don't want to go to de bad place. Dere ain't but two places to go to, Heaven and hell, and I'se tryin' to head for Heaven. Folkses says dat when Old Dives done so bad he had to go to de bad place, a dog was sot at his heels for to keep him in dar. No Mam, if it's de Good Lawd's will to let me git to Heaven, I is sho gwine to keep out of hell, if I kin.

"Goodbye, Missy. Next time you comes fetch me a garlic tab to keep de conjure spells 'way from me," was Addie's parting request.

PLANTATION LIFE AS VIEWED BY AN EX-SLAVE

EMMA VIRGEL, Age 73
1491 W. Broad Street
Athens, Georgia

Written by:
Grace McCune
Athens

Edited by:
Sarah H. Hall
Athens

and

John N. Booth
District Supervisor
Federal Writers' Project
Residencies 6 & 7
Augusta, Ga.
[Date Stamp: MAY 13 1938]

EMMA VIRGEL

Hurrying for shelter from a sudden shower, the interviewer heard a cheerful voice singing "Lord I'se Comin' Home," as she rushed up the steps of Aunt Emma's small cabin. Until the song was ended she quietly waited on the tiny porch and looked out over the yard which was attractive with roses and other old-fashioned flowers; then she knocked on the door.

Dragging footsteps and the tap, tap of a crutch sounded as Aunt Emma approached the door. "Come in out of dat rain, chile, or you sho' will have de pneumony," she said. "Come right on in and set here by my fire. Fire feels mighty good today. I had to build it to iron de white folkses clothes." Aunt Emma leaned heavily on her crutch as she wielded the iron with a dexterity attainable only by long years of experience. Asked if her lameness and use of a crutch made her work difficult, she grinned and answered: "Lawsy chile, I'se jus' so used to it, I don't never think 'bout it no more. I'se had to wuk all of my life, no matter what was in de way." The comfort, warmth and cheer of the small kitchen encouraged intimate conversation and when Aunt Emma was asked for the story of her childhood days and her recollections of slavery, she replied: "I was too little to 'member much, but I'se heared my Ma tell 'bout dem days.

"My Pa and Ma was Louis and Mary Jackson. Dey b'longed to Marse John Montgomery, way down in Oconee County. Marse John didn't have no wife den, 'cause he didn't git married 'til atter de War. He had a big place wid lots of slaves. He was sho' good to 'em, and let 'em have plenty of evvything. De slave quarters was log cabins wid big fireplaces, whar dey done de cookin'. Dey had racks to hang pots on to bile and dey baked in ovens set on de harth (hearth). Dat was powerful good eatin'. Dey had a big old gyarden whar dey raised plenty of corn, peas, cabbages, potatoes, collards, and turnip greens. Out in de fields dey growed mostly corn, wheat, and cotton. Marster kep' lots of chickens, cows, hogs, goats, and sheep; and he fed 'em all mighty good.

"Marster let his slaves dance, and my Ma was sho' one grand dancer in all de breakdown's. Dey give 'em plenty of toddy and Niggers is dancers f'um way back yonder while de toddy lasts.

"Slaves went to deir Marster's meetin's and sot in de back of de church. Dey had to be good den 'cause Marster sho' didn't 'low no cuttin' up 'mongst his Niggers at de church. Ma said he didn't believe in whuppin' his Niggers lessen it jus' had to be done, but den dey knowed he was 'round dar when he did have to whup 'em.

"Ma said when dey had big baptizin's in de river dey prayed and shouted and sung 'Washin' 'way my Sins,'— 'Whar de Healin' Water Flows,' and 'Crossin' de River Jerdan.' De white preacher baptized de slaves and den he preached—dat was all dere was to it 'ceppen de big dinner dey had in de churchyard on baptizin' days.

"When slaves died, dey made coffins out of pine wood and buried 'em whar de white folkses was buried. If it warn't too fur a piece to de graveyard, dey toted de coffin on three or four hand sticks. Yessum, hand sticks, dat's what day called 'em. Dey was poles what dey sot de coffin on wid a Nigger totin' each end of de poles. De white preacher prayed and de Niggers sung 'Hark f'um de Tomb.'

"Ma said she had a grand big weddin'. She wore a white swiss dress wid a bleachin' petticoat, made wid heaps of ruffles and a wreath of flowers 'round her head. She didn't have no flower gals. Pa had on a long, frock tail, jim swinger coat lak de preacher's wore. A white preacher married 'em in de yard at de big house. All de Niggers was dar, and Marster let 'em dance mos' all night.

"I was de oldest of Ma's 10 chillun. Dey done all gone to rest now 'ceptin' jus' de three of us what's lef in dis world of trouble. Yessum, dere sho' is a heap of trouble here.

"Atter de War, Ma and Pa moved on Mr. Bill Marshall's place to farm for him and dar's whar I was born. Dey didn't stay dar long 'fore dey moved to Mr. Jim Mayne's place away out in de country, in de forks of de big road down below Watkinsville. I sho' was a country gal. Yessum, I sho' was. Mr. Mayne's wife was Mrs. Emma Mayne and she took a lakin' to me 'cause I was named Emma. I stayed wid her chilluns all de time, slep' in de big house, and et dar too, jus' lak one of dem, and when dey bought for dey chillun dey bought for me too.

"Us wore homespun dresses and brass toed shoes. Sometimes us would git mighty mad and fuss over our games and den Miss Emma would make us come in de big house and set down. No Ma'am, she never did whup us. She was good and she jus' talked to us, and told us us never would git to Heb'en lessen us was good chillun. Us played games wid blocks and jumped de rope and, when it was warm, us waded in de crick. Atter I was big 'nough, I tuk de white chillun to Sunday School, but I didn't go inside den—jus' waited on de outside for 'em. I never got a chanct to go to school none, but de white chilluns larnt me some.

"Marse Jim was mighty good to de Niggers what wukked for him, and us all loved him. He didn't 'low no patterollers or none of dem Ku Kluxers neither to bother de Niggers on his place. He said he could look atter 'em his own self. He let 'em have dances, and evvy Fourth of July he had big barbecues. Yessum, he kilt hogs, goats, sheep and sometimes a cow for dem barbecues. He believed in havin' plenty to eat.

"I 'members dem big corn shuckin's. He had de mostes' corn, what was in great big piles put in a circle. All de neighbors was axed to come and bring deir Niggers. De fus' thing to do was to 'lect a gen'ral to stand in de middle of all dem piles of corn and lead de singin' of de reels. No Ma'am, I don't 'member if he had no shuck stuck up on his hat or not, and I can't ricollec' what de words of de reels was, 'cause us chillun was little den, but de gen'ral he pulled off de fus' shuck. Den he started singin' and den dey all sung in answer to him, and deir two hands a-shuckin' corn kep' time wid de song. As he sung faster, dey jus' made dem shucks more dan fly. Evvy time de gen'ral would speed up de song, de Niggers would speed up deir corn shuckin's. If it got dark 'fore dey finished, us chillun would hold torch lights for 'em to see how to wuk. De lights was made out of big pine knots what would burn a long time. Us felt mighty big when us was 'lowed to hold dem torches. When dey got done shuckin' all de corn, dey had a big supper, and Honey, dem was sho' some good eatments—barbecue of all sorts—jus' thinkin' 'bout dem pies makes me hongry, even now. Ma made 'em, and she couldn't be beat on chicken pies and sweet potato pies. Atter dey done et and drunk all dey wanted, Marse Jim would tell 'em to go to it. Dat was de word for de gen'ral to start up de dancin', and dat lasted de rest of de night; dat is if dey didn't all fall out, for old time corn shuckin' breakdowns was drag-outs and atter all dem 'freshments, hit sho' kept somebody busy draggin' out dem what fell out. Us chillun was 'lowed to stay up long as us wanted to at corn shuckin's, and sometimes us would git out and try to do lak de grown-up Niggers. Hit was de mos' fun.

"Dey went huntin' and fishin' and when dey cotch or kilt much, dey had a big supper. I 'members de fus' time I ever cooked 'possum. Ma was sick in de bed, and de mens had done been 'possum huntin'. Ma said I would jus' have to cook dem 'possums. She told me how to fix 'em and she said to fix 'em wid potatoes and plenty of butter and red pepper. Den she looked at me right hard and said dat dey had better be jus' right. Dat skeered me so I ain't never been so I could eat no 'possum since den. Yessum, dey was cooked jus' right, but cookin' 'em jus' once when I was skeered cured me of de taste for eatin' 'possum.

"Us chillun didn't git out and go off lak dey does dese days. Us stayed dar on de plantation. In winter us had to wear plenty of clothes, wid flannel petticoats and sich lak, and us stayed in by de fire. Big boys had clothes made out of jeans, but little boys wore homespun shirts. On hot days us jus' wore one piece of clothes, a sort of shirt what was made long and had a yoke in it.

"Dey made me use snuff to cure my sore eyes when I was little, and I never could quit usin' it no more. When I was 'bout 15, Ma and Pa moved to Athens and I went to wuk for Mr. Joe Webb's fambly. I wukked for 'em for 30 years and raised all deir chillun. Dey was all mighty good to me and seed dat I had plenty of evvything. I would still be dar, but de old folkses all done died out and gone to dey rest and de younguns done married and lef' here.

"I was wukkin' right in de house wid 'em when I 'cided to git married. Yes Ma'am, I sho' done had one swell elegant weddin'. Jus' evvything heart could ask for. I married at my Ma's house, but my white folkses was all right dar, and dey had done fixed de house up pretty wid flowers all over it. Dey give me my white flannel weddin' dress and it was sho' pretty, but dey warn't nothin' lackin' 'bout my second day dress. My white folkses bought dat too,—It was a bottle green silk. Lawsy, but I was sho' one dressed up bride. It was 8 o'clock dat night when de preacher got finished wid tyin' dat knot for me and Sam Virgel. My sister and her fellow stood up wid us and us had a big crowd at our weddin' supper. Dere was one long table full of our white folkses, 'sides all de Niggers, and I jus' never seed so much to eat. My white folkses said dat Emma jus' had to have plenty for her weddin' feast and dey evermore did lay out good things for dat supper, and dem Niggers sho' did hide dat chicken and cake away lak dey hadn't never seed none before.

"I wukked on for de Webbs 'til dey was all gone. De old folks is in Heb'en whar I 'spects to see 'em some day when de Lord done called me home. De younguns moved away, but I still loves 'em evvyone, 'cause dey looked atter old Emma so good when dey was here. Us never had no chillun and Sam done been gone to his res' long years ago. I'se jus' a-wukkin and a-waitin 'til I gits called to go too. I don't have plenty all de time now lak I used to, and nobody here looks atter old Emma no more, but I makes out.

"I'se mighty glad it rained if dat's what sont you to my door. It's been nice to talk wid white folkses again. I wisht I had somepin' nice for you! Let me cut you a bunch of my flowers?" She carefully placed her iron on the hearth and hobbled out in the yard. The May shower had been followed by sunshine as she handed her guest a huge bouquet of roses, Aunt Emma bowed low. "Goodbye, Missy," she said, "please come back to see me."

United States. Work Projects Administration

[HW: Dist. 7
Ex-Slave #110]
Adella S. Dixon

INTERVIEW WITH RHODUS WALTON, EX-SLAVE, Age 84
[Date Stamp: MAY 8 1937]

RHODUS WALTON

Ten years before the Emancipation Proclamation was signed, a son was born to Antony and Patience Walton who lived in Lumpkin, Stewart County, Ga. When this son, Rhodus, was three weeks old, his mother, along with the three younger children, was sold. His father and the thirteen sons and daughters that she left behind were never seen again. His parents' birthplace and the name they bore before moving to the Walton home are unknown to Rhodus and he never was able to trace his family even after "freedom."

The Walton plantation, home of Mr. Sam B. Walton who purchased his mother, was a very large one with the "Big House" on an elevation near the center. The majestic colonial home with its massive columns was seen for miles around and from its central location the master was able to view his entire estate.

Approximately one block from the planter's home, the "quarters" were clustered. These were numerous log-houses with stick-and-clay chimneys in which the slave families dwelt. Each house was composed of one room sparsely furnished. The beds were corded with rope and as large families were stressed, it was often necessary for several members to sleep on the floor. There was an open fireplace at which family meals were prepared. Equipment consisted of an iron pot suspended by a hanger and a skillet with long legs that enabled the cook to place fire beneath it. Bread known as "ash cake" was sometimes cooked on the hot coals.

The auction block was located not far from this old home. Here Rhodus Walton with other young children watched slaves emerge from boxcars, where they had been packed so closely that there was no room to sit, to be sold to the highest bidder. This was one of his most vivid recollections.

As Rhodus' father did not come to this home with his family, he knows nothing of him. Except for brief intervals his mother worked in the house where cotton and wool were spun into thread and then woven into cloth from which the slaves' clothing was made. An elder sister nursed the master's smaller children. Rhodus' first duties were to drive the cows to and from the pastures and to keep the calves from annoying the milkers.

His master was a very cruel man whose favorite form of punishment was to take a man (or woman) to the edge of the plantation where a rail fence was located. His head was then placed between two rails so that escape was impossible and he was whipped until the overseer was exhausted. This was an almost daily occurrence, administered on the slightest provocation.

Saturday was the only afternoon off and Christmas was the only vacation period, but one week of festivities made this season long remembered. Many "frolics" were given and everyone danced where banjoes were available; also, these resourceful people secured much of their music from an improvised fiddle fashioned from a hand saw. Immediately after these festivities, preparations began for spring planting. New ground was cleared; old land fertilized and the corn fields cleared of last year's rubbish.

Courtship began at a later age than is customary now but they were much more brief. Gifts to one's sweetheart were not permitted, but verses such as:

> Roses are red,
> Violets blue,
> I don't love
> No one but you

were invariably recited to the loved one. Young negro men always "cocked" their hats on one side of their heads when they became interested in the other sex. Marriages were performed by the master. Common law situations did not exist.

Serious illnesses were not frequent and home remedies compounded of roots and herbes usually sufficed. Queensy's light root, butterfly roots, scurry root, red shank root, bull tongue root were all found in the woods and the teas made from their use were "cures" for many ailments. Whenever an illness necessitated the services of a physician, he was called. One difference in the old family doctor and those of today was the method of treatment. The former always carried his medicine with him, the latter writes prescriptions. The fee was also much smaller in olden times.

Food was distributed weekly in quantities according to the size of the family. A single man would receive:

1 pk. meal	on Sunday
1 qt. syrup	flour (seconds)
3 ½ lbs. meat	Holidays—July 4th and Christmas fresh meat.

Peas, pepper grass, polk salad were plentiful in the fields. Milk and "pot likker" could be had from the big house when desired, although every family cooked for itself. Saturday afternoon was the general fishing time and each person might catch as many as he needed for his personal use.

The slaves did most of the weaving on the plantation, but after the cloth was woven the problem of giving it color presented itself. As they had no commercial dye, certain plants were boiled to give color. A plant called indigo, found in the cotton patch, was the chief type of dye, although thare was another called copperas. The dresses made from this material were very plain.

Walton believes in most of the old signs and superstitions because he has "watched them and found that they are true." The continuous singing of a whipporwill near a house is a sign of death, but if an iron is placed in the fire and allowed to remain there, the bird will fly away.

When the news of the war finally reached the plantation, the slaves followed the progress with keen interest and when battles were fought near Columbus, and firing of guns was heard, they cried joyfully—"It ain't gonna be long now." Two of their master's sons fought in the Confederate Army, but both returned home before the close of the war. One day news came that the Yankee soldiers were soon to come, and Walton began to hide all valuables. The slaves were sent to the cemetery to dig very deep graves where all manner of food was stored. They were covered like real graves and wooden slabs placed at either end. For three days before the soldiers were expected, all the house servants were kept busy preparing delicacies with which to tempt the Yankees and thus avoid having their place destroyed. In spite of all this preparation, they were caught unawares and when the "blue coats" were seen approaching, the master and his two sons ran. The elder made his way to the woods; the younger made away on "Black Eagle" a horse reputed to run almost a mile a minute. Nearly everything on the place was destroyed by these invaders. One bit of information has been given in every interview where Northern soldiers visited a plantation, they found, before coming, whether the Master was mean or kind and always treated him as he had treated his slaves. Thus Mr. Walton was "given the works" as our modern soldiers would say.

When the war ended the slaves were notified that they were free. Just before Rhodus' family prepared to move, his mother was struck on the head by a drunken guest visiting at the "big house." As soon as she regained consciousness, the family ran off without communicating with an elder sister who had been sold to a neighbor the previous year. A year later, news of this sister reached them through a wagoner who recognized the small boys as he passed them. He carried the news to the family's new residence back to the lost sister and in a few weeks she arrived at Cuthbert to make her home with her relatives.

For the past 9 years Rhodus has been unable to work as he is a victim of a stroke on his left side; both sides have been ruptured, and his nerves are bad. He attributes his long life to his faith in God.

[HW: Dist. 5
Ex-slave #111
(Ross)]

AN ACCOUNT Of SLAVERY RELATED BY WILLIAM WARD—EX-SLAVE
[Date Stamp: 10-8-1937]

WILLIAM WARD

In a small one-room apartment located on one of Atlanta's back streets lives William Ward, an ex-slave, whose physical appearance in no way justifies his claim to being 105 years of age. He is about five ft. in height with a rather smooth brown complexion. What hair he has is gray. He moves about like a much younger person. For a person of his age his thoughts and speech are remarkably clear.

On a bright sunny afternoon in September this writer had an opportunity of talking with Mr. Ward and in the course of the conversation some very interesting things were learned regarding the institution of slavery and its customs. Ward took a dip of snuff from his little tin box and began his story by saying that he is the son of Bill and Leana Ward who were brought to this country from Jamaica, B.W.I. The first thing he remembers was the falling of the stars in 1833. From that time until he was 9 years old he played around the yard with other slave children. Then his parents were sent back to Jamaica by their master, the former Governor Joseph E. Brown. While he was in bondage he carried the name of his masters instead of Ward, his parents' name.

From the age of 9 until he was old enough to do heavy work, he kept the master's yard clean.

Although Mr. Brown owned between 50 and 75 slaves, he had no plantation but hired his slaves out to other men who needed more help but were not able to own as many slaves as their work required.

Mr. Ward and his fellow slaves lived in one-room houses in the rear of the master's home. The furnishings consisted of a bed which was known as a "Grand Rascal" due to its peculiar construction. The mattress made in the form of a large bag was stuffed with hat and dried grass.

At daybreak each morning they were called from these crude beds to prepare for the day's work. Breakfast, which consisted of white bacon, corn bread, and imitation coffee, was served before they left for the scene of their day's work. Incidentally the slaves under Mr. Brown's ownership never had any other form of bread than corn bread.

This imitation coffee was made by putting corn meal in a pan, parching it until it reached a deep golden brown and steeping it in boiling water. At noon, dinner was brought to them in the field in wash tubs placed on carts drawn by oxen. Dinner consisted of fat meat, peas and corn bread. Often all laundry was done in these same tubs.

The only time that this diet ever varied was at Christmas time when the master had all slaves gathered in one large field. Then several hogs were killed and barbecued.

Everyone was permitted to eat as much as he could, but was forbidden to take anything home. When some one was fortunate enough to catch a possum or a coon, he had a change of food.

On Sundays the slaves were permitted to have a religious meeting of their own. This usually took place in the back yard or in a building dedicated for this purpose. They sang spirituals which gave vent to their true feelings. Many of these songs are sung today. There was one person who did the preaching. His sermon was always built according to the master's instructions which were that slaves must always remember that they belonged to their masters and were intended to lead a life of loyal servitude. None of the slaves believed this, although they pretended to believe because of the presence of the white overseer. If this overseer was absent sometimes and the preacher varied in the text of his sermon, that is, if he preached exactly what he thought and felt, he was given a sound whipping.

Mr. Brown was a kind person and never mistreated his slaves, although he did furnish them with the whip for infractions of rules such as fighting, stealing, visiting other plantations without a "pass", etc. Ward vividly recalls that one of the soundest thrashings he ever got was for stealing Mr. Brown's whisky. His most numerous offenses were fighting. Another form of punishment used in those days was the stocks, such as those used in early times in England. Serious offenses like killing another person was also handled by the master who might hang him to a tree by the feet or by the neck, as he saw fit.

Few slaves ever attempted to escape from Mr. Brown, partially because of his kindliness and partically because of the fear inspired by the pack of blood hounds which he kept. When an escaped slave was caught he was returned to his master and a sound beating was administered.

As far as marriage was concerned on the Brown estate, Mr. Brown, himself placed every two individuals together that he saw fit to. There was no other wedding ceremony. If any children were born from the union, Mr. Brown named them. One peculiarity on the Brown estate was the fact that the slaves were allowed no preference or choice as to who his or her mate would be. Another peculiarity was these married couples were not permitted to sleep together except when the husband received permission to spend the night with his wife. Ward is the father of 17 children whose whereabouts he does not know.

At this point Ward began to smile, and when he was asked the cause of his mirth, he replied that he was thinking about his fellow slaves beliefs in conjuring one another. This was done by putting some sort of wild berries in the person's food. What he can't understand is why some of this black magic was not tried on the white people since they were holding the Negroes as slaves.

Ward recalls vividly Sherman's march through Georgia. When Sherman reached the present site of Hapeville, he bombarded Atlanta with cannon, afterwards marching through and burning the city. The white residents made all sorts of frantic attempts to hide their money and other valuables. Some hiding places were under stumps of trees and in sides of hills. Incidentally Sherman's army found quite a bit of the hidden wealth. Slaves were never allowed to talk over events and so very few, if any, knew about the war or its results for them before it actually happened. At the time that Sherman marched through Atlanta, Ward and other slaves were living in an old mansion at the present site of Peachtree and Baker Streets. He says that Sherman took him and his fellow slaves as far as Virginia to carry powder and shot to the soldiers. He states that he himself did not know whether Sherman intended to keep him in slavery or free him. At the close of the war, his master, Mr. Brown, became ill and died later. Before His death he informed the slaves that they could remain on his property or go where they wanted to. Ward was taken to Mississippi where he remained in another form of slavery (Peonage System) for 40 years. He remembers when Atlanta was just a few hills without any buildings. Some of the buildings he worked on are the Herman Building and the original Kimball House, a picture of which is attached.

He attributes his old age to his belief in God and living a sane life. Whenever he feels bad or in low spirits, a drink of coffee or a small amount of whisky is enough to brace him. He believes that his remedy is better than that used in slavery which consisted mainly of pills and castor oil.

With a cheerful good-bye, Ward asked that the writer stop in to see him again; said that he would rather live in the present age under existing conditions than live in slavery.

United States. Work Projects Administration

Driskell
JWL 10-12-37

[MR. WILLIAM WARD]

WILLIAM WARD

Following is Mr. William Ward's description of the bed called "The Grand Rascal."

"De beds dat all o' de slaves slept in wus called 'Grand Rascals'. Dey wus made on de same order as a box. De way dey made 'em wus like dis: dey took four strips of narrow wood, each one of 'em 'bout a foot wide, an' den dey nailed 'em together so dat dey wus in de shape of a square. Den dey nailed a bottom onto dis square shape. Dis bottom wus called de slats. When dis wus finished dey set dis box on some legs to keep it off'n de floor, an' den dey got busy wid de mattress. Dey took ol' oat sacks an' filled 'em wid straw an' hay an' den dey put dis in de box an' slept on it. Dere wusn't no springs on dese bunks an' everybody had a hard time sleepin'.

"De real name of dese wus 'Sonova-Bitches' but de slaves called 'em 'Grand Rascals' 'cause dey didn't want people to hear 'em use a bad word.

"After Sherman come through Atlanta he let de slaves go, an' when he did, me an' some of de other slaves went back to our ol' masters. Ol' man Gov. Brown wus my boss man. After de war wus over Ol' man Gordon took me an' some of de others out to Mississippi. I stayed in peonage out dere fer 'bout forty years. I wus located at jes' 'bout forty miles south of Greenwood, an' I worked on de plantations of Ol' man Sara Jones an' Ol' man Gordon.

"I couldn't git away 'cause dey watched us wid guns all de time. When de levee busted dat kinda freed me. Man, dey was devils; dey wouldn't 'low you to go nowhere—not even to church. You done good to git sumpin' to eat. Dey wouldn't give you no clothes, an' if you got wet you jes' had to lay down in whut you got wet in.

"An', man, dey would whup you in spite of de devil. You had to ask to git water—if you didn't dey would stretch you 'cross a barrel an' wear you out. If you didn't work in a hurry dey would whup you wid a strap dat had five-six holes in it. I ain't talkin' 'bout whut I heard—I'm talkin' 'bout whut I done see'd.

"One time dey sent me on Ol' man Mack Williams' farm here in Jasper County, Georgia. Dat man would kill you sho. If dat little branch on his plantation could talk it would tell many a tale 'bout folks bein' knocked in de head. I done seen Mack Williams kill folks an' I done seen 'im have folks killed. One day he tol' me dat if my wife had been good lookin', I never would sleep wid her again 'cause he'd kill me an' take her an' raise chilluns off'n her. Dey uster take women away fum dere husbands an' put wid some other man to breed jes' like dey would do cattle. Dey always kept a man penned up an' dey used 'im like a stud hoss.

"When you didn't do right Ol' Mack Williams would shoot you or tie a chain 'roun your neck an' throw you in de river. He'd git dem other niggers to carry dem to de river an' if dey didn't he'd shoot 'em down. Any time dey didn't do whut he said he would shoot 'em down. He'd tell 'em to "Ketch dat nigger", an' dey would do it. Den he would tell 'em to put de chain 'roun dere neck an' throw 'em in de river. I ain't heard dis—I done seen it.

"In 1927 I wus still in peonage but I wus back in Mississippi on Gordon's farm. When de levee broke in May of dat same year I lost my wife an' three chilluns. I climbed a tree an' stayed dere fer four days an' four nights. Airplanes dropped food an' when I got ready to eat I had to squeeze de water out of de bread. After four days I got out of de tree an' floated on logs down de river 'till I got to Mobile, Alabama, an' I wade fum dere to Palmetto, Georgia, where I got down sick. De boss mans dere called Gov. Harden an' he sent de Grady Hospital examiners down dere an' got me an' I been in Atlanta since dat time."

United States. Work Projects Administration

Willie H. Cole
10-8-37

THE STORY OF AN EX-SLAVE
[MRS. LULA WASHINGTON, Age 84]

LULA WASHINGTON

Mrs. Lula Washington was born a slave. She claims to be eighty-four years old.

Mrs. Washington was confined to bed because of a recent accident in which she received a broken leg.

She is the mother of twenty-three children of which only two are living. She lives in one room at 64 Butler St., N.E. with one of her daughters. Since the death of her husband several years ago she has been making her living as a dray-women, driving a mule and wagon.

Following are some of the events she remembers. "Ah wuz born in Randolph, Alabama on de plantation of Marster John Terrell, de sixth child of my mammy and pappy".

"When ah wuz six years old marster John sold me an' my sister, Lize and brother, Ben to Marster Charlie Henson."

"Marster Charlie wuz good to his niggers.

"He never whipped dem 'less dey done somethin'

awful bad, like stealin chickens or slipping off de plantation without permission."

"It wuz funny, de white folks would whipped de niggers for stealin' but if dey saw a hog in de woods, dey would make the niggers catch de hog an kill him an hide him under dey bushes. Den at night de niggers would hafta' go down to de spring, build a fire, heat water an skin de hog."

"De man on de plantation next to us' shore wuz mean to his niggers, Marster Jim Roberts wus his name. He would take his niggers an strip there clothes to dere waist an' lay dem 'cross a barrel an beat dem 'til the blood run. Den he would pore salt water on de sore places."

"Oh 'member one time he tied two wimmen by dere thumbs to a limb of a tree for blessin' out the missus."

"Us had plenty to eat and plenty to wear, calico dresses an' brogan shoes. Sometimes dere misses would give the wimmen some of her old clothes".

"All de niggers on Marster Charlie's plantation had to work in de field 'cept Malindy Lu, a Mulatto nigger gal. Marster Charlie kept her in de house to take care of Missus Jane, dat wuz Marster Charlie wife."

"One thing 'bout de mulatto niggers, wuz, dey thought dey wuz better than de black niggers. I guess it wuz 'cause dey was half white. Dere wuz a bad feelin' 'tween the mulatto slaves an de black ones."

Asked, how did the slaves marry? She replied, "Ah jest don't 'member seeing any marry 'cause ah wuz so small. Ah wuz jest eleven years old de time of de war but ah' members hearing some of dem say dat when two slaves wanted to git married dey would hafta get permission from dere marster. Den dey would come 'fore de marster an' he would have dem to jump over a broom an den 'nounce dem married."

"When de Yankees come thru" de white folks told us to go down to de swamp an hide cause dey would git us. When de war wuz over de white folks told us we wuz free."

"Marster Terrell gave my mammy an pappy a oxcart an mule an a bushel of meal. Den my pappy an mammy come got me an my sister an' brother. Den we come from Randolph, Alabama to Georgia."

"Sometimes I wish I wuz back in slavery, times is so hard."

Mrs. Washington's chief concern now is getting her old-age pension.

United States. Work Projects Administration

Slave Narratives

PLANTATION LIFE AS VIEWED BY AN EX-SLAVE

GREEN WILLBANKS, Age 77
347 Fairview Street
Athens, Georgia

Written by:
Mrs. Sadie B. Hornsby
Athens

Edited by:
Mrs. Sarah H. Hall
Athens

and

John N. Booth
District Supervisor
Federal Writers' Project
Residencies 6 & 7
Augusta, Georgia

Sept. 19, 1938

GREEN WILLBANKS

Fairview Street, where Green Willbanks lives is a section of shabby cottages encircled by privet hedges.

As the visitor carefully ascended the shaky steps to his house a mulatto man, who was sitting on the veranda, quickly arose. "Good morning," he said, "Yes mam, this is Green Willbanks. Have a seat in the swing." The porch furniture was comprised of a chair, a swing, and a long bench. Green is tall, slender, and stooped; a man with white hair and grizzled face. A white broadcloth shirt, white cotton trousers, blue socks, and low-cut black shoes made up his far from immaculate costume.

The old man's eyes brightened when he was asked to give the story of his life. His speech showed but little dialect, except when he was carried away by interest and emotion, and his enunciation was remarkably free from Negroid accent.

"I don't mind telling you what I know," he began, "but I was such a little chap when the war ended that there's mighty little I can recollect about slavery time, and it seems that your chief interest is in that period. I was born on a plantation the other side of Commerce, Georgia, in Jackson County. My Ma and Pa were Mary and Isom Willbanks; they were raised on the same plantation where I was born. Ma was a field hand, and this time of the year when work was short in the field—laying-by time, we called it—and on rainy days she spun thread and wove cloth. As the thread left the spinning wheel it went on a reel where it was wound into hanks, and then it was carried to the loom to be woven into cloth. Pa had a little trade; he made shoes and baskets, and Old Boss let him sell them. Pa didn't make shoes for the slaves on our plantation; Old Boss bought them ready-made and had them shipped here from the West.

"Me and Jane, Sarah, Mitchell, and Willie were the five children in our family. Oh! Miss, I was not big enough to do much work. About the most I done was pick up chips and take my little tin bucket to the spring to get a cool, fresh drink for Old Miss. Us children stayed 'round the kitchen and drunk lots of buttermilk. Old Miss used to say, 'Give my pickaninnies plenty of buttermilk.' I can see that old churn now; it helt about seven or eight gallons.

"Our houses? Slaves lived in log cabins built the common way. There was lots of forest pine in those days. Logs were cut the desired length and notches put in each end so they would fit closely and have as few cracks as possible, when they stacked them for a cabin. They sawed pine logs into blocks and used a frow to split them into planks that were used to cover the cracks between the logs. Don't you know what a frow is? That's a wooden wedge that you drive into a pine block by hitting it with a heavy wooden mallet, or maul, as they are more commonly called. They closed the cracks in some of the cabins by daubing them with red mud. The old stack chimneys were made of mud and sticks. To make a bed, they first cut four posts, usually of pine, and bored holes through them with augers; then they made two short pieces for the head and foot. Two long pieces for the sides were stuck through the auger holes and the bedstead was ready to lay on the slats or cross pieces to hold up the mattress. The best beds had heavy cords, wove crossways and lengthways, instead of slats. Very few slaves had corded beds. Mattresses were not much; they were made of suggin sacks filled with straw. They called that straw 'Georgia feathers.' Pillows were made of the same things. Suggin cloth was made of coarse flax wove in a loom. They separated the flax into two grades; fine for the white folks, and coarse for the Negroes.

"The only one of my grandparents I can bring to memory now is Grandma Rose on my Pa's side. She was some worker, a regular man-woman; she could do any kind of work a man could do. She was a hot horse in her time and it took an extra good man to keep up with her when it came to work.

"Children were not allowed to do much work, because their masters desired them to have the chance to grow big and strong, and therefore they had few opportunities to earn money of their own. I never did own any money during slavery days, but I saw plenty of ten cent greenbacks (shinplasters).

"White children and slave children played around the plantation together but they were not allowed to fight. They had to be on friendly terms with each other.

"What about our food? The biggest thing we had was buttermilk, some sweet milk, and plenty of cornbread, hog meat, and peas. As a rule we had wheat bread once a week, usually on Sunday. All kinds of fruits were plentiful in their seasons. Each slave family was permitted to have separate garden space, in fact, Old Boss insisted that they work their own gardens, and they raised plenty of vegetables. Grown folks had rabbits and 'possums but I never did get much 'quainted with them. We fished in the cricks and rills 'round the plantation and brought in lots of hornyheads and perch. You never saw any hornyheads? Why they is just fish a little bigger and longer than minnows and they have little horns on their heads. We caught a good many eels too; they look like snakes, but folks call them eels. I wasn't much 'quainted with them fish they brought from way down South; they called them mullets.

"The kitchen was a separate log house out in the back yard. The fireplace, where the cooking was done, took up one end of the kitchen, and there was a rack acrost it to hang the cook-pots on for biling. Baking and frying was done in ovens and heavy iron skillets that sat on trivets so coals could be piled underneath, as well as over the lids.

"The long shirts slave boys wore in summer were straight like a meal sack open at both ends, with holes in the sides for your arms to go through. You stuck your head in one end and it came out the other; then you were fully dressed for any whole summer day. These summer shirts were made of thin osnaburg. Our winter clothes were made of woolen cloth called merino. Old Boss kept enough sheep to provide plenty of wool and some mighty good food. Slave children had no extra or special clothes for Sunday; they wore the same kind of gowns, or long shirts, seven days a week. Old Boss provided brass-toed brogans for winter, but we never thought of such a thing as shoes to wear in hot weather.

"My owners were Marse Solomon and his wife, Miss Ann Willbanks. We called them Old Boss and Old Miss. As I saw it, they were just as good as they could be. Old Boss never allowed nobody to impose on his slave children. When I was a little chap playing around the big house, I would often drop off to sleep the minute I got still. Good Old Boss would pick me up and go lay me on his own bed and keep me there 'til Ma come in from the field.

"Old Boss and Old Miss had five children. The boys were Solomon, Isaac, James, and Wesley. For the life of me I can't bring to memory the name of their only daughter. I guess that's because we frolicked with the four boys, but we were not allowed to play with Little Miss.

"It was a right decent house they lived in, a log house with a fine rock chimney. Old Boss was building a nice house when the war come on and he never had a chance to finish it. The log house was in a cedar grove; that was the style then. Back of the house were his orchards where fruit trees of every kind we knew anything about provided plenty for all to eat in season as well as enough for good preserves, pickles, and the like for winter. Old Boss done his own overseeing and, 'cording to my memory, one of the young bosses done the driving.

"That plantation covered a large space of land, but to tell you how many acres is something I can't do. There were not so many slaves. I've forgot how they managed that business of getting slaves up, but I do know we didn't get up before day on our place. Their rule was to work slaves from sunup to sundown. Before they had supper they had a little piddlin' around to do, but the time was their own to do as they pleased after they had supper. Heaps of times they got passes and went off to neighboring plantations to visit and dance, but sometimes they went to hold prayer-meetings. There were certain plantations where we were not permitted to go and certain folks were never allowed on our place. Old Boss was particular about how folks behaved on his place; all his slaves had to come up to a certain notch and if they didn't do that he punished them in some way or other. There was no whipping done, for Old Boss never did believe in whipping slaves.

"None of the slaves from our place was ever put in that county jail at Jefferson. That was the only jail we ever heard of in those days. Old Boss attended to all the correction necessary to keep order among his own slaves. Once a slave trader came by the place and offered to buy Ma. Old Boss took her to Jefferson to sell her on the block to that man. It seemed like sales of slaves were not legal unless they took place on the trading block in certain places, usually in the county site. The trader wouldn't pay what Old Boss asked for her, and Old Miss and the young bosses all objected strong to his selling her, so he brought Ma back home. She was a fine healthy woman and would have made a nice looking house girl.

"The biggest part of the teaching done among the slaves was by our young bosses but, as far as schools for slaves was concerned, there were no such things until after the end of the war, and then we were no longer slaves. There were just a few separate churches for slaves; none in our part of the country. Slaves went to the same church as their white folks and sat in the back of the house or in a gallery. My Pa could read the Bible in his own way, even in that time of slavery; no other slave on our place could do that.

"Not one slave or white person either died on our plantation during the part of slavery that I can bring to memory. I was too busy playing to take in any of the singing at funerals and at church, and I never went to a baptizing until I was a great big chap, long after slavery days were over.

"Slaves ran off to the woods all right, but I never heard of them running off to no North. Paterollers never came on Old Boss' place unless he sont for them, otherwise they knowed to stay off. They sho was devils in sheeps' clothing; that's what we thought of them paterollers. Slaves worked all day Saddays when there was work to be done, but that night was their free time. They went where they pleased just so Old Boss gave them a pass to protect them from paterollers.

"After slaves went to church Sunday they were free the rest of the day as far as they knowed. Lots of times they got 'em a stump speaker—usually a Negro—to preach to them. There were not as many preachers then as now.

"'Bout Christmas Day? They always had something like brandy, cider, or whiskey to stimulate the slaves on Christmas Day. Then there was fresh meat and ash-roasted sweet 'taters, but no cake for slaves on our place, anyhow, I never saw no cake, and surely no Santa Claus. All we knowed bout Christmas was eating and drinking. As a general thing there was a big day's work expected on New Years Day because we had to start the year off right, even if there was nothing for the slaves to do that day but clean fence corners, cut brush and briers, and burn off new ground. New Years Day ended up with a big old pot of hog jowl and peas. That was for luck, but I never really knowed if it brought luck or not.

"Well, yes, once a year they had big cornshuckings in our section and they had generals to lead off in all the singing; that was done to whoop up the work. My Pa was one of the generals and he toted the jug of liquor that was passed 'round to make his crowd hustle. After the corn was shucked the crowd divided into two groups. Their object was to see which could reach the owner of the corn first and carry him where he wanted to go. Usually they marched with him on their shoulders to his big house and set him down on his porch, then he would give the word for them to all start eating the good things spread out on tables in the yard. There was a heap of drinking done then, and dancing too—just all kinds of dancing that could be done to fiddle and banjo music. My Pa was one of them fiddlers in his young days. One of the dances was the cotillion, but just anybody couldn't dance that one. There was a heap of bowing and scraping to it, and if you were not 'quainted with it you just couldn't use it.

"When any of the slaves were bad sick Old Boss called in his own family doctor, Dr. Joe Bradbury. His plantation hit up against ours. The main things they gave for medicine them days was oil and turpentine. Sometimes folks got black snakeroot from the woods, biled it, and gave the tea to sick folks; that was to clean off the stomach. Everybody wore buckeyes 'round their necks to keep off diseases for we never knowed nothing about asefetida them days; that came later.

"When the Yankees came through after the surrender Old Boss and Old Miss hid their valuables. They told us children, 'Now, if they ask you questions, don't you tell them where we hid a thing.' We knowed enough to keep our mouths shut. We never had knowed nothing but to mind Old Boss, and we were scared 'cause our white folks seemed to fear the Yankees.

"Old Boss had done told slaves they were free as he was and could go their own way, but we stayed on with him. He provided for Pa and give him his share of the crops he made. All of us growed up as field hands.

"Them night-riders were something else. They sho did beat on Negroes that didn't behave mighty careful. Slaves didn't buy much land for a long time after the war because they didn't have no money, but schools were set up for Negroes very soon. I got the biggest part of my education in West Athens on Biggers Hill. When I went to the Union Baptist School my teacher was Professor Lyons, the founder of that institution.

"When me and Molly Tate were married 50 years ago we went to the church, because that was the cheapest place to go to have a big gathering. Molly had on a common, ordinary dress. Folks didn't dress up then like they does now; it was quite indifferent. Of our 10 children, 8 are living now and we have 14 grandchildren. Six of our children live in the North and two have remained here in Athens. One of them is employed at Bernstein's Funeral Home and the other works on the university campus. I thanks the Lord that Molly is still with me. We bought this place a long time ago and have farmed here ever since. In fact, I have never done nothing but farm work. Now I'm too old and don't have strength to work no more.

"I thinks Abraham Lincoln was a all right man; God so intended that we should be sot free. Jeff Davis was all right in his way, but I can't say much for him. Yes mam, I'd rather be free. Sho! Give me freedom all the time. Jesus said: 'If my Son sets you free, you shall be free indeed.'

"When I jined the church, I felt like I was rid of my burden. I sot aside the things I had been doing and I ain't never been back to pick 'em up no more. I jined the Baptist church and have been teaching a class of boys every Sunday that I'm able to go. I sho am free from sin and I lives up to it.

"I wonder if Molly's got them sweet 'taters cooked what I dug this morning. They warn't much 'count 'cause the sun has baked them hard and it's been so dry. If you is through with me, I wants to go eat one of them 'taters and then lay this old Nigger on the bed and let him go to sleep."

United States. Work Projects Administration

[HW: Dist 5]
Josephine Lowell

[HW: ELIZA WILLIAMSON]

[TR: This interview contained many handwritten edits; where text was transposed or meaning was significantly changed, it has been noted.]

ELIZA WILLIAMSON

Just a few recollections of life in slavery time, as told me by [TR: illegible] who was Eliza Taliaferro Williamson, daughter of Dickerson and Polly Taliaferro. My mother was born at Mt. Airy, North Carolina, near the Virginia line, and always went to school, across the line, in Virginia. Her grandfather was John Taliaferro, slave holder, tobacco raiser, and farmer. The Negro quarters were near the main or Big House. Mother said that great-grandfather would go to the back door each night and call every slave to come in for family prayer. They came and knelt in the Big House, while old marster prayed. Mother said it was like a camp-meeting when he died—wailing and weeping by the Negroes for their old Marster. She said the slaves had the same food that the white family had and the same warm clothes for winter. All clothing, bed sheeting, table linen, towels, etc. were hand woven. They raised sheep for wool, and flax for linen, but I don't know where they got the cotton they used. The work of the house and farm was divided as with a big family. Some of the women cooked, sewed, wove, washed, milked, but was never sent to the field.

None of the Toliver family believed in women working in the field. When each of great-grandfather's children married, he or she was given a few slaves. I think he gave my grandfather, Dickerson Taliaferro, three slaves, and these he brought with him to Georgia when they settled in Whitfield County.

My grandfather was a member of the Legislature from Whitfield County for two terms. He was as gentle with his slaves as a father would have been, and was never known to abuse one of them. One of his slaves, who was a small boy at the close of the War, stayed with my grandfather until he was a grown man, then after a few years away from home, came home to old Marster to die. This is the picture of good slave holders, but sad to say all were not of that type. [TR: deleted: 'See next sheet for'] a picture of horror, which was also told me by my mother. [TR: deleted: 'The thought of it'] was like a nightmare to my childish mind.

The Story of little Joe.

[TR: deleted: 'Mother said there were'] two families lived on farms adjacent to her father. They were the two Tucker brothers, tobacco raisers. One of the wives, Polly, or Pol, as she was called, hated the family of her husband's brother because they were more affluent than she liked them to be. It [HW: Her jealousy] caused the two families to live in disagreement.

Little Joe belonged to Pol's family, and was somewhere between ten and fourteen years old. Mother said Pol made Joe work in the field at night, and forced him to sing so they would know he wasn't asleep. He wore nothing in summer but an old shirt made of rough factory cloth which came below his knees. She said the only food Pol would give him was swill [HW: scraps] from the table—handed to him out the back door. Mother said Pol had some kind of impediment in her speech, which caused her to say 'ah' at the close of a sentence. So, when she called Joe to the back door to give him his mess of scraps, she would say, "Here, Joe, here's your truck, ah." Mother was a little girl then, and she and grandmother felt so sorry for Joe that they would bake baskets of sweet potatoes and slip [TR: 'to the field to give him' replaced with illegible text ending 'in the field']. She said he would come through the corn, almost crawling, so Pol wouldn't see him, and take the sweet potatoes in the tail of his shirt and scuttle back through the tall stuff where he might hide and eat it them.

She had a Negro woman who had a baby (and there may have been other women) but this Negro woman was not allowed to see her baby except just as a cow would be let in to her calf at certain times during the day, [TR: 'then' replaced by ??] she had to go to the field and leave it alone. Mother said that Pol either threw or kicked the baby into the yard because it cried, and it died. I don't know why the authorities didn't arrest her, but she may have had an alibi, or some excuse for the death of the child.

The Burning of the Tobacco Barn

The [HW: other] Tucker brother had made a fine crop of tobacco that year, more than a thousand dollars worth in his big barn. Pol made one of her slaves go with her, [HW: when] and she set fire to the tobacco barn of her brother-in-law's barn, and not being able to get away [HW: unable to escape] before the flames [HW: brought] a crowd, she hid in the grass, right near the path where the people were running to the fire. She had some kind of stroke, perhaps from fright, or pure deviltry which 'put her out of business'. I wish I could remember whether it killed her or just made a paralytic of her, but this is a true story.

PLANTATION LIFE AS VIEWED BY AN EX-SLAVE

FRANCES WILLINGHAM, Age 78
288 Bridge Street
Athens, Georgia

Written by:
Sadie B. Hornsby
Athens

Edited by:
Sarah H. Hall
Athens

Leila Harris
Augusta

and

John N. Booth
District Supervisor
Federal Writers' Project
Residencies 6 & 7

FRANCES WILLINGHAM

The interviewer arrived at Frances Willingham's address on a sultry July morning, and found a fat and very black Negress sweeping the sidewalk before the three-room frame house. There was no front yard and the front steps led up from the sidewalk into the house. A vegetable garden was visible at the rear of the lot. The plump sweeper appeared to be about five feet tall. Her wooly white hair was plaited in tiny braids, and she wore a brown print dress trimmed in red and blue. A strand of red beads encircled her short neck, and a blue checked coat and high topped black shoes completed her costume. Asked if Frances Willingham was at home, the woman replied: "Dis is her you is a-talkin' to. Come right in and have a seat."

When Frances was asked for the story of her life, her daughter who had doubtless been eavesdropping, suddenly appeared and interrupted the conversation with, "Ma, now don't you git started 'bout dem old times. You knows your mind ain't no good no more. Tomorrow your tongue will be runnin' lak a bell clapper a-talkin' to yourself." "Shut your big mouth, Henrietta." Frances answered. "I been sick, and I knows it, but dere ain't nothin' wrong wid my mind and you knows it. What I knows I'se gwine to tell de lady, and what I don't know I sho' ain't gwine tell no lie about. Now, Missus, what does you want to know? Don't pay no 'tention to dis fool gal of mine 'cause her mouth is big as dis room.

"I was born way off down in Twiggs County 'bout a mile from de town of Jeffersonville. My Pa and Ma was Otto and Sarah Rutherford. Our Mist'ess, dat was Miss Polly, she called Ma, Sallie for short. Dere was nine of us chillun, me and Esau, Harry, Jerry, Bob, Calvin, Otto, Sallie and Susan. Susan was our half-sister by our Pa's last marriage. Us chillun never done much but play 'round de house and yards wid de white chillun. I warn't but four years old when dey made us free." Henrietta again interrupted, "See dere, I told you she don't know what she's a-talkin' 'bout."

Frances ignored the interruption and continued: "Us lived in log cabins what had jus' one room wid a stick and mud chimbly at de end. Our bedsteads was made out of rough planks and poles and some of 'em was nailed to de sides of de cabins. Mattress ticks was made out of osnaburg and us filled 'em wid wheat straw in season. When dat was used up us got grass from de fields. Most any kind of hay was counted good 'nough to put in a slave's mattress. Dey let us mix some cotton wid de hay our pillows was stuffed wid.

"My grandmas lived on another plantation. I 'members once Grandma Suck, she wes my Ma's mammy, come to our house and stayed one or two days wid us. Daddy's Ma was named Puss. Both my grandmas was field hands, but Ma, she was a house gal 'til she got big enough to do de cyardin' and spinnin'. Aunt Phoebie done de weavin' and Aunt Polly was de seamster. All de lak of dat was done atter de craps was done laid by.

"No Ma'am, nobody never give slave chillun no money in dem times. I never had none 'til atter us had done been give our freedom. I used to see Old Marster countin' of it, but de slaves never did git none of dat money.

"Our Old Marster was a pow'ful rich man, and he sho' b'lieved in givin' us plenty to eat. It warn't nothin' fine, but it was good plain eatin' what filled you up and kept you well. Dere was cornbread and meat, greens of all sorts, 'taters, roas'en-ears and more other kinds of veg'tables dan I could call up all day. Marster had one big old gyarden whar he kept most evvything a-growin' 'cept cabbages and 'matoes. He said dem things warn't fittin' for nobody to eat. Marster let Daddy go huntin' enough to fetch in lots of 'possums, coons, rabbits, and squirrels. Us cooked 'em 'bout lak us does now, only us never had no stoves den, and had to do all de cookin' in open fireplaces in big old pots and long handled skillets what had big old heavy lids. I'se seed Ma clean many a 'possum in hot ashes. Den she scalded him and tuk out his innards. She par-boiled and den baked him and when she fetched him to de table wid a heap of sweet 'taters 'round him on de dish, dat was sho' somepin good to eat. Daddy done his fishin' in Muddy Crick 'cause slaves wern't 'lowed to leave de plantation for nothin' lak dat.

"Summertimes us wore homespun dresses, made wid full skirts sewed on to tight fittin' waisties what was fastened down de back wid buttons made out of cows and rams horns. Our white petticoat slips and pantalettes was made on bodices. In winter us wore balmorals what had three stripes 'round de bottom, and over dem us had on long sleeved ap'ons what was long as de balmorals. Slave gals' pantalettes warn't ruffled and tucked and trimmed up wid lace and 'broidery lak Miss Polly's chilluns' was. Ours was jus' made plain. Grown folks wore rough brogans, but me, I wore de shoes what Miss Polly's chillun had done outgrowed. Dey called 'em Jackson shoes, 'cause dey was made wid a extra wide piece of leather sewed on de outside so as when you knocked your ankles 'gainst one another, it wouldn't wear no holes in your shoes. Our Sunday shoes warn't no diffunt from what us wore evvyday.

[TR: HW sidenote: 'durable', regarding Jackson Shoes]

"Marse Lish Jones and his wife—she was Miss Polly—was our Marster and Mist'ess. Dey sho' did love to be good to deir little Niggers. Dey had five chillun of deir own, two gals and three boys. Dey was: Mary, Anna Della, Steve, John, and Bob. 'Bout deir house! Oh, Missus, dat was somepin to see for sho'. It was a big old fine two-story frame house wid a porch 'cross de front and 'round both sides. Dere was five rooms on de fust floor and three upstairs. It sho' did look grand a-settin' back dar in dat big old oak grove.

"Old Marster had a overseer but he never had no car'iage driver 'cause he loved to drive for hisself so good. Oh Lord! How big was dat plantation? Why, it must have been as big as from here to town. I never did know how many slaves Marster had, but dat old plantation was plumb full of 'em. I ain't never seed Old Marster do nothin' 'cept drive his car'iage, walk a little, and eat all he wanted to. He was a rich man, and didn't have to do nothin'.

"Our overseer got all de slaves up 'fore break of day and dey had to be done et deir breakfast and in de field when de sun riz up. Dat sun would be down good 'fore dey got to de house at night. I never seed none of de grown folks git whupped, but I sho' got a good beatin' myself one time. I had done got up on top of de big house porch and was a-flappin' my arms and crowin' lak a rooster. Dey told me to come on down, but I wouldn't mind nobody and kept on a-crowin' and a-flappin', so dey whupped me down.

"Dey had jails in Jeffersonville, but dem jails was for white folks what didn't be-have deirselfs. Old Marster, de overseer, and de patterollers kept de slaves straight. Dey didn't need no jails for dem.

"I ain't never been to school a day in my life, 'cause when I was little, Niggers warn't 'lowed to larn to read and write. I heared Ma say de colored preacher read out of de Bible, but I never seed him do it, 'cause I never went to church none when I was a chap. Colored folks had deir own church in a out settlement called John De Baptist.

Dat's whar all de slaves went to meetin'. Chilluns was 'lowed to go to baptizin's. Evvybody went to 'em. Dey tuk dem converts to a hole in de crick what dey had got ready for dat purpose. De preacher went fust, and den he called for de converts to come on in and have deir sins washed away.

"Our Marster sot aside a piece of ground 'long side of his own place for his Niggers to have a graveyard. Us didn't know nothin' 'bout no fun'rals. When one of de slaves died, dey was put in unpainted home-made coffins and tuk to de graveyard whar de grave had done been dug. Dey put 'em in dar and kivvered 'em up and dat was all dey done 'bout it.

"Us heared a plenty 'bout patterollers beatin' up Niggers what dey cotched off deir Marsters' plantations widout no passes. Sometimes dey cotched one of our Marster's slaves and sometimes dey didn't, but dey was all time on deir job.

"When slaves come in from de fields at night de 'omans cleant up deir houses atter dey et, and den washed and got up early next mornin' to put de clothes out to dry. Mens would eat, set 'round talkin' to other mens and den go to bed. On our place evvybody wukked on Saddays 'til 'bout three or four o'clock and if de wuk was tight dey wukked right on 'til night lak any other day. Sadday nights de young folks got together to have deir fun. Dey danced, frolicked, drunk likker, and de lak of dat. Old Marster warn't too hard on 'em no time, but he jus' let 'em have dat night to frolic. On Sunday he give dem what wanted 'em passes to go to church and visit 'round.

"Christmas times, chilluns went to bed early 'cause

dey was skeered Santa Claus wouldn't come. Us carried our stockin's up to de big house to hang 'em up. Next mornin' us found 'em full of all sorts of good things, 'cept oranges. I never seed nary a orange 'til I was a big gal. Miss Polly had fresh meat, cake, syrup puddin' and plenty of good sweet butter what she 'lowanced out to her slaves at Christmas. Old Marster, he made syrup by de barrel. Plenty of apples and nuts and groundpeas was raised right dar on de plantation. In de Christmas, de only wuk slaves done was jus' piddlin' 'round de house and yards, cuttin' wood, rakin' leaves, lookin' atter de stock, waitin' on de white folks and little chores lak dat. Hard work started again on de day atter New Year's Day. Old Marster 'lowed 'em mighty little rest from den 'til atter de craps was laid by.

"Course Marster let his slaves have cornshuckin's, cornshellin's, cotton pickin's, and quiltin's. He had grove atter grove of pecan, chestnut, walnut, hickor'nut, scalybark, and chinquapin trees. When de nuts was all gathered, Old Marster sold 'em to de big men in de city. Dat was why he was so rich. Atter all dese things was gathered and tended to, he give his slaves a big feast and plenty to drink, and den he let 'em rest up a few days 'fore dey started back to hard wuk.

"I never seed but one marriage on Old Marster's plantation, and I never will forgit dat day. Miss Polly had done gimme one of little Miss Mary's sho' 'nough pretty dresses and I wore it to dat weddin', only dey never had no real weddin'. Dey was jus' married in de yard by de colored preacher and dat was all dere was to it.

"Ma used to tell us if us didn't be-have Raw Head and Bloody Bones would come git us and take us off. I tried to see him but I never did. Grown folks was all time skeerin' chillun. Then us went to bed at night, us used to see ghosties, what looked lak goats tryin' to butt us down. Ma said I evermore used to holler out in my sleep 'bout dem things I was so skeered of.

[HW sidenote: Home remedies]

"White folks was mighty good and kind when deir slaves got sick. Old Marster sont for Dr. 'Pree (DuPree) and when he couldn't git him, he got Dr. Brown. He made us swallow bitter tastin' powders what he had done mixed up in water. Miss Polly made us drink tea made out of Jerusalem oak weeds. She biled dem weeds and sweetened de tea wid syrup. Dat was good for stomach trouble, and us wore elder roots strung 'round our necks to keep off ailments.

"Mercy me! I'se seed plenty of dem yankees a-gwine and comin'. Dey come to our Marster's house and stole his good mules. Dey tuk what dey wanted of his meat, chickens, lard and syrup and den poured de rest of de syrup out on de ground. Atter de war was over Niggers got so rowdy dem Ku Kluxers come 'long to make 'em be-have deirselfs.' Dem Niggers and Kluxers too jus' went hog wild.

"What did Niggers have to buy no land wid, when dey never had no money paid 'em for nothin' 'til atter dey was free? Us jus' stayed on and wukked for Old Marster, 'cause dere warn't no need to leave and go to no other place. I was raised up for a field hand, and I ain't never wukked in no white folks house.

"Me I'se sho' glad Mr. Lincoln sot us free. Iffen it was still slav'ry time now old as I is, I would have to wuk jus' de same, sick or no. Now I don't have to ax nobody what I kin do. Dat's why I'se glad I'se free.

"Now, 'bout my marriage; I was a-living in Putnam County at dat time, and I got married up wid Green Willingham. He had come dar from Jasper County. I didn't have no weddin'. Ma jus' cooked a chicken for us, and I was married in a white dress. De waist had ruffles 'round de neck and sleeves. Us had 17 chilluns in all, seven boys and 10 gals, dere was 19 grandchillun and 21 great grandchillun. Dey ain't all of 'em livin', and my old man, he's done been daid a long time ago."

Henrietta again made her appearance and addressed her mother: "Hush your mouth Ma, for you knows you ain't got all dem chillun. I done told de lady you ain't got your right mind." Frances retorted: "You shut up your mouth, Henrietta. I is so got my right mind, and I knows how many chillun of mine dere was. One thing sho' you is got more mouth dan all de rest of my chillun put together."

The interviewer closed her notebook and took her departure, leaving Frances dozing in her chair.

United States. Work Projects Administration

[HW: Dist-1-2
Ex-slave #114
(Mrs. Stonestreet)]

ADELINE WILLIS—EX-SLAVE
[Date Stamp: MAY 8 1937]

ADELINE WILLIS

Who is the oldest ex-slave in Wilkes County? This question was answered the other day when the quest ended on the sunny porch of a little cottage on Lexington Road in Washington-Wilkes, for there in a straight old-fashioned split-bottom chair sat "Aunt" Adeline Willis basking in the warm October sunshine. She is remarkable for her age—she doesn't know just exactly how old she is, from all she tells and what her "white folks" say she is around a hundred. Her general health is good, she spends her days in the open and tires only on the days she cannot be out in her place in the sun. She has the brightest eyes, her sight is so good she has never had to wear glasses; she gets around in the house and yard on her cane. Her memory is excellent, only a time or two did she slowly shake her head and say apologetically—"Mistress, it's been so long er go, I reckon I done forgot".

From her long association with white people she uses very little Negro dialect and always refers to her Mother as "Mother", never as Ma or Mammy as most Negroes do. This is very noticable.

Her mother was Marina Ragan, "cause she belonged to the Ragans," explained Aunt Adeline, "and she was born on the Ragan Plantation right down on Little River in Greene County" (Georgia). When Marina's "young Mistress" married young Mr. Mose Wright of Oglethorpe County, she took Marina to her new home to be her own servant, and there is where Adeline was born. The place was known as the Wright Plantation and was a very large one.

Adeline doesn't remember her father, and strange to say, she cannot recall how many brothers and sisters she had though she tried hard to name them all. She is sure, however, there were some older and some younger, "I reckon I must er come along about the middle", she said.

After a little while Aunt Adeline was living far back in the past and talked freely—with questions now and then to encourage her reminiscences, she told many interesting things about her life as a slave.

She told about the slaves living in the Quarters—log houses all in a long row near the "white folks' house", and how happy they were. She couldn't remember how many slaves were on the plantation, but was sure there were many: "Yas'm, my Marster had lots of niggers, jest how many, I don't know, but there sho' was a sight of us". They were given their allowance of "rations" every week and cooked their own meals in their cabins. They had good, plain, home-raised things to eat—"and we was glad to get it too. We didn't have no fancy fixings, jest plain food". Their clothes were made by Negro sewing women out of cloth spun and woven right there in the Quarters. All the little dresses were made alike. "When they took a notion to give us striped dresses we sho' was dressed up. I never will forget long as I live, a hickory stripe—(that's what they called stripes in them days)—dress they made me, it had brass buttons at the wrist bands. I was so proud of that dress and felt so dressed up in it I jest strutted er round with it on", and she chuckled over the recollection of that wonderful dress she wore so long ago.

When asked what was the very first thing she remembered, Aunt Adeline gave a rather surprising answer: "The first thing I recollect is my love for my Mother—I loved her so and would cry when I couldn't be with her, and as I growed up I kept on loving her jest that a-way even after I married and had children of my own."

The first work she did was waiting in the house. Before she could read her mistress taught her the letters on the newspapers and what they spelled so she could bring them the papers they wanted. Her mother worked in the field: she drove steers and could do all kinds of farm work and was the best meat cutter on the plantation. She was a good spinner too, and was required to spin a broach of "wool spinning" every night. All the Negro women had to spin, but Aunt Adeline said her mother was specially good in spinning wool and "that kind of spinning was powerful slow". Thinking a moment, she added: "And my mother was one of the best dyers anywhere 'round, and I was too. I did make the most colors by mixing up all kinds of bark and leaves. I recollect the prettiest sort of a lilac color I made with maple bark and pine bark, not the outside pine bark, but that little thin skin that grows right down next to the tree—it was pretty, that color was."

Aunt Adeline thinks they were more fortunate than any other little slaves she knew because their marster had a little store right there where he would give them candy every now and then—bright pretty sticks of candy. She remembers one time he gave them candy in little tin cups, and how proud of those cups they were. He never gave them money, but out of the store they could get what money bought so they were happy. But they had to have whippings, "yas'um, good er bad we got them whippings with a long cowhide kept jest fer that. They whipped us to make us grow better, I reckon".

Although they got whippings a-plenty they were never separated by sale. "No mam, my white folks never believed in selling their niggers", said Aunt Adeline, and related an incident proving this. "I recollect once my oldest brother done something Marster didn't like an' he got mighty mad with him an' said 'Gus, I'm goin' ter sell you, I ain't a-goin' to keep you no longer'. Mistress spoke up right quick and said: 'No you ain't a-goin' to sell Gus, neither, he's nussed and looked after all our oldest chillun, and he's goin' to stay right here'. And that was the last of that, Gus was never sold—he went to war with his young Marster when he went and died up there in the war cause he was homesick, so Marster come back and said."

Aunt Adeline was surprised when asked if the Doctor ever was called in to see her or any of the slaves when they were sick back in slavery days—in fact she was a bit indignant as she answered; "*No mam*, I was born, growed up, married, had sixteen children and never had no Doctor with me 'til here since I got so old". She went on to say that her white folks looked after their Negroes when they were sick.

They were given tonics and things to keep them well so sickness among them was rare. No "store-bought" medicines, but good old home-made remedies were used. For instance, at the first sniffle they were called in and given a drink of fat lightwood tea, made by pouring boiling water over finely split kindling—"that" explained Aunt Adeline, "was cause lightwood got turpentine in it". In the Springtime there was a mixture of anvil dust (gathered up from around the anvil in the blacksmith's shop) and mixed with syrup, and a teaspoon full given every morning or so to each little piccaninny as they were called up in the "white folks' yard". Sometimes instead of this mixture they were given a dose of garlic and whisky—all to keep them healthy and well.

There was great rejoicing over the birth of a Negro baby and the white folks were called upon to give the little black stranger a name.

Adeline doesn't remember anything about the holidays and how they were spent, not even Christmas and Thanksgiving, but one thing she does remember clearly and that is: "All my white folks was Methodist folks, and they had fast days and no work was done while they was fastin' and prayin'. And we couldn't do no work on Sunday, no mam, everybody had to rest on that day and on preachin' days everybody went to church, white and black to the same church, us niggers set up in the gallery that was built in the white folks' church for us".

There wasn't any time for play because there was so much work to do on a big plantation, but they had good times together even if they did have so much to do.

Before Adeline was grown her "young Mistress," Miss Mary Wright, married Mr. William Turner from Wilkes County, so she came to the Turner Plantation to live, and lived there until several years after the War. Adeline hadn't been in her new home long before Lewis Willis, a young Negro from the adjoining plantation, started coming to see her. "Lewis come to see me any time 'cause his Marster, Mr. Willis, give him a pass so he wasn't scared to be out at night 'count of the Patterollers. They didn't bother a nigger if he had a pass, they sho' did beat him." [HW: ?]

When Adeline was fourteen years old she and Lewis married, or rather it was like this: "We didn't have no preacher when we married, my Marster and Mistess said they didn't care, and Lewis's Master and Mistress said they didn't care, so they all met up at my white folks' house and had us come in and told us they didn't mind our marryin'. My Marster said, 'Now you and Lewis wants to marry and there ain't no objections so go on and jump over the broom stick together and you is married'. That was all there was to it and we was married. I lived on with my white folks and he lived on with his and kept comin' to see me jest like he had done when he was a courtin'. He never brought me any presents 'cause he didn't have no money to buy them with, but he was good to me and that was what counted."

Superstition and signs still have a big place in the life of this woman even after a hundred long years. She has outlived or forgotten many she used to believe in, but still holds fast to those she remembers. If a rooster crows anywhere near your door somebody is coming "and you might as well look for 'em, 'cause that rooster done told you". When a person dies if there is a clock in the room it must be stopped the very minute of death or it will never be any more good—if left ticking it will be ruined. Every dark cloudy day brings death—"Somebody leaving this unfriendly world today". Then she is sure when she "feels sadness" and doesn't know why, it a sign somebody is dying "way off somewhere and we don't know it". Yes, she certainly believes in all the signs she remembers even "to this good day", as she says.

When asked about the war Aunt Adeline said that times were much harder then: "Why we didn't have no salt—jest plain salt, and couldn't get none them days. We had to get up the dirt in the smokehouse where the meat had dripped and 'run it' like lye, to get salt to put on things—yas'm, times was sho' hard and our Marster was off in war all four years and we had to do the best we could. We niggers wouldn't know nothing about it all if it hadn't a been for a little old black, sassy woman in the Quarters that was a talkin' all the time about 'freedom'. She give our white folks lots of trouble—she was so sassy to them, but they didn't sell her and she was set free along with us. When they all come home from the war and Marster called us up and told us we was free, some rejoiced so they shouted, but some didn't, they was sorry. Lewis come a runnin' over there an' wanted me and the chillun to go on over to his white folks' place with him, an' I wouldn't go—*No mam*, I wouldn't leave my white folks. I told Lewis to go on and let me 'lone, I knowed my white folks and they was good to me, but I didn't know his white folks. So we kept living like we did in slavery, but he come to see me every day. After a few years he finally 'suaded me to go on over to the Willis place and live with him, and his white folks was powerful good to me. After a while, tho' we all went back and lived with my white folks and I worked on for them as long as I was able to work and always felt like I belonged to 'em, and you know, after all this long time, I feel like I am their's."

"Why I live so long, you asking? 'Cause I always been careful and took good care of myself, eat a plenty and stayed out in the good fresh open air and sunshine when I could—and then I had a good husband that took care of me." This last reason for her long life was added as an afterthought and since Lewis, her husband, has been dead these forty years maybe those first named causes were the real ones. Be that as it may, Aunt Adeline is a very remarkable old woman and is most interesting to talk with.

FEDERAL WRITERS' PROJECTS
Augusta-Athens
Supervisor: Miss Velma Bell

EXCERPTS FROM SLAVE INTERVIEWS
UNCLE WILLIS
[Date Stamp: APR 8 1937]

[TR: Also in combined interviews as Willis Bennefield.]

UNCLE WILLIS

"Uncle Willis" lived with his daughter, Rena, who is 74 years old. "I his baby," said Rena. "All dead but me and I ain't no good for him now, 'cause I kain't tote nothin'."

When asked where her father was, Rena looked out over the blazing cotton field and called:

"Pap! Oh—pappy! Stop pickin' cotton and come in awhile. Dey's some ladies wants to see you."

Uncle Willis hobbled slowly to the cabin, which was set in the middle of the cotton patch. He wore clean blue overalls, obviously new. His small, regular features had high cheekbones. There was a tuft of white hair on his chin, and his head was covered with a "sundown" hat.

"Mawnin," he said. "I bin sick. So I thought I might git some cotton terday."

Willis thinks he is 101 years old. He said: "I was 35 years old when freedom declared." He belonged to a doctor in Burke County, who, Willis at first said, had three or four plantations. Later he stated that the good doctor had five or six places, all in Burke County.

"I wuk in de fiel'," he went on: "and I drove de doctor thirty years. He owned 300 slaves. I never went to school a day in my life, 'cept Sunday school, but I tuk de doctor's sons four miles ev'y day to school. Guess he had so much business in hand he thought de chillun could walk. I used to sit down on de school steps 'till dey turn out. I got way up de alphabet by listenin', but when I went to courtin' I forgot all dat."

Asked what his regular duties were, Willis answered with pride:

"Marster had a ca'yage and a buggy too. My father driv' de doctor. Sometimes I was fixin' to go to bed, and had to hitch up my horse and go five or six mile. I had a regular saddle horse, two pair of horses for ca'yage. Doctor were a rich man. Richest man in Burke County. He made his money on his farm. When summertime come, I went wid him to Bath, wheh he had a house on Tena Hill. We driv' down in de ca'yage. Sundays we went to church when Dr. Goulding preach. De darkies went in de side do'. I hear him preach many times."

Asked about living conditions on the plantation, Willis replied:

"De big house was set in a half acre yard. 'Bout fifty yards on one side was my house, and fifty yards on de yudder side was de house o' Granny, a woman what tended de chillun and had charge o' de yard when we went to Bath." Willis gestured behind him. "Back yonder was de quarters, half a mile long; dey wuz one room 'crost, and some had shed room. When any of 'em got sick, Marster would go round to see 'em all."

As to church, Willis said:

"I belongst to Hopeful Church. Church people would have singin' and prayin' and de wicked people would have dancin' and singin'." Willis chuckled. "At dat time I wuz a regular dancer! I cut de pigeon wing high enough! Not many cullud peoples know de Bible in slavery time. We had dances, and prayers, and sing, too. We sang a song, 'On Jordan's stormy banks I stand, and cast a wishful eye.'"

"How about marriages?" Willis was asked.

"Colored preacher marry 'em. You had to get license and give it to de preacher and he marry 'em. When de men on our plantation had wives on udder plantations, dey call 'em broad wives."

"Did you give your wife presents when you were courting?" he was asked.

"I went to courtin' and never give her nuthin' till I marry her."

As to punishments, Willis said that slaves were whipped as they needed it, and as a general rule the overseer did the whipping.

"When derky wouldn't take whippin' from de overseer," he said, "he had to ca'y dem to de boss; and if we needed any brushin' de marster brush 'em. Why, de darkies would whip de overseer!"

Willis was asked to describe how slaves earned money for personal use, and replied:

"Dey made dey own money. In slavery time, if you wanted four-five acre of land to plant you anything on, marster give it to you and whatever dat land make, it belong to you. You could take dat money and spend it any way you wanted. Still he give you somethin' to eat and clothe you, but dat patch you mek cotton on, sometimes a whole bale, dat money yours."

Willis thought the plantation house was still there, "but it badly wounded," he said. "Dey tell me dere ain't nobuddy living in it now. It south of Waynesboro."

"When de soldiers come thoo'," continued Willis, "dey didn't burn dat place, but dey went in dere and took out ev'yting dey want and give it to de cullud people. Dey kep' it till dey got free. De soldiers tuk de doctor's horses and ca'y 'em off. Got in de crib and tek de corn. Got in de smoke 'ouse and tek de meat out. Old Marssa bury his money and silver in an iron chist. Dey tuk it 300 yards away to a clump o' trees and bury it. It tuk fo' men to ca'y it. Dere was money widout mention in dat chist! After de soldiers pass thoo' dey went down and got it back."

"What did you do after freedom was declared?"

Willis straightened up.

"I went down to Augusta to de Freedman's Bureau to see if twas true we wuz free. I reckon dere was over a hundred people dere. De man got up and stated to de people: 'You all is jus' as free as I am. You ain't got no mistis and no marster. Work when you want.' On Sunday morning Old Marster sont de house gal and tell us to all come to de house. He said:

'What I want to send for you all is to tell you dat you are free. You hab de privilege to go anywheh you want, but I don't want none o' you to leave me now. I wants you-all to stay right wid me. If you stay, you mus' sign to it.'

I asked him:

'What you want me to sign for? I is free.'

'Dat will hold me to my word and hold you to yo' word,' he say.

"All my folks sign it, but I wouldn't sign. Marster call me up and say: 'Willis, why wouldn't you sign?' I say: 'If I is already free, I don't need to sign no paper. If I was workin' for you and doin' for you befo' I got free, I kin do it still, if you wants me to stay wid you.'

"My father and mother tried to git me to sign, but I wouldn't sign. My mother said: 'You oughter sign. How you know Marster gwine pay?' I say: 'Den I kin go somewheh else.'

"Marster pay first class hands $15.00 a month, other hands $10.00, and den on down to five and six dollars. He give rations like dey always have. When Christmus' come, all come up to be paid off. Den he calls me. Ask whar is me? I was standin' roun' de corner of de house. 'Come up here, Willis,' he say. 'You didn't sign dat paper but I reckon I hab to pay you too.' He paid me and my wife $180.00. I said: 'Well, you-all thought he wouldn't pay me, but I got my money too.'

"I stayed to my marster's place one year after de war, den I lef' dere. Nex' year I decided I would quit dere and go somewheh else. It was on account o' my wife. You see, Marster bought her off, as de highes' bidder, down in Waynesboro, and she ain't seen her mother and father for fifteen years. When she got free, she went down to see 'em. Waren't willin' to come back. T'was on account o' Mistis and her. Dey bofe had chilluns, five-six year old. De chilluns had disagreement. Mistis slap my gal. My wife sass de Mistis. But my marster, he wuz as good a man as ever born. I wouldn't have lef' him for nobody, just on account of his wife and her fell out."

"What did your master say when you told him you were going to leave? Was he sorry?"

"I quit and goes over three miles to another widow lady's house, and mek bargain wid her," said Willis. "I pass right by de do'. Old boss sittin' on de pi—za. He say: 'Hey, boy, wheh you gwine?' I say: 'I 'cided to go.' I wuz de fo'man' o' de plow-han' den. I saw to all de looking up, and things like dat. He say: 'Hold on dere.' He come out to de gate. 'tell you what I give you to stay on here. I give you five acre of as good land as I got, and $30.00 a month, to stay here and see to my bizness.'"

Willis paused a moment, thinking back on that long distant parting.

"I say," he went on, "'I can't, marster. It don't suit my wife 'round here. She won't come back. I can't stay.'

"He turn on me den, and busted out crying. 'I didn't tho't I could raise up a darky dat would talk dat-a-way,' he said. Well, I went on off. I got de wagon and come by de house. Marster say: 'Now, you gwine off but don't forget me, boy. Remember me as you always done.' I said: 'All right.'"

Willis chewed his tobacco reflectively for a few minutes, spat into the rosemary bush and resumed his story.

"I went over to dat widow lady's house and work. Along about May I got sick. She say: 'I going send for de doctor.' I say: 'Please ma'am, don't do dat.' (I thought maybe he kill me 'cause I lef' him.) She say: 'Well, I gwine send fo' him.' I in desprut condition. When I know anything, he walk up in de do'. I was laying' wid my face toward de do', and I turn over.

"Doctor come up to de bed. 'Boy, how you gettin' on?' 'I bad off,' I say. He say: 'see you is. Yeh.' Lady say: 'Doctor, whut you think of him?' Doctor say: 'Mistis, it mos' too late, but I do all I kin.' She say: 'Please do all you kin, he 'bout de bes' han' I got.'

"Doctor fix up med'cine and tole her to give it to me.

"She say: 'Uncle Will, tek dis med'cine. I 'fraid to tek it. 'Fraid he wuz tryin' to kill me. Den two men, John and Charlie, come in. Lady say: 'Get dis med'cine in Uncle Will.' One o' de men hold my hand and dey gag me and put it in me. Nex' few days I kin talk and ax for somethin' to eat so I git better. (I say: "Well, he didn't kill me when I tuk de med'cine!')

"I stayed dere wid her," continued Willis. "Nex' year I move right back in two miles, other side wheh I always live, wid anudder lady. I stay dere three year. Got along all right. When I lef' from there, I lef' dere wid $300.00

and plenty corn and hog. Everything I want, and three hundred cash dollars in my pocket!"

It was plain that in his present status of relief ward, Uncle Willis looked back on that sum of money as a small fortune. He thought about it awhile, spat again, and went on:

"Fourth year I lef and went down to anudder place near de Creek. I stay dere 33 years in dat one place."

"Uncle Willis, did you ever see the doctor again?"

"He die 'fore I know it," he replied. "I was 'bout fifteen miles from him, and by de time I year o' his death, he bury on plantation near de creek."

Willis was asked about superstitions and answered with great seriousness:

"Eve'ybuddy in de worl' hab got a sperrit what follow 'em roun' and dey kin see diffrunt things. In my sleep I hab vision."

"Pappy, tell de ladies 'bout de hant," urged Aunt Rena from her post in the doorway, and Willis took up the story with eagerness:

"One night I was gwine to a lady's store, ridin' a horse. De graveyard was 100 yards from de road I wuz passin'. De moon was shinin' bright as day. I saw somethin' comin' out of dat graveyard. It come across de road, right befo' me. His tail were draggin' on de ground—a long tail. He had hair on both sides of him, layin' down on de road. He crep' up. I pull de horse dis way. He move too. I yell out: 'What in de name o' God is dat?' And it turn right straight around and went back to de graveyard.

I went on to de lady's house and done my shoppin'. I tell you I wuz skeered, 'cause I was sho' I would see it going back, but I never saw it. De horse was turrible skeered of it. It looked like a Maryno sheep and it had a long, swishy tail."

Uncle Willis was asked if he had ever seen a person "conjured" and he answered:

"Dey is people in de worl' got sense enough to kill out de conjur in anybuddy, but nobuddy ever conjur me. I year 'um say, if a person conjur you, you'll git somethin' in you dat would kill you."

Asked to what he attributed his long, healthy life, Willis raised his head with a preaching look and replied:

"I tell you, Missis, 'zactly what I believe, I bin tryin' to serve God ever since I come to be a man of family. I bin tryin' to serve de Lawd 79 years, and I live by precept of de word. Until today nobuddy can turn me away from God business. I am a man studying my gospel, I ain't able to go to church, but I still keep serving God."

[TR: Return visit]

A week later Uncle Willis was found standing in his cabin door.

"Do you want to ride to the old plantation to-day?" he was asked. His vitality was almost too low for him to grasp the invitation.

"I'se mighty weak to-day," he said in a feeble voice. "I don't feel good for much."

"Where is Aunt Rena?" he was asked. "Do you think she would mind your taking an automobile trip?"

"She gone to town on de bus, to see de Fambly Welfare."

"Have you had breakfast?"

"I had some coffee, but I ain't eat none."

"Well, come on, Uncle Willis. We'll get you some breakfast and then we'll take you to the plantation and take your picture in the place where you were born, 101 years ago."

Uncle Willis appeared to be somewhat in a daze as he padlocked the cabin door, put on his "sundown" hat, took up his stout stick and tottered down the steps. He wore a frayed sweater with several layers of shirts showing at the cuffs. On the way he recalled the first railroad train that passed through Burke County.

"I kinder skeered," he recollected. "We wuz all 'mazed to see dat train flying' long 'thout any horses. De people wuz all afraid."

"Had you heard of airplanes before you saw one, Uncle Willis?"

"Yes, ma'am. I yeared o' dem but you couldn't gimme dis car full o' money to fly. Dey's too high off de ground. I never is gwine in one!"

Uncle Willis was deposited on the porch of one of the remaining slave cabins to eat his "breakkus," while his kidnapers sought over hill and field for "The big house," but only two cabins and the chimney foundations of a large burned dwelling rewarded the search.

The old ex-slave was posed in front of the cabin, to one side of the clay and brick chimney, and took great pleasure in the ceremony, rearing his head up straight so that his white beard stuck out.

The brutal reality of finding the glories of the plantation forever vanished must have been a severe blow for the old man. Several times on the way back he wiped tears from his eyes. Once again at his cabin in the cottonfield, his vitality reasserted itself, and he greeted his curious dusky neighbors with the proud statement.

"Dey tuk me when I was bred and born! I ain't ax no better time!"

Willis' farewell words were:

"Goo'bye! I hopes you all gits to Paradise!"

United States. Work Projects Administration

[HW: Dist 1-2
Ex-Slave #116]

EX-SLAVE INTERVIEW

CORNELIA WINFIELD, Age 82
Richmond County
1341 Ninth Street
Augusta, Georgia

BY: (Mrs.) Margaret Johnson—Editor
Federal Writers' Project
Augusta, Georgia
[Date Stamp: MAY 8 1937]

CORNELIA WINFIELD

Cornelia Winfield, 1341 Ninth Street, was born in Crawford, Oglethorpe County, Georgia March 10, 1855. Her father, being the same age as her master, was given to him as a little boy. They grew up together, playing games, and becoming devoted to each other. When her master was married her father went to his home with him and became the overseer of all the slaves on the plantation. "My father and mother wuz house servants. My marster served my father's plate from his own table and sent it to him, every meal. He had charge of the work shop, and when marster was away he always stayed at the Big House, to take care of my Missis and the children. My mother was a seamstress and had three younger seamsters under her, that she taught to sew. We made the clothes for all the house servants and fiel' hans. My mother made some of the clothes for my marster and missis. My mother was a midwife too, and useter go to all the birthings on our place. She had a bag she always carried and when she went to other plantations she had a horse and buggy to go in.

"All the slaves on our place wuz treated well. I never heard of any of 'em bein' whipped. I was ten years old when freedom come, and I always knowed I wuz to belong to one of marster's daughters. After freedom my father and mother worked on just the same for marster. When my father died, marster's fam'ly wanted him buried in the fam'ly lot but I wanted him to lie by my mother."

Cornelia's husband was a Methodist preacher, and she lived with him to celebrate their Golden Wedding. During the last years of his life they lived in Augusta. For sixteen years she washed all the blankets for the Fire Department, and did some of the washing for the firemen. Cornelia is now 82 years of age, but her memory is good and her mind active; and she is extremely loquacious. She is quite heavy, and crippled, having to use a crutch when she walks. Her room was clean, but over-crowded with furniture, every piece of which has recently been painted. Of the wardrobe in her room Cornelia told the following story. "All the planks eny of our family was laid out on, my father kep'. When he came to Augusta he brought all these planks and made this here wardrobe. When the fire burnt me out, this here wardrobe was the only thing in my house that was saved."

During the past summer she put up quantities of preserves, pickles and canned fruits. These she sells in a little shop-room adjoining her house, and when the weather permits, on the steps of the Post Office.

Cornelia can read, and spends much of time reading the Bible but she learned to read after "Freedom." She is greatly interested to tell of the "best families" she has worked for and the gifts she has received from them.

United States. Work Projects Administration

[HW: Dist. 5
Ex-Slave #117]
E. Driskell
Whitley
1-20-37

GEORGE WOMBLE
EX-SLAVE
[Date Stamp: MAY 8 1937]

GEORGE WOMBLE

One of the relics of Slavery is George Womble. From all appearances Mr. Womble looks to be fifty-three years of age instead of the ripe old age of ninety-three that he claims. He is about five and one-half or six feet in height, weighs one-hundred and seventy-five pounds or more, and has good sight and hearing in addition to a skin that is almost devoid of any wrinkle. Besides all of this he is a clear thinker and has a good sense of humor. Following is an account of the experiences of Mr. Womble as a slave and of the conditions in general on the plantations where he lived:

"I was born in the year of 1843 near the present site of what is now known as Clinton, Georgia. The names of my parents were Patsy and Raleigh Ridley. I never saw my father as he was sold before I was old enough to recognize him as being my father. I was still quite young when my mother was sold to a plantation owner who lived in New Orleans, La. As she was being put on the wagon to be taken away I heard her say: "Let me see my poor child one more time because I know I'll never see him again". That was the last I ever saw or heard of her. As I had no brothers or sisters or any other relatives to care for me my master, who was Mr. Robert Ridley, had me placed in his house where I was taught to wait tables and to do all kinds of house work. Mr. Ridley had a very large plantation and he raised cotton, corn, oats, wheat, peas, and live stock. Horses and mules were his specialty—I remember that he had one little boy whose job was to break these animals so that they could be easily sold. My job was to wait tables, help with the house cleaning, and to act as nurse maid to three young children belonging to the master. At other times I drove the cows to and from the pasture and I often helped with the planting in the fields when the field hands were rushed. Out of the forty-odd slaves that were held by the Ridleys all worked in the field with the exception of myself and the cook whose name was Harriet Ridley." Continuing, Mr. Womble says: "I believe that Mr. Ridley was one of the meanest men that ever lived. Sometimes he whipped us, especially us boys, just to give himself a little fun. He would tie us in such a way as to cause our bodies to form an angle and then he preceeded to use the whip. When he had finished he would ask: "Who do you belong to?" and we had to answer; "Marse Robert". At other times he would throw us in a large tank that held about two-thousand gallons of water. He then stood back and laughed while we struggled to keep from drowning."

"When Marse Robert died I was still a small boy. Several months after his death Mrs. Ridley gave the plantation up and took her share of the slaves (ten in number) of which I was one, and moved to Tolbert County, Georgia near the present location of Talbottom, Georgia.

The other slaves and the plantation were turned over to Marse Robert's relatives. After a few months stay in this place I was sold to Mrs. Ridley's brother, Enoch Womble. On the day that I was sold three doctors examined me and I heard one of them say: "This is a thoroughbred boy. His teeth are good and he has good muscles and eyes. He'll live a long time." Then Mr. Womble said: "He looks intelligent too. I think I'll take him and make a blacksmith out of him." And so to close the deal he paid his sister five-hundred dollars for me."

According to Mr. Womble his new master was even meaner than the deceased Mr. Ridley. He was likewise a plantation owner and a farmer and as such he raised the same things that Mr. Ridley did with the exception of the horses and the mules. In all there were about five-hundred acres to the plantation. There were six children in the Womble family in addition to Mr. Womble and his wife, and they all lived in a large one-storied frame house. A large hickory tree grew through the center of the porch where a hole had been cut out for its growth.

Mr. Womble says that his reputation of being an excellent house boy had preceded him, and so here too he was put to work in the master's house where he helped with the cooking, washed the dishes, cleaned the house, and also acted as nurse for the younger white children. In addition to this, he was also required to attend to the cows. He remembers how on one night at a very late hour he was called by the master to go and drive the cows from the pasture as the sleet and snow might do them more harm than good. He was so cold that on the way back from the pasture he stopped at the pig pens where he pushed one or two of them out of the spots where they had lain so that he could squat there, and warm his feet in the places left warm by their bodies. To add to his discomfort the snow and sleet froze in his long hair and this made him even more miserable than ever.

Mr. Womble was asked to tell what time he had to arise in the morning to be at his day's work, and he replied that sometimes he didn't even go to sleep as he had to keep one hand on the baby crib to keep it from crying. Most of the time he got up at four o'clock in the morning, and went to the kitchen where he helped the cook prepare breakfast. After this was done, and he had finished waiting on the master and his family he started to clean the house. When he had finished this, he had to take care of the younger Womble children, and do countless the other things to be done around a house. Of the other slaves, Mr. Womble says: "None of them ever suffered from that disease known as "mattress fever". They all got up long before day, and prepared their breakfasts and then before it was light enough to see clearly they were standing in the field holding their hoes and other implements—afraid to start work for fear that they would cover the cotton plants with dirt because they could'nt see clearly due to the darkness." An overseer was hired by the master to see that the work was done properly. If any of the slaves were careless about their work they were made to take off their clothes in the field before all the rest and then a sound whipping was administered. Field hands also get whippings when they failed to pick the required three-hundred pounds of cotton daily. To avoid a whipping for this they sprinkled the white sand of the fields on the dew soaked cotton and at the time it was weighed they were credited with more pounds than they had actually picked. Around ten or eleven o'clock in the morning they were all allowed to go to the cook house where they were given dinner by the plantation cook. By one o'clock they were all back in the field where they remained until it was too dark to see clearly, and then they were dismissed by the overseer after he had checked the number of pounds of cotton that they had picked.

The slaves knew that whenever Mr. Womble hired a new overseer he always told the prospect that if he could'nt handle the slaves his services would not be needed. The cook had heard the master tell a prospective overseer this and so whenever a new one was hired the slaves were quick to see how far they could go with him. Mr. Womble says that an overseer had to be a very capable man in order to keep his job as overseer on the Womble plantation because if the slaves found out that he was afraid of them fighting him (and they did sometimes) they took advantage of him so much so that the production dropped and the overseer either found himself trying to explain to his employer or else looking for another job. The master would never punish a slave for beating an overseer with his fists stated Mr. Womble.

During rainy weather the slaves shucked corn, piled manure in the barns, and made cloth. In the winter season the men split rails, built fences, and dug ditches, while the women did the weaving and the making of cloth. These slaves who were too old to work in the fields remained at home where they nursed the sick slaves (when there was sickness) and attended to the needs of those children who were too young for field work. Those children who were still being fed from their mother's breasts were also under the care of one of these old persons. However, in this case the mothers were permitted to leave the field twice a day (once between breakfast and dinner and once between dinner and supper) so that these children could be fed.

At times Mr. Womble hired some of his slaves out to work by the day for some of the other nearby plantation owners. Mr. Geo. Womble says that he was often hired out to the other white ladies of the community to take care of their children and to do their housework. Because of his ability to clean a house and to handle children he was in constant demand.

The men worked every day in the week while the women were given Saturday afternoon off so that they might do their personal work such as the washing and the repairing of their clothing etc. The women were required to do the washing and the repairing of the single men's clothing in addition to their own. No night work was required of any of them except during the winter when they were given three cuts of thread to card, reel, and spin each night.

There were some days when the master called them all to his back yard and told them that they could have a frolic. While they danced and sang the master and his family sat and looked on. On days like the Fourth of July and Christmas in addition to the frolic barbecue was served and says Mr. Womble: "It was right funny to see all of them dancing around the yard with a piece of meat in one hand and a piece of bread in the other.

Mr. Womble stated further that clothes were given to all the slaves once a year. An issue for the men usually consisted of one or two pairs of pants and some shirts, underwear, woolen socks, and a pair of heavy brogans that had been made of horse hide. These shoes were reddish in appearance and were as stiff as board according to Mr. Womble. For special wear the men were given a garment that was made into one piece by sewing the pants and shirt together. This was known as a "roundabout". The women were given one or two dresses that had been made of the same material as that of the men's pants. As the cloth that these clothes were made of was very coarse and heavy most of them lasted until the time for the next issue. None of the clothing that the slaves wore was bought. After the cloth had been made by the slaves who did all the spinning and the weaving the master's wife cut the clothes out while the slave women did the sewing. One of the men was a cobbler and it was he who made all of the shoes for slave use. In the summer months the field hands worked in their bare feet regardless of whether they had shoes or not. Mr. Womble says that he was fifteen years of age when he was given his first pair of shoes. They were a pair of red boots and were so stiff that he needed help to get them on his feet as well as to get them off. Once when the master had suffered some few financial losses the slaves had to wear clothes that were made of crocus material. The children wore sacks after holes had been cut out for their heads and arms. This garment looked like a slightly lengthened shirt in appearance. A dye made from red clay was used to give color to these clothes.

The bed clothing consisted of bagging sacks and quilts that were made out of old clothes.

At the end of the week all the field hands met in the master's backyard where they were given a certain amount of food which was supposedly enough to last for a week. Such an issue was made up of three pounds of fat meat, one peck of meal, and one quart of black molasses. Mr. Womble was asked what the slaves did if their allowance of food ran out before the end of the week, and he replied in the following manner: "If their food gave out before the time for another issue they waited until night and then one or two of them would go to the millhouse where the flour and the meal was kept. After they had succeeded in getting in they would take an auger and bore a hole in the barrel containing the meal. One held the sack while the other took a stick and worked it around in the opening made by the auger so as to make the meal flow freely. After their bags were filled the hole was stopped up, and a hasty departure was made. Sometimes when they wanted meat they either went to the smoke house and stole a ham or else they would go to the pen where the pigs were kept and take a small pig out. When they got to the woods with this animal they proceeded to skin and clean it (it had already been killed with a blow in the head before they left the pen). All the parts that they did not want were either buried or thrown in the nearby river. After going home all of this meat was cooked and hidden. As there was danger in being caught none of this stolen meat was ever fried because there was more danger of the odor of frying meat going farther away than that odor made by meat being boiled." At this point Mr. Womble stated that the slaves were taught to steal by their masters. Sometimes they were sent to the nearby plantations to steal chickens, pigs, and other things that could be carried away easily. At such times the master would tell them that he was not going to mistreat them and that he was not going to allow anyone else to mistreat them and that by taking the above mentioned things they were helping him to be more able to take care of them.

At breakfast the field hands ate fried meat, corn bread, and molasses. When they went to the house for dinner they were given some kind of vegetable along with pot liquor and milk. When the days work was done and it was time for the evening meal there was the fried meat again with the molasses and the corn bread. Mr. Womble says that they ate this kind of food every day in the week. The only variation was on Sunday when they were given the seconds of the flour and a little more molasses so that they might make a cake. No other sweetening was used except the molasses.

As for Mr. Womble and the cook they fared better as they ate the same kind of food that the master and his family did. He remembers how he used to take biscuits from the dishes that were being sent to the masters table. He was the waiter and this was an easy matter. Later he took some of these biscuits and sold them to the other little boys for a nickle each. Neither the master or the slaves had real coffee. They all drank a type of this beverage that had been made by parching bran or meal and then boiled in water.

The younger children were fed from a trough that was twenty feet in length. At meal time each day the master would come out and supervise the cook whose duty it was to fill the trough with food. For breakfast the milk and bread was all mixed together in the trough by the master who used his walking cane to stir it with. At dinner and supper the children were fed pot liquor and bread and sometimes milk that had been mixed together in the same manner. All stood back until the master had finished stirring the food and then at a given signal they dashed to the trough where they began eating with their hands. Some even put their mouths in the trough and ate. There were times when the master's dogs and some of the pigs that ran round the yard all came to the trough to share these meals. Mr. Womble states that they were not permitted to strike any of these animals so as to drive them away and so they protected their faces from the tongues of the intruders by placing their hands on the sides of their faces as they ate. During the meal the master walked from one end of the trough to the other to see that all was as it should be. Before Mr. Womble started to work in the master's house he ate as the other children for a short time. Some of the times he did not have enough food to eat and so when the time came to feed the cows he took a part of their food (a mixture of cotton seed, collard stalks, and small ears of corn) and ate it when night came. When he started working in the house regularly he always had sufficient food from then on.

All the food that was eaten was grown on the plantation in the master's gardens. He did not permit the slaves to have a garden of their own neither could they raise their own chickens and so the only time that they got the chance to enjoy the eating of chicken was when they decided to make a special trip to the master's poultry yard.

The housing facilities varied with the work a slave was engaged in on the Womble plantation according to Mr. Womble. He slept in the house under the dining-room table all of the time. The cook also slept in the house of her owner. For those who worked on the fields log cabins (some distance behind the master's house.) were provide [sic]. Asked to describe one of these cabins Mr. Womble replied: "They were two roomed buildings made out of logs and daubed with mud to keep the weather out. At one end there was a chimney that was made out of dried mud, sticks and stones. The fireplace was about five or six feet in length and on the inside of it there were some hooks to hang the pots from when there was cooking to be done.

"There was only one door and this was the front one. They would'nt put a back door in a cabin because it would be easy for a slave to slip out of the back way if the master or the overseer came to punish an occupant. There were one or two small openings cut in the back so that they could get air."

"The furniture was made by the blacksmith", continued Mr. Womble. "In one corner of the room there was a large bed that had been made out of heavy wood. Rope that ran from side to side served as the springs while the mattress was a large bag that had been stuffed with wheat straw. The only other furnishings were a few cooking utensils and one or two benches." As many as four families lived in one of these cabins although the usual number to a cabin was three families. There was one other house where the young children were kept while their parents worked in the fields.

Most of the sickness on the Womble plantation was due to colds and fever. For the treatment of either of these ailments the master always kept a large can filled with a mixture of turpentine and caster oil. When anyone complained of a cold a dose of this oil was prescribed. The master gave this dose from a very large spoon that always hung from the can. The slaves also had their own home made remedies for the treatment of different ailments. Yellow root tea and black-hall tea were used in the treatment of colds while willow tea was used in the treatment of fever. Another tea made from the droppings of sheep was used as a remedy for the measles. A doctor was always called when anyone was seriously ill. He was always called to attend those cases of childbirth. Unless a slave was too sick to walk he was required to go to the field and work like the others. If, however, he was confined to his bed a nurse was provided to attend to his needs.

On Sundays all of the slaves were allowed to attend the white church where they listened to the services from the rear of the church. When the white minister was almost through he would walk back to where the slaves sat and tell them not to steal their master's chickens, eggs, or his hogs and their backs would not be whipped with many stripes. After this they were dismissed and they all left the church wondering what the preacher's sermon meant. Some nights they went to the woods and conducted their own services. At a certain spot they all knelt and turned their faces toward the ground and then they began moaning and praying. Mr. Womble says that by huddling in this circle and turning their voices toward the ground the sound would not travel very far.

None of them ever had the chance to learn how to read and write. Some times the young boys who carried the master's children's books to and from school would ask these children to teach them to write but as they were afraid of what their father might do they always refused. On the adjoining plantation the owner caught his son teaching a little slave boy to write.

He was furious and after giving his son a severe beating he then cut the thumb and forefinger off of the slave. The only things that were taught the slaves was the use of their hands. Mr. Womble says that all the while that he was working in the master's house they still found the time for him to learn to be a blacksmith.

When a male slave reached the age of twenty-one he was allowed to court. The same was true of a girl that had reached the age of eighteen. If a couple wished to marry they had to get permission from the master who asked each in turn if they wished to be joined as man and wife and if both answered that they did they were taken into the master's house where the ceremony was performed. Mr. Womble says that he has actually seen one of these weddings and that it was conducted in the following manner: "A broom was placed in the center of the floor and the couple was told to hold hands. After joining hands they were commanded to jump over the broom and then to turn around and jump back.

"After this they were pronounced man and wife." A man who was small in stature was never allowed to marry a large, robust woman. Sometimes when the male slaves on one plantation were large and healthy looking and the women slaves on some nearby plantation looked like they might be good breeders the two owners agreed to allow the men belonging to the one visit the women belonging to the other, in fact they encouraged this sort of thing in hopes that they would marry and produce big healthy children. In such cases passes were given freely.

All of the newly born babies were named by the master. "The only baptisms that any of us get was with a stick over the head and then we baptised our cheeks with our tears," stated Mr. Wombly.

Continuing, Mr. Wombly stated that the slaves on the

Womble plantation were treated more like animals rather than like humans. On one or two occasions some of them were sold. At such a time those to be sold were put in a large pen and then they were examined by the doctors and prospective buyers and later sold to the highest bidder the same as a horse or a mule. They were sold for various reasons says Mr. Womble. His mother was sold because she was too hard to rule and because she made it difficult to discipline the other slaves.

Mr. Womble further reported that most of his fellow slaves believed in signs. They believed that if a screech owl or a "hoot" owl came near a house and made noises at night somebody was going to die and instead of going to heaven the devil would get them. "On the night that old Marse Ridley died the screech owls like to have taken the house away," he says.

There was always a great amount of whipping on this plantation. This was practically the only form of punishment used. Most of them were whipped for being disobedient or for being unruly. Mr. Womble has heard his master say that he would not have a slave that he could not rule and to be sure that the slaves held him and his family in awe he even went so far as to make all of them go and pay their respects to the newly born white children on the day after their birth. At such a time they were required to get in line outside of the door and then one by one they went through the room and bowed their heads as they passed the bed and uttered the following words: "Young Marster" or if the baby was a girl they said: "Young Mistress". On one occasion Mr. Womble says that he has seen his master and a group of other white men beat an unruly slave until his back was raw and then a red hot iron bar was applied to his back. Even this did not make the slave submissive because he ran away immediately afterwards. After this inhuman treatment any number of the slaves ran away, especially on the Ridley plantation. Some were caught and some were not. One of the slaves on the Womble plantation took his wife and ran away. He and his wife lived in a cave that they found in the woods and there they raised a family. When freedom was declared and these children saw the light of day for the first time they almost went blind stated Mr. Womble.

Mr. Womble says that he himself has been whipped to such an extent by his master, who used a walking cane, that he had no feeling in his legs. One other time he was sent off by the master and instead of returning immediately he stopped to eat some persimmons. The master came upon him at the tree and started beating him on the head with a wagon spoke. By the time he reached the house his head was covered with knots the size of hen eggs and blood was flowing from each of them.

The slaves on the Womble plantation seldom if ever came in contact with the "Paddle-Rollers" who punished those slaves who had the misfortune to be caught off of their plantations without passes. In those days the jails were built for the white folks because the masters always punished the slaves when they broke any of the laws exclaimed Mr. Womble.

Several years before the war Mr. Wombly was sold to Mr. Jim Wombly, the son of Mr. Enoch Wombly. He was as mean as his father or meaner, Mr. Wombly says that the first thing that he remembers in regard to the war was to hear his master say that he was going to join the army and bring Abe Lincoln's head back for a soap dish.

He also said that he would wade in blood up to his neck to keep the slaves from being freed. The slaves would go to the woods at night where they sang and prayed. Some used to say; "I knew that some day we'll be free and if we die before that time our children will live to see it."

When the Yankees marched through they took all of the silver and gold that had been hidden in the wall on the Womble plantation. They also took all of the live stock on the plantation, most of which had been hidden in the swamps. These soldiers then went into the house and tore the beds up and poured syrup in the mattresses. At the time all of the white people who lived on the plantation were hiding in the woods. After the soldiers had departed (taking these slaves along who wished to follow) Mrs. Womble went back into the house and continued to make the clothes and the bandages that were to be used by the Confederate Soldiers.

After the slaves were set free any number of them were bound over and kept, says Mr. Womble. He himself was to remain with the Womble family until he reached the age of twenty-one. When this time came Mr. Womble refused to let him go. However, Mrs. Womble helped him to escape but he was soon caught one night at the home of an elderly white lady who had befriended him. A rope was tied around his neck and he was made to run the entire way back to the plantation while the others rode on horse back. After a few more months of cruel treatment he ran away again. This time he was successful in his escape and after he had gone what he considered a safe distance he set up a blacksmith shop where he made a living for quite a few years. Later one of the white men in that community hired him to work in his store. After a number of years at this place he decided to come to Atlanta where he has been since.

Mr. Womble concluded by saying that he has been able to reach his present age because he has never done any smoking or drinking. An old lady once told him not to use soap on his face and he would not wrinkle. He accounts for his smooth skin in this manner.

United States. Work Projects Administration

[HW: Dist. 5
Ex. Slave #118
E. Driskell]

SLAVERY AS SEEN THROUGH THE EYES OF
HENRY WRIGHT—EX-SLAVE, Age 99

HENRY WRIGHT

In Atlanta among that ever decreasing group of persons known as ex-slaves there is an old Negro man named Henry Wright. Although Mr. Wright is 99 years of age his appearance is that of a much younger man. He is about 5 feet in height; his dark skin is almost free of wrinkles and his head is thickly covered with gray hair. His speech and thought indicate that he is very intelligent and there is no doubt that he still possesses a clear and active mind.

As he noisily puffed on a battered old pipe he related the following tale of his experiences in slavery and of conditions in general as he saw them at that time.

Mr. Wright was born on the plantation of Mr. Phil House. This plantation was located near the present site of Buckhead, Ga. His parents were Henry Wright and Margaret House. In those days it was customary for slaves to carry the name of their owners. His father was owned by Mr. Spencer Wright and his mother was owned by Mr. Phil House. Both of these slave owners lived in the same district. His grandparents, Kittie and Anite House also belonged to Mr. Phil House and it was they who told him how they had been sold like cattle while in Virginia to a speculator (slave dealer) and brought to Decatur, Ga. where they were sold to Mr. House.

Mr. Wright lived with his mother on the House plantation for several years then he was given to Mr. George House, the brother of Phil House, as a wedding present. However, he saw his parents often as they were all allowed "passes" so that they might visit one another.

According to Mr. Wright, his master was a very rich man and a very intelligent one. His plantation consisted of about three or four hundred acres of land on which he raised cotton, cane, corn, vegetables and live stock. Although he was not very mean to his slaves or "servants" as he called them, neither did his kindness reach the gushing or overflowing stage.

On this plantation there were a large number of slaves, some of whom worked in "Old Marster's" (as Mr. House was called) house and some of whom worked in the fields.

As a youngster Mr. Wright had to pick up chips around the yard, make fires and keep the house supplied with water which he got from the well. When he was ten years of age he was sent to the field as a plow-boy. He remembers that his mother and father also worked in the fields. In relating his experience as a field hand Mr. Wright says that he and his fellow slaves were roused each morning about 3 o'clock by the blowing of a horn. This horn was usually blown by the white overseer or by the Negro foreman who was known among the slaves as the "Nigger Driver." At the sounding of the horn they had to get up and feed the stock. Shortly after the horn was blown a bell was rung and at this signal they all started for the fields to begin work for the day. They were in the field long before the sun was up. Their working hours were described as being from "sun to sun." When the time came to pick the cotton each slave was required to pick at least 200 lbs. of cotton per day. For this purpose each was given a bag and a large basket. The bag was hung around the neck and the basket was placed at the end of the row. At the close of the day the overseer met all hands at the scales with the lamp, the slate and the whip. If any slave failed to pick the required 200 lbs. he was soundly whipped by the overseer. Sometimes they were able to escape this whipping by giving illness as an excuse. Another form of strategy adopted by the slaves was to dampen the cotton or conceal stones in the baskets, either of which would make the cotton weigh more.

Sometimes after leaving the fields at dark they had to work at night—shucking corn, ginning cotton or weaving. Everyday except Sunday was considered a work day. The only form of work on Sunday was the feeding of the live stock, etc.

When Mr. Wright was asked about the treatment that was given the house slaves in comparison to that given the field slaves, he replied with a broad grin that "Old Marster" treated them much the same as he would a horse and a mule. That is, the horse was given the kind of treatment that would make him show off in appearance, while the mule was given only enough care to keep him well and fit for work. "You see," continued Mr. Wright, "in those days a plantation owner was partially judged by the appearance of his house servants." And so in addition to receiving the discarded clothes of "Old Marster" and his wife, better clothing was bought for the house slaves.

The working hours of the house slave and the field slave were practically the same. In some cases the house slaves had to work at night due to the fact that the master was entertaining his friends or he was invited out and so someone had to remain up to attend to all the necessary details.

On the plantation of Mr. House the house slaves thought themselves better than the field slaves because of the fact that they received better treatment. On the other hand those slaves who worked in the fields said that they would rather work in the fields than work in the house because they had a chance to earn spending money in their spare or leisure time. House servants had no such opportunity.

In bad weather they were not required to go to the fields—instead they cut hedges or did other small jobs around the house. The master did not want them to work in bad weather because there was too much danger of illness which meant a loss of time and money in the end.

Mr. House wanted his slaves to learn a trade such as masonry or carpentry, etc., not because it would benefit the slave, says Mr. Wright, but because it would make the slave sell for more in case he had "to get shet (rid) of him." The slaves who were allowed to work with these white mechanics, from whom they eventually learned the trade, were eager because they would be permitted to hire themselves out. The money they earned could be used to help buy their freedom, that is, what money remained after the master had taken his share. On the other hand the white mechanic had no particular objection to the slaves being there to help him, even though they were learning the trade, because he was able to place all the hard work on the slave which made his job easier. Mr. Wright remembers how his grandfather used to hire his time out doing carpentry work, making caskets and doing some masonry. He himself can plaster, although he never hired out during slavery.

Clothing was issued once per year usually around September. An issue consisted mostly of the following: 1 pair of heavy shoes called "Negro Brogans." Several homespun shirts, woolen socks and two or three pairs of jeans pants. The women were either given dresses and underskirts that were already made or just the plain cloth to make these garments from. Some of their clothing was bought and some was made on the plantation. The wool socks were knitted on the plantation along with the homespun which was woven there. The homespun was dyed by placing it in a boiling mixture of green walnut leaves or walnut hulls. In the event that plaid material was to be made the threads were dyed the desired color before being woven. Another kind of dye was made from the use of a type of red or blue berry, or by boiling red dirt in water (probably madder). The house slaves wore calico dresses or sometimes dresses made from woolen material.

Often this clothing was insufficient to meet the individual needs. With a broad smile and an almost imperceptible shake of his old gray head Mr. Wright told how he had worked in the field without shoes when it was so cold until the skin cracked and the blood flowed from these wounds. He also told how he used to save his shoes by placing them under his arm and walking barefooted when he had a long distance to go. In order to polish these shoes a mixture of soot and syrup was used.

The young slave children wore a one-piece garment with holes cut for the head and arms to go through. In appearance it resembled a slightly long shirt.

As Mr. House did not give blankets, the slaves were required to make the necessary cover by piecing together left over goods. After this process was completed, it was padded with cotton and then dyed in much the same way as homespun. After the dyeing was completed the slave was the owner of a new quilt.

The food that the slaves ate [**TR: was] all raised on the plantation. At the end of each week each slave was given 3 lbs. of meat (usually pork), 1 peck of meal and some syrup. Breakfast and dinner usually consisted of fried meat, corn bread and syrup. Vegetables were usually given at dinner time. Sometimes milk was given at supper. It was necessary to send the meals to the field slaves as they were usually too far away from the house to make the trip themselves. For this purpose there was a woman who did all the cooking for the field hands in a cook house located among the slave cabins.

Mr. House permitted his slaves to have a garden and chickens of their own. In fact, he gave each of them land, a small plot of ground for this purpose. The benefit of this was twofold as far as the slave was concerned. In the first place he could vary his diet. In the second place he was able to earn money by selling his produce either in town or to "Old Marster." Sometimes Old Marster took the produce to town and sold it for them. When he returned from town the money for the sale of this produce was given to the slave. Mr. Wright says that he and all the other slaves felt that they were being cheated when the master sold their goods. Mr. House also permitted his slaves to hunt and fish both of which were done at night for the most part.

Coffee was made by parching meal and then placing it in boiling water. To sweeten this coffee, syrup was used. One delicacy that he and the other slaves used to have on Sunday was biscuit bread which they called "cake bread."

All children who were too young to work in the field were cared for by some old slave woman who was too old to go to the field. She did all of their cooking, etc. The diet of these children usually consisted of pot liquor, milk, vegetables and in rare cases, meat. Mr. Wright laughed here as he stated that these children were given long handled spoons and were seated on a long bench before a trough out of which they all ate like little pigs. Not a slave ever suffered the pangs of hunger on the plantation of Mr. George House.

The houses or cabins of the slaves were located a short distance in the rear of "Old Marster's" house. These houses were usually made from logs—the chinks being closed with mud. In some cases boards were used on the inside of the cabin to keep the weather out, but according to Mr. Wright, mud was always the more effective. The floor was usually covered with boards and there were two or three windows to each cabin, shutters being used in place of glass. The chimney and fireplace were made of mud, sticks and stones. All cooking was done on the fireplace in iron utensils, which Mr. Wright declares were a lot better than those used today. For boiling, the pots hung from a long hook directly above the fire. Such furniture as each cabin contained was all made by the slaves. This furniture usually consisted of a wooden bench, instead of a chair, and a crude bed made from heavy wood. Slats were used in the place of springs. The mattress was made stuffing a large bag with wheat straw. "This slept as good as any feather bed" says Mr. Wright. Candles were used to furnish light at night.

On this plantation each family did not have an individual cabin. Sometimes as many as three families shared a cabin, which of course was rather a large one. In this case it was partitioned off by the use of curtains.

Besides having to take care of the young children, these older slaves were required to care for those slaves who were ill. Mr. House employed a doctor to attend his slaves when their cases seemed to warrant it. If the illness was of a minor nature he gave them castor oil, salts or pills himself. Then, too, the slaves had their own home remedies. Among these were different tonics made from "yarbs" (herbs), plasters made from mustard, and whisky, etc. Most illnesses were caused by colds and fevers. Mr. Wright says that his two brothers and his sister, all of whom were younger than he, died as a result of typhoid fever.

Even with all the hardships that the slaves had to suffer they still had time to have fun and to enjoy themselves, Mr. Wright continued. At various times Mr. House permitted them to have a frolic. These frolics usually took place on such holidays as 4th of July, Christmas or "laying-by time", after the cultivating of the crops was finished and before gathering time. During the day the master provided a big barbecue and at night the singing and dancing started. Music was furnished by slaves who were able to play the banjo or the fiddle. The slaves usually bought these instruments themselves and in some cases the master bought them. "In my case," declared Mr. Wright, "I made a fiddle out of a large sized gourd—a long wooden handle was used as a neck, and the hair from a horse's tail was used for the bow. The strings were made of cat-gut. After I learned to play this I bought a better violin." Sometimes the slaves slipped away to the woods to indulge in a frolic. As a means of protection they tied ropes across the paths where they would be less likely to be seen. These ropes were placed at such a height as to knock a man from his horse if he came riding up at a great speed. In this way the master or the overseer was stopped temporarily, thereby giving the slaves time to scamper to safety. In addition to the presents given at Christmas (candy and clothing) the master also gave each family half a gallon of whisky. This made the parties more lively. One of the songs that the slaves on the House plantation used to sing at their parties runs as follows:

> "Oh, I wouldn't have a poor girl,
> (another version says, "old maid")
> And I'll tell you the reason why,
> Her neck's so long and stringy,
> I'm afraid she'd never die."

On Sundays Mr. House required all of his slaves to attend church. All attended a white church where they sat in the back or in the balcony. After preaching to the white audience, the white pastor turned his attention to the slaves. His sermon usually ran: "Obey your master and your mistress and the Lord will love you." Sometimes a colored preacher was allowed to preach from the same rostrum after the white pastor had finished. His sermon was along similar lines because that is what he had been instructed to say. None of the slaves believed in the sermons but they pretended to do so.

Marriages were usually performed by the colored preacher although in most cases it was only necessary for the man to approach "Old Marster" and tell him that he wanted a certain woman for his wife. "Old Marster" then called the woman in question and if she agreed they were pronounced man and wife. If the woman was a prolific breeder and if the man was a strong, healthy-looking individual she was forced to take him as a husband whether she wanted to or not.

When Mr. Wright was asked if he had ever been arrested and placed in jail for any offense while he was a slave he replied that in those days few laws, if any, applied to slaves. He knows that it was against the law for anyone to teach a slave to write because on one occasion his father who had learned to do this with the help of his master's son was told by the master to keep it to himself, because if the men of the community found out that he could write they would cut his fingers or his hand off. Horse stealing or house burning was another serious crime. On the House plantation was a mulato slave who was to have been given his freedom when he reached the age of 21. When this time came Mr. House refused to free him and so an attempt was made to burn the House mansion. Mr. Wright remembers seeing the sheriff come from town and take this slave. Later they heard on the plantation that said slave had been hanged.

For the most part punishment consisted of severe whipping sometimes administered by the slaves' master and sometimes by the white men of the community known as the Patrol. To the slaves this Patrol was known as the "Paddle" or "Paddie-Rollers." Mr. Wright says that he has been whipped numerous times by his master for running away. When he was caught after an attempted escape he was placed on the ground where he was "spread-eagled," that is, his arms and feet were stretched out and tied to stakes driven in the ground. After a severe beating, brine water or turpentine was poured over the wounds. This kept the flies away, he says. Mr. House did not like to whip his slaves as a scarred slave brought very little money when placed on the auction block. A slave who had a scarred back was considered as being unruly. Whenever a slave attempted to escape the hounds were put on his trail. Mr. Wright was caught and treed by hounds several times. He later found a way to elude them. This was done by rubbing his feet in the refuse material of the barnyard or the pasture, then he covered his legs with pine tar. On one occasion he managed to stay away from the plantation for 6 months before he returned of his own accord. He ran away after striking his master who had attempted to whip him. When he returned of his own accord his master did nothing to him because he was glad that he was not forever lost in which case a large sum of money would have been lost. Mr. Wright says that slave owners advertised in the newspapers for lost slaves, giving their description, etc. If a slave was found after his master had stopped his advertisements he was placed on the block and sold as a "stray." While a fugitive he slept in the woods, eating wild berries, etc. Sometimes he slipped to the plantation of his mother or that of his father where he was able to secure food.

He took a deep puff on his pipe and a look of satisfaction crossed his face as he told how he had escaped from the "Paddle Rollers." It was the "Paddle-Rollers" duty to patrol the roads and the streets and to see that no slave was out unless he had a "pass" from his master. Further, he was not supposed to be any great distance away from the place he had been permitted to go. If a slave was caught visiting without a "pass" or if at any time he was off his plantation without said "pass" and had the misfortune to be caught by the "Paddle-Rollers" he was given a sound whipping and returned to his master.

When the Civil War began all the slaves on the House plantation grew hopeful and glad of the prospect of being set free. Mr. House was heard by some of the slaves to say that he hoped to be dead the day Negroes were set free. Although the slaves prayed for their freedom they were afraid to even sing any type of spiritual for fear of being punished.

When the Yankee troops came through near the House plantation they asked the slaves if their master was mean to them. As the answer was "no" the soldiers marched on after taking all the livestock that they could find. At the adjoining plantation where the master was mean, all property was burned. Mr. House was not present for when he heard of the approach of Sherman he took his family, a few valuables and some slaves and fled to Augusta. He later joined the army but was not wounded. However, his brother, Phil House, lost a leg while in action.

Mr. Wrights says that he witnessed one battle which was fought just a few miles beyond his plantation near Nancy's Creek. Although he did not officially join the Yankee army he cooked for them while they were camped in his vicinity.

When freedom was declared he says that he was a very happy man. Freedom to him did not mean that he could quit work but that he could work for himself as he saw fit to. After he was freed he continued working for his master who was considerably poorer than he had ever been before. After the war things were in such a state that even common table salt was not available. He remembers going to the smokehouse and taking the dirt from the floor which he later boiled. After the boiling process of this water which was now salty was used as a result of the dripping from the meats which had been hung there to be smoked in the "good old days."

After seven years of share-cropping with his former master Mr. Wright decided to come to Atlanta where he has been since. He attributes his ripe old age to sane and careful living. In any case he says that he would rather be free than be a slave but—and as he paused he shook his head sadly—"In those days a man did not have to worry about anything to eat as there was always a plenty. It's a lot different now."

United States. Work Projects Administration

[HW: Dist. 6
Ex-Slave #119 v.3]

"MAMMY DINK"
[HW: DINK WALTON YOUNG], Age 96

Place of birth:
On the Walton plantation, near old Baughville,
Talbot County, Georgia

Date of Birth: About 1840

Present residence:
Fifth Avenue, between 14th and 15th Streets,
Columbus, Georgia

Interviewed: August 1, 1936

DINK WALTON YOUNG

Dink Walton Young, better known as "Mammy Dink", is one of the oldest ex-slaves living in Muscogee County. She was born the chattel of Major Jack Walton, the largest ante-bellum planter and slave-holder of Talbot County, a man who owned several hundred Negroes and ten thousand or more acres of land. As a child, "Mammy Dink" was "brung up" with the Walton white children, often joining and playing with them in such games as "Mollie Bright", "William Trembletoe", and "Picking up Sticks".

The boys, white and black, and slightly older than she, played "Fox" and "Paddle-the-Cat" together. In fact, until the white boys and girls were ten or twelve years of age, their little Negro playmates, satellites, bodyguards, "gangs", and servants, usually addressed them rather familiarly by their first names, or replied to their nicknames that amounted to titles of endearment. Thus, Miss Susie Walton—the later Mrs. Robert Carter—was "Susie Sweet" to a host of little Negro girls of her age. Later on, of course, this form of familiarity between slave child and white child definitely ceased; but for all time there existed a strong bond of close friendship, mutual understanding, and spirit of comradeship between the Whites and Blacks of every plantation. As an example, Pat Walton, aged 18, colored and slave, "allowed" to his young master in 1861: "Marse Rosalius, youse gwine to de war, ain't yer?" and without waiting for an answer, continued: "So is Pat. You knows you ain't got no bizness in no army 'thout a Nigger to wait on yer an keep yer outa devilment, Marse Rosalius. Now, doen gin me no argyment, Marse Rosalius, case ise gwine 'long wid yer, and dat settles it, sah, it do, whether you laks it or you don't lak it." Parenthetically, it might be here inserted that this speech of Pat's to his young master was typical of a "style" that many slaves adopted in "dictating" to their white folks, and many Southern Negroes still employ an inoffensive, similar style to "dominate" their white friends.

According to "Mammy Dink", and otherwise verified, every time a Negro baby was born on one of his plantations, Major Dalton gave the mother a calico dress and a "bright, shiny", silver dollar.

All Walton slaves were well fed and clothed and, for a "drove" of about fifty or sixty little "back-yard" piccaninnies, the Waltons assumed all responsibility, except at night. A kind of compound was fenced off for "dese brats" to keep them in by day.

When it rained, they had a shelter to go under; play-houses were built for them, and they also had see-saws, toys, etc. Here, their parents "parked dese youn-guns" every morning as they went to the fields and to other duties, and picked them up at night. These children were fed about five times a day in little wooden trough-like receptacles. Their principal foods were milk, rice, pot-licker, vegetables and corn dumplings; and they stayed so fat and sleek "dat de Niggers calt 'em Marse Major's little black pigs."

The average weekly ration allowed an adult Walton slave was a peck of meal, two "dusters" of flour (about six pounds), seven pounds of flitch bacon, a "bag" of peas, a gallon of grits, from one to two quarts of molasses, a half pound of green coffee—which the slave himself parched and "beat up" or ground, from one to two cups of sugar, a "Hatful" of peas, and any "nicknacks" that the Major might have—as extras.

Many acres were planted to vegetables each year for the slaves and, in season, they had all the vegetables they could eat, also Irish potatoes, sweet potatoes, roasting ears, watermelons and "stingy green" (home raised tobacco). In truth, the planters and "Niggers" all used "stingy green", there then being very little if any "menufro" (processed tobacco) on the market.

The standard clothes of the slaves were: jeans in the winter for men and women, cottonades and osnabergs for men in the summer, and calicos and "light goods" for the women in the summer time. About 75% of the cloth used for slaves' clothing was made at home.

If a "Nigger come down sick", the family doctor was

promptly called to attend him and, if he was bad off, the Major "sat up" with him, or had one of his over-seers do so.

Never in her life was "Mammy Dink" whipped by any of the Waltons or their over-seers. Moreover, she never knew a Negro to be whipped by a white person on any of the dozen or more Walton plantations. She never "seed" a pataroler in her life, though she "has heard tell dat Judge Henry Willis, Marses Johnnie B. Jones, Ned Giddens, Gus O'Neal, Bob Baugh, an Jedge Henry Collier rid as patarolers" when she was a girl.

When the Yankee raiders came through in '65, "Mammy Dink" was badly frightened by them. She was also highly infuriated with them for "stealin de white fokes' things", burning their gins, cotton and barns, and conducting themselves generally as bandits and perverts.

In 1875, the year of the cyclone "whooch kilt sebenteen fokes twixt Ellesli (Ellerslie) and Talbotton", including an uncle of her's. "Mammy Dink" was living at the Dr. M.W. Peter's place near Baughville. Later, she moved with her husband—acquired subsequent to freedom—to the Dr. Thomas D. Ashford's place, in Harris County, near Ellerslie. There, she lost her husband and, about thirty-five years ago, moved to Columbus to be near Mrs. John T. Davis, Jr., an only daughter of Dr. Ashford, to whom she long ago became very attached.

When interviewed, "Mammy Dink" was at Mrs. Davis' home, "jes piddlin 'round", as she still takes a pride in "waiting on her white fokes."

Naturally, for one of her age, the shadows are lengthening. "Mammy Dink" has never had a child; all her kin are dead; she is 96 and has no money and no property, but she has her memories and, "thank Gawd", Mrs. Davis—her guardian-angel, friend and benefactress.

United States. Work Projects Administration

Whitley,
4-29-37
Ex-Slave #119

MAMMY DINK IS DEAD
[HW: (From Columbus News—Record of Dec-8-1936)]

MAMMY DINK

Mammy Dink, who cooked and served and gained pure joy through faithful service, has gone to the Big House in the skies. She lacked but a few years of a hundred and most of it was spent in loving service. She was loyal to the families she worked for and was, to all practical intents, a member of the family circle. She was 94 or 95 when she passed away—Mammy was about to lose track of mere age, she was so busy with other things—and she was happily at work to within a week of her death. She was an institution in Columbus, and one of the best known of the many faithful and loyal colored servants in this city.

Mammy Dink—her full name, by the way, was Dink Young—started out as a cook in a Talbot county family and wound up her career as cook for the granddaughter of her original employer. She was first in service in the home of Dr. M.W. Peters, in Talbot county, and later was the cook in the family of Dr. T.R. Ashford, at Ellerslie, in Harris county. Then, coming to Columbus, she was cook in the home of the late Captain T.J. Hunt for some 20 years.

For the last 27 years she had been cook for Mrs. John T. Davis, just as she had been cook in the home of her father, Dr. Ashford, and her grandfather, Dr. Peters.

Mammy, in leisure hours, used to sit on the coping at the Sixteenth street school, and watch the world go by. But her greatest joy was in the kitchen.

The Davis family was devoted to the faithful old servant. A week ago she developed a severe cold and was sent to the hospital. She passed away Saturday night—the old body had given out. The funeral service was conducted yesterday afternoon from St. Philips colored church in Girard. She was buried in a churchyard cemetery, two or three miles out, on the Opelika road. The white people who were present wept at the departure of one who was both servant and friend.

Thus passes, to a sure reward, Mammy Dink, whose life was such a success.

[HW: *Mammy Dink died Saturday night, Dec. 5th, 1936*]

COMBINED INTERVIEWS

United States. Work Projects Administration

[HW: Dist 1-2
Ex-Slave #24]

FEDERAL WRITERS' PROJECTS,
Augusta-Athens
Supervisor: Miss Velma Bell
[Date Stamp: MAY 8 1937]

EXCERPTS FROM SLAVE INTERVIEWS

[ADELINE]

"Aunt Adeline," an ex-slave of Wilkes County, Georgia, thinks she is "around a hundred." Her first memory is, in her own words, "my love for my mother. I loved her so! I would cry when I couldn't be with her. When I growed up, I kep' on loving her jes' that-a-way, even after I married and had children of my own."

Adeline's mother worked in the field, drove steers, and was considered the best meat cutter on the plantation. The slave women were required to spin, and Adeline's mother was unusually good at spinning wool, "and that kind of spinning was powerful slow," added the old woman. "My mother was one of the best dyers anywhere around. I was too. I made colors by mixing up all kinds of bark and leaves. I made the prettiest sort of lilac color with maple bark and pine bark—not the outside pine bark, but that little thin skin that grows right down next to the tree." Adeline remembers one dress she loved: "I never will forget it as long as I live. It was a hickory stripe dress they made for me, with brass buttons at the wrist bands. I was so proud of that dress and felt so dressed up in it, I just strutted!"

She remembers the plantation store and the candy the master gave the Negro children. "Bright, pretty sticks of candy!" Tin cups hold a special niche in her memory. But there were punishments, too. "Good or bad, we got whippings with a long cowhide kept just for that. They whipped us to make us grow better, I reckon!"

Asked about doctors, Adeline replied:

"I was born, growed up, married and had sixteen children and never had no doctor till here since I got so old!"

Plantation ingenuity was shown in home concoctions and tonics. At the first sniffle of a cold, the slaves were called in and given a drink of fat lightwood tea, made by pouring boiling water over split kindling. "'Cause lightwood got turpentine in it," explained Adeline. She said that a springtime tonic was made of anvil dust, gathered at the blacksmith's shop, mixed with syrup. This was occasionally varied with a concoction of garlic and whiskey!

Adeline adheres to traditional Negro beliefs, and concluded her recountal of folklore with the dark prediction: "Every gloomy day brings death. Somebody leaving this unfriendly world to-day!"

[EUGENE]

Another version of slavery was given by Eugene, an Augusta Negro. His mother was brought to Augusta from Pennsylvania and freed when she came of age. She married a slave whose master kept a jewelry store. The freed woman was required to put a guardian over her children. The jeweler paid Eugene's father fifty cents a week and was angry when his mother refused to allow her children to work for him. Eugene's mother supported her children by laundry work. "Free colored folks had to pay taxes," said Eugene, "And in Augusta you had to have a pass to go from house to house. You couldn't go out at night in Augusta after 9 o'clock. They had a bell at the old market down yonder, and it would strike every hour and half hour. There was an uptown market, too, at Broad and McKinne."

Eugene told of an old Negro preacher, Ned Purdee, who had a school for Negro children in his back yard, in defiance of a law prohibiting the education of Negroes. Ned, said Eugene, was put in jail but the punishment of stocks and lashes was not intended to be executed. The sympathetic jailor told the old man: "Ned, I won't whip you. I'll just whip down on the stock, and you holler!" So Ned made a great noise, the jailor thrashed about with his stick, and no harm was done.

Eugene touched on an unusual angle of slavery when he spoke of husbands and wives discovering that they were brother and sister. "They'd talk about their grandfathers and grandmothers, and find out that they had been separated when they were children," he said.

"When freedom was declared, they called the colored people down to the parade ground. They had built a big stand, and the Yankees and some of the leading colored men made addresses. 'You are free now. Don't steal. Work and make a living. Do honest work. There are no more masters. You are all free.' He said the Negro troops came in, singing:

> "Don't you see the lightning?
> Don't you hear the thunder?
> It isn't the lightning,
> It isn't the thunder,
> It's the buttons on
> The Negro uniforms!"

[MARY]

Mary is a tiny woman, 90 years old. "I'd love to see some of the white folks boys and girls," she said, smiling and showing a set of strong new teeth. "We had school on our plantation, and a Negro teacher named Mathis, but they couldn't make me learn nothin'. I sure is sorry now!"

Mary's plantation memories, in contrast to those of slaves who remember mostly molasses and corn-pone, include tomato rice, chickens, baked, fried and stewed. "And chicken pies!" Mary closed her eyes. "Don't talk about 'em! I told my grand children last week, I wanted to eat some old-time potato pie!"

They played "peep-squirrel," Mary remembered. "I never could put up to dance much, but none could beat me runnin'. "Peep Squirrel" was a game we made up on the plantation. The girls peeped out, then ran by the men, and they'd be caught and twirled around. They said I was like a kildee bird, I was so little and could run so fast! They said I was married when I was 17 years old. I know it was after freedom. I had the finest kind of marrying dress that my father bought for me. It had great big grapes hanging down from the sleeves and around the skirt." Mary sighed. "I wish't I had-a kep' it for my children to saw!"

[RACHEL]

Rachel's master called his people "servants", not Negroes or slaves. "He de bes' marster in de worl'," said Rachel. "I love his grave!"

Rachel nursed her aunt's children while the mother acted as nurse for "de lady's baby whut come fum Russia wid de marster's wife." The czarina was godmother for the ambassador's baby. "Marster bin somewheh in de back part o' de worl'." explained the old woman, "You see, he wuz de guv'nor. He knowed all de big people, senetras and all." Rachel laughed. "I was a old maid when I married," she said. "De broom wuz de law. All we hadder do was step over de broom befo' witnesses and we wuz marry!"

[LAURA]

"As far as I kin rekellec'," said Laura, "my mother was give." She could not remember her age, but estimated that she might be 75 years old. Her native dignity was evident in her calm manner, her neat clothing and the comfortable, homelike room. "Dey say in dem days," she continued, "when you marry, dey give you so many colored people. My mother, her brother and her aunt was give to young Mistis when she marry de Baptis' preacher and come to Augusta. When dey brought us to Augusta, I wuz de baby. Round wheh de barracks is now, was de Baptis' parsonage. My mother was a cook. I kin remember de Yankees comin' down Broad Street. Dey put up wheh de barracks is on Reynolds Street. Dey ca'yed me to de fairground. De man was speakin'. I thought it wuz up in de trees, but I know now it muster been a platform in bushes. Mistis say to me: 'Well, Laura, what did you see?' I say: 'Mistis, we is all free.' I such a lil' chile she jus' laugh at me for saying sich a thing. When I was sick, she nuss me good."

Laura remembered a long house with porches on Ellis Street, "running almost to Greene," between 7th and 8th, where slaves were herded and kept for market day. "Dey would line 'em up like horses or cows," she said, "and look in de mouf' at dey teeth. Den dey march 'em down together to market, in crowds, first Tuesday sale day."

[MATILDA]

In contrast to the pleasant recollections of most of the ex-slaves, Matilda gave a vivid picture of the worst phase of plantation life on a Georgia plantation. She had been plowing for four years when the war started.

"I wuz in about my thirteen when de war end," she mumbled, "Fum de fus' overseer, dey whu-op me to show me how to wuk. I wuk hard, all de time. I never had no good times. I so old I kain't rekellec' my marster's name. I kain't 'member, honey. I had too hard time. We live in, a weather-board house, jus' hulled in. We had to eat anyting dey give us, mos'ly black 'lasses in a great big ole hogshead. When de war gwine on, we had to live on rice, mos'ly, what dey raise. We had a hard time. Didn't know we wuz free for a long time. All give overseer so mean, de slaves run away. Dey gits de blood-houn' to fin' 'em. Dey done dug cave in de wood, down in de ground, and hide dere. Dey buckle de slave down to a log and beat de breaf' outter dem, till de blood run all over everywhere. When night come, dey drug 'em to dey house and greases 'em down wid turpentine and rub salt in dey woun's to mek 'em hurt wuss. De overseer give de man whiskey to mek him mean. When dey whu-op my mother, I crawl under de house and cry."

One of Matilda's younger friends, listening, nodded her head in sympathy.

"When Matilda's mind was clearer she told us terrible stories," she said. "It makes all the rest of us thankful we weren't born in those times."

Matilda was mumbling end weeping.

"Dey wuz mean overseer," she whispered. "But dey wuz run out o' de country. Some white ladies in de neighborhood reported 'um and had 'um run out."

[EASTER]

"Aunt Easter" is from Burke County. Her recollections are not quite so appalling as Matilda's, but they are not happy memories.

"Dey didn' learn me nothin' but to churn and clean up house. 'Tend day boy, churn dat milk, spin and cyard dat roll."

Asked if the slaves were required to go to Church, Easter shook her head.

"Too tired. Sometime we even had to pull fodder on Sunday. Sometime we go to church, but all dey talk about wuz obeyin' Massa and obeyin' Missus. Befo' we went to church, we had to git up early and wash and iron our clo'es."

Easter's brother was born the day Lee surrendered. "Dey name him Richmond," she said.

[CARRIE]

Carrie had plenty to eat in slavery days. "I'd be a heap better off if it was dem times now," she said, "My folks didn't mistreet de slaves. When freedom come, de niggers come 'long wid dere babies on dey backs and say I wuz free. I tell 'em I already free! Didn't mek no diffrunce to me, freedom!"

[MALINDA]

Malinda would gladly exchange all worldly possessions and freedom to have plantation days back again. She owns her home and has a garden of old-fashioned flowers, due to her magic "growing hand."

"I belonged to a preacher in Ca'lina," said Malinda. "A Baptis' preacher. My fambly wasn't fiel' han's, dey wuz all house servants. Marster wouldn't sell none o' his slaves. When he wanted to buy one, he'd buy de whole fambly to keep fum having 'em separated."

Malinda and her sister belonged to the young girls. "Whar'ever da young Mistises visited, we went right erlong. My own mammy tuk long trips wid ole Mistis to de Blue Ridge Mountings and sometimes over de big water." Malinda said the slaves danced to "quills," a homemade reed instrument. "My mammy wuz de bes' dancer on de planteshun," asserted the old woman. "She could dance so sturdy, she could balance a glass of water on her head and never spill a drap!"

[AMELIA]

Amelia, like many of the old slaves in Augusta today, came from South Carolina.

"I put on a hoopskirt one time," she said. "I wanted to go to church wid a hoop on. I such a lil' gal, all de chillun laugh at me, playin' lady. I take it off and hide it in de wood."

Amelia remembered her young mistresses with affection. "Dey wuz so good to me," she said, "dey like to dress me up! I was a lil' gal wid a tiny wais'. Dey put corsets on me and lace me up tight, and then dey take off all dey medallion and jewelry and hang 'em roun' my neck and put long sash on me. I look pretty to go to dance. When I git back, I so tired I thow myself on de bed and sleep wid dat tight corset on me!"

United States. Work Projects Administration

FOUR SLAVES INTERVIEWED
by
MAUDE BARRAGAN, EDITH BELL LOVE, RUBY LORRAINE RADFORD

ELLEN CAMPBELL

1030 Brayton Street, Augusta, Ga., Born 1846.

Ellen Campbell lives in a little house in a garden behind a picket fence. Ellen is a sprightly, erect, black woman ninety years old. Beady little eyes sparkled behind her glasses as she talked to us. Her manner is alert, her mind is very keen and her memory of the old days very clear. Though the temperature was in the high nineties she wore two waists, and her clothes were clean and neatly patched. There was no headcloth covering the fuzzy grey wool that was braided into innumerable plaits.

She invited us into her tiny cabin. The little porch had recently been repaired, while the many flowers about the yard and porch gave evidence of constant and loving care to this place which had been bought for her long ago by a grandson who drove a "hack." When she took us into the crowded, but clean room, she showed us proudly the portrait of this big grandson, now dead. All the walls were thickly covered with framed pictures of different members of her family, most of whom are now dead. In their midst was a large picture of Abraham Lincoln.

"Dere's all my chillun. I had fo' daughter and three 'grands', but all gone now but one niece. I deeded de place to her. She live out north now, but she send back de money fer de taxes and insurance and to pay de firemens."

Then she proudly pointed out a framed picture of herself when she was young.

"Why Auntie, you were certainly nice looking then."

Her chest expanded and her manner became more sprightly as she said, "I wus de pebble on de beach den!"

"And I suppose you remember about slavery days?"

"Yes ma'm, I'm ninety years old—I wus a grown 'oman when freedom come. I 'longed to Mr. William Eve. De plantachun was right back here—all dis land was fields den, slap down to Bolzes'."

"So you remember a lot about those times?"

She laughed delightedly. "Yas'm. I 'longed to Miss Eva Eve. My missus married Colonel Jones. He got a boy by her and de boy died."

"You mean Colonel Jones, the one who wrote books?"

"Yas'm. He a lawyer, too, down to de Cote House. My missus was Mrs. Carpenter's mother, but she didn't brought her here."

"You mean she was her step-mother?"

"Yas'm, dat it. I go to see dem folks on de hill sometime. Dey good to me, allus put somepen in mah hands."

"What kind of work did you do on the plantation?"

"When I wus 'bout ten years old dey started me totin' water—you know ca'in water to de hands in de field. 'Bout two years later I got my first field job, 'tending sheep. When I wus fifteen my old Missus gib me to Miss Eva—you know she de one marry Colonel Jones. My young missus wus fixin' to git married, but she couldn't on account de war, so she brought me to town and rented me out to a lady runnin' a boarding house. De rent was paid to my missus. One day I wus takin' a tray from de outdoor kitchen to de house when I stumbled and dropped it. De food spill all over de ground. De lady got so mad she picked up a butcher knife and chop me in de haid. I went runnin' till I come to de place where my white folks live. Miss Eva took me and wash de blood out mah head and put medicine on it, and she wrote a note to de lady and she say, 'Ellen is my slave, give to me by my mother. I wouldn't had dis happen to her no more dan to me. She won't come back dere no more.'"

"Were you ever sold during slavery times, Aunt Ellen?"

"No'm. I wa'nt sold, but I knows dem whut wus. Jedge Robinson he kept de nigger trade office over in Hamburg."

"Oh yes, I remember the old brick building."

"Yas'm, dat it. Well, all de colored people whut gonner be sold was kept dere. Den dey brung 'em over to de market and put 'em up fer sale. Anybody fixin' to buy 'em, 'zamines 'em to see if dey all right. Looks at de teef to tell 'bout de age."

"And was your master good to you, Auntie?"

"I'll say dis fer Mr. William Eve—he de bes' white man anywhere round here on any dese plantachuns. Dey all own slaves. My boss would feed 'em well. He wus killin' hogs stidy fum Jinury to March. He had two smoke-houses. Dere wus four cows. At night de folks on one side de row o' cabins go wid de piggins fer milk, and in de mawnin's dose on de odder side go fer de piggins o' milk."

"And did you have plenty of other things to eat?"

"Law, yas'm. Rations wus given out to de slaves; meal, meat and jugs o' syrup. Dey give us white flour at Christmas. Every slave family had de gyrden patch, and chickens. Marster buy eggs and chickens fum us at market prices."

"Did the overseers ever whip the slaves or treat them cruelly?"

"Sometimes dey whup 'em—make 'em strip off dey shirt and whup 'em on de bare skin. My boss had a white overseer and two colored men dey call drivers. If dey didn't done right dey dus whup you and turn you loose."

"Did the Eves have a house on the plantation, too?"

"No'm, dey live in town, and he come back and fo'th every day. It warn't but three miles. De road run right fru de plantachun, and everybody drive fru it had to pay toll. Dat toll gate wus on de D'Laigle plantachun. Dey built a house fer Miss Kitty Bowles down by de double gate where dey had to pay de toll. Dat road where de Savannah Road is."

When asked about war times on the plantation Ellen recalled that when the Northern troops were around Waynesboro orders were sent to all the masters of the nearby plantations to send ten of their best men to build breastworks to hold back the northern advance.

"Do you remember anything about the good times or weddings on the plantation?"

She laughed delightedly. "Yas'm. When anybody gwine be married dey tell de boss and he have a cake fix. Den when Sunday come, atter dey be married, she put on de white dress she be married in and dey go up to town so de boss see de young couple."

"Den sometimes on Sadday night we have a big frolic. De nigger frum Hammond's place and Phinizy place, Eve place, Clayton place, D'Laigle place all git togedder fer big dance and frolic. A lot o' de young white sports used to come dere and push de nigger bucks aside and dance wid de wenches."

"What happened, Auntie, if a slave from one plantation wanted to marry a slave from another?"

She laughed significantly. "Plenty. Old Mr. Miller had a man name Jolly and he wanner marry a woman off anudder plantachun, but Jolly's Marster wanna buy de woman to come to de plantachun. He say, 'Whut's fair fer de goose is fair fer de gander.' When dey couldn't come to no 'greement de man he run away to de woods. Den dey sot de bloodhounds on 'im. Dey let down de rail fence so de hounds could git fru. Dey sarch de woods and de swamps fer Jolly but dey neber find him.

"De slaves dey know whar he is, and de woman she visit him. He had a den down dere and plenty o' grub dey take 'im, but de white folks neber find him. Five hundred dollars wus what Miller put out for whomsover git him."

"And you say the woman went to visit him?"

"Yes, Ma'm. De woman would go dere in de woods wid him. Finally one night when he was outer de swamp he had to lie hidin' in de ditch all night, cross from de nigger hospital. Den somebody crep' up and shot him, but he didn't die den. Dey cay'ed his [TR: sic] crost to de hospital and he die three days later."

"What about church? Did you go to church in those days?"

"Yas'm, we used to go to town. But de padderolas wus ridin' in dem days, and you couldn't go off de plantachun widout a pass. So my boss he build a brick church on de plantachuhn, and de D'Laigles build a church on dere's."

"What happened if they caught you off without a pass?"

"If you had no pass dey ca'y you to de Cote House, and your marster hadder come git you out."

"Do you remember anything about the Yankees coming to this part of the country?"

At this her manner became quite sprightly, as she replied, "Yas'm, I seen 'em comin' down de street. Every one had er canteen on he side, a blanket on his shoulder, caps cocked on one side de haid. De cavalry had boots on and spurros on de boots. First dey sot de niggers free on Dead River, den dey come on here to sot us free. Dey march straight up Broad Street to de Planters' Hotel, den dey camped on Dead River, den dey camped on de river. Dey stayed here six months till dey sot dis place free. When dey campin' on de river bank we go down dere and wash dey clo'es fer a good price. Dey had hard tack to eat. Dey gib us de hard tack and tell us to soak it in Water, and fry it in de meat gravy. I ain't taste nothing so good since. Dey say, 'Dis hard tack whut we hadder lib on while we fightin' to sot you free."

RACHEL SULLIVAN

1327 Reynolds Street, Augusta, Ga., Born 1852.

We found Rachel Sullivan sitting on the porch of a two room house on Reynolds Street. She is a large, fleshy woman. Her handmade yellow homespun was baggy and soiled, and her feet were bare, though her shoes were beside her rocker.

We approached her cautiously. "Auntie, we heard you were one of the slaves who used to live on Governor Pickens' place over near Edgefield."

"Yas'm, Yas'm. I shore wus. He gin us our chu'ch—de one over yonder on de Edgefield road. No'm you can't see it fum de road. You has to cross de creek. Old Marster had it pulled out de low ground under de brush arbor, and set it dere."

"And what did you do on the plantation, Auntie?"

"I wus a nu's gal, 'bout 'leben years old. I nu'sed my

Auntie's chillun, while she nu'sed de lady's baby whut come from Russia wid de Marster's wife—nu'sed dat baby fum de breas's I mean. All de white ladies had wet nusses in dem days. Her master had just returned from Russia, where he had been ambassador. Her baby had the czarina for a godmother."

"And so you used to look after you aunt's children?"

"Yas'm. I used to play wid 'em in de big ground wid de monuments all around."

"Miss Lucy Holcome was Governor Pickens' second wife, wasn't she?"

"Musta wus, ma'm."

"And were you born on the plantation at Edgefield?"

"I wus born at Ninety-six. Log Creek place was Marster's second place. Oh, he had plantachuns everywhere, clear over to Alabama. He had overseers on all de places, ma'm."

"Did the overseers whip you or were they good?"

"Overseers wus good. Dey better been good to us, Marster wouldn't let 'em been nothin' else. And Marster wus good. Lawdy, us had de bes' Marster in de world. It wus great times when he come to visit de plantachun. Oh Lord, when de Governor would come—dey brung in all de sarvants. Marster call us 'sarvants', not 'niggers.' He say 'niggers wuk down in de lagoons.' So when de Governor come dey brung in all de sarvants, and all de little chillun, line 'em's up whar Marster's cai'age gwine pass. And Marster stop dere in de lane and 'zamine us all to see is us all right. He de bes' Marster in de world. I love his grave!"

"Den he'd talk to de overseer. Dere was Emmanuel and Mr. DeLoach. He gib 'em a charge. Dey couldn't whup us or treat us mean."

"How many slaves did your Master have, Auntie?"

"Oh, I don't know 'xactly—over a thousand in all I reckon. He had plantachuns clear over to Alabama. Marster wus a world manager! Lordy, I luv my Marster. Dere wus 'bout seventy plower hands, and 'bout a hunnard hoe hands."

"Did your master ever sell any of the slaves off his plantation?"

"No'm—not 'less dey did wrong. Three of 'em had chillun by de overseer, Mr. Whitefield, and Marster put 'em on de block. No ma'm he wouldn't tolerate dat. He say you keep de race pure. Lawdy, he made us lib right in dem time."

"And what did he do to the overseer?"

"He sont him off—he sont him down to de low place."

"I guess you had plenty to eat in those good old days?"

"Oh, yes ma'm—dey's kill a hunnard hogs."

"And what kind of houses did you have?"

"Des like dis street—two rows facin' each odder, only dey wus log houses."

"Did they have only one room?"

"Yas'm. But sometimes dey drap a shed room down if dere wus heap o' chullun.'

"Did you have a good time at Christmas?"

"Oh yas'm. No matter where Marster wus—crost de water er ennywhere he send us a barrel o' apples, and chestnuts—dey had chestnuts in dem days—and boxes o' candy. He sont 'em to 'Manuel and Mr. DeLoach to gib out."

"So your master would sometimes be across the water?"

"Lawdy, yas'm, he be dere somewhere in de back part o' de world. You see he wus gov'nur. He knowed all de big people—Mr. Ben Tillman and all—he was senetra."

"Auntie do you remember seeing any of the soldiers during the war?"

"Does I? Law honey! Dey come dere to de plantachun 'bout ten o'clock after dey surrender. Oh and dey wus awful, some of 'em wid legs off or arms off. De niggers took all de mules and put 'em down in de sand field. Den dey took all de wimmens and put 'em in de chillun's house. And dey lef' a guard dere to stand over 'em, and tell him not to git off de foot. You know dey didn't want put no temptation in de way o' dem soldiers."

"What kind of work did some of the slave women do?"

"Everything. I had a one-legged auntie—she was de seamster. She sew fum one year end to de odder. Anodder auntie wus a loomer."

"And where did you go to church?"

"We went to de Salem Chu'ch. Yas'm we all go to chu'ch. Marster want us to go to chu'ch. We sit on one side—so—and dey sit over dere. Dey wus Methodis'. My mother was Methodis', but dey gib her her letter when freedom come."

"How about dances, Auntie? Did they have dances and frolics?"

"Yassum, on Sadday night. But boys had to git a pass when dey go out or de Padderola git 'em."

"So you had a happy time in those days, eh?"

"Lawdy, yas'm. If de world would done now like dey did den de world wouldn't be in such a mess. I gwine on eighty-five, but I wish de young ones wus raise now like I was raise. Marster taught us to do right."

"How many children have you?"

"I had 'leben—seben livin now." Then she laughed. "But I wus ole maid when I git married."

"I wus twenty years old! In dem days all dey hadder do to git married wus step over de broom."

"Step over the broom. Didn't your master have the preacher come and marry you?"

"Lawdy, no'm. De broom wus de law!" Then she laughed. "Jus' say you wanner be married and de couple git together 'fore witnesses and step ober de broom."

"Do you remember when freedom came?"

"Lawdy yas'm. Mr. DeLoach come riding up to de plantachun in one o' dem low-bellied ca'yages. He call to Jo and James—dem de boys what stay round de house to bring wood and rake de grass and sich—he sont Jo and Jim down to all de fields to tell all de hands to come up. Dey unhitch de mules fum de plows and come wid de chains rattlin', and de cotton hoers put dey hoes on dey shoulders—wid de blades shinin' in de sun, and all come hurrying to hear what Mr. DeLoach want wid'em. Den he read de freedom warrant to 'em. One man so upset he start runnin' and run clear down to de riber and jump in."

EUGENE WESLEY SMITH
1105 Robert Street, Augusta, Ga., Born 1852

Eugene is 84 years old. He has thin features, trembling lips and a sparse beard. His skin is a deep brown, lined and veined. His legs showing over white socks are scaly. His hands are palsied, but his mind is intelligent. He shows evidences of association with white people in his manner of speech, which at times is in the manner of white persons, again reverting to dialect.

Eugene stated that his father was a slave who belonged to Steadman Clark of Augusta, and acted as porter in Mr. Clark's jewelry store on Broad Street. His grandmother came from Pennsylvania with her white owners. In accordance with the laws of the state they had left, she was freed when she came of age, and married a man named Smith. Her name was Louisa. Eugene's "Arnt" married a slave. As his mother was free, her children were free, but Eugene added:

"She had put a Guardian over us, and Captain Crump was our guardian. Guardians protected the Negro children who belonged to them."

To illustrate that children were considered the property of the mothers' owners, he added that his uncle went to Columbia County and married a slave, and that all of her children belonged to her master.

Mr. Clark, who owned Eugene's father, paid him 50¢

a week, and was angry when Louisa refused to allow her children to work for him.

"He was good in a way," admitted Eugene, "Some masters were cruel to the colored people, but a heap of white people won't believe it.

"I was too little to do any work before freedom. I just stayed with my mother, and ran around. She did washing for white folks. We lived in a rented house. My father's master, Mr. Clark, let him come to see us sometimes at night. Free colored folks had to pay taxes. Mother had to pay taxes. Then when they came of age, they had to pay taxes again. Even in Augusta you had to have a pass to go from house to house. They had frolics. Sometimes the white people came and looked at 'em having a good time. You couldn't go out at night in Augusta after 9 o'clock. They had a bell at the old market down yonder, and it would strike every hour and every half hour. There was an uptown market, too, at Broad and McKinne."

Asked about school, Eugene said:

"Going to school wasn't allowed, but still some people would slip their children to school. There was an old Methodist preacher, a Negro named Ned Purdee, he had a school for boys and girls going on in his back yard. They caught him and put him in jail. He was to be put in stocks and get so many lashes every day for a month. I heard him tell many times how the man said: 'Ned, I won't whip you. I'll whip on the stock, and you holler.' So Ned would holler out loud, as if they were whipping him. They put his feet and hands in the holes, and he was supposed to be whipped across his back."

"I read in the paper where a lady said slaves were never sold here in Augusta at the old market, but I saw them selling slaves myself. They put them up on something like a table, bid 'em off just like you would horses or cows. Dey was two men. I kin rekellect. I know one was called Mr. Tom Heckle. He used to buy slaves, speculating. The other was named Wilson. They would sell your mother from the children. That was the reason so many colored people married their sisters and brothers, not knowing until they got to talking about it. One would say, 'I remember my grandmother,' and another would say, "that's *my* grandmother," then they'd find out they were sister and brother.

"Speculators used to steal children," said Eugene. "I saw the wagons. They were just like the wagons that came from North Carolina with apples in. Dey had big covers on them. The speculators had plantations where they kept the children until they were big enough to sell, and they had an old woman there to tend to those children."

"I was a butler." (A dreamy look came into Eugene's old eyes.) "So I were young. I saw a girl and fell in love with her, and asked her to marry me. 'Yes,' she said, 'when I get grown!' I said, 'I am not quite grown myself.' I was sixteen years old. When I was twenty-one years old I married her in my father's house. My mother and father were dead then. I had two sisters left, but my brothers were dead too."

"I quit butling when I got married. They was enlarging the canal here. It was just wide enough for the big flats to go up with cotton. They widened it, and I went to work on dat, for $1.25 a day. They got in some Chinese when it was near finished, but they wasn't any good. The Irishmen wouldn't work with niggers, because they said they could make the job last eight years—the niggers worked too fast. They accomplished it in about four years.

"After working on the canal, I left there and helped dig the foundations of Sibley Mill. The raceway, the water that run from canal to river, I helped dig that. Then after that, I went to Mr. Berckmans and worked for him for fifty years. All my children were raised on his place. That's how come my boy do garden work now. I worked for 50¢ a day, but he give me a house on the place. He 'lowed me to have chickens, a little fence, and a garden. He was very good to us. That was Mr. P.J. Berckmans. I potted plants all day long. I used to work at night. I wouldn't draw no money, just let them keep it for me. After they found out I could read and write and was an honest fellow, they let me take my work home, and my children helped me make the apple grass and plum grass, and mulberry grass. A man come and told me he would give me $60 a month if I would go with him, but I didn't I couldn't see hardly at all then—I was wearing glasses. Now, in my 84th year, I can read the newspaper, Bible and everything without glasses. My wife died two years ago." (Tears came into Eugene's eyes, and his face broke up) "We lived together 62 years!"

Asked if his wife had been a slave, Eugene answered that she was but a painful effort of memory did not reveal her owner's name.

"I do remember she told me she had a hard time," he went on slowly. "Her master and misses called themselves 'religious people' but they were not good to her. They took her about in the barouche when they were visiting. She had to mind the children. They had a little seat on the back, and they'd tie her up there to keep her from falling off. Once when they got to a big gate, they told her to get down and open it for the driver to go through, not knowing the hinges was broken. That big gate fell on her back and she was down for I don't know how long. Before she died, she complained of a pain in her back, and the doctor said it must have been from a lick when she was a child.

"During the war there were some Southern soldiers went through. I and two friends of mine were together. Those soldiers caught us and made us put our hands down at our knees, and tied 'em, and run the stick through underneath.

"It was wintertime. They had a big fire. They pushed us nearer and nearer the fire, until we hollered. It was just devilment. They was having fun with us, kept us tied up about a half hour. There was a mulatto boy with us, but they thought he was white, and didn't bother him. One time they caught us and threw us up in blankets, way up, too—I was about 11 years old then."

Asked about church, Eugene said:

"We went to bush meetings up on the Sand Hill out in the woods. They didn't have a church then."

Eugene's recollections were vivid as to the ending of the war:

"The Northern soldiers come to town playing Yankee Doodle. When freedom come, they called all the white people to the courthouse first, and told them the darkies was free. Then on a certain day they called all the colored people down to the parade ground. They had built a big stand, and the Yankees and some of our leading colored men got up and spoke, and told the Negroes:

"You are free now. Don't steal. Now work and make a living. Do honest work, make an honest living to support yourself and children. No more masters. You are free."

Eugene said when the colored troops come in, they sang:

> "Don't you see the lightning?
> Don't you hear the thunder?
> It isn't the lightning,
> It isn't the thunder,
> But its the button on
> The Negro uniforms!

"The slaves that was freed, and the country Negroes that had been run off, or had run away from the plantations, was staying in Augusta in Guv'ment houses, great big ole barns. They would all get free provisions from the Freedmen's Bureau, but people like us, Augusta citizens, didn't get free provisions, we had to work. It spoiled some of them. When the small pox come, they died like hogs, all over Broad Street and everywhere."

WILLIS BENNEFIELD
Hephzibah, Ga., Born 1835.

[TR: *"Uncle Willis" in individual interviews.*]

"Uncle Willis" lives with his daughter Rena Berrian, who is 74 years old. "I his baby," said Rena, "all dead but me, and I ain't no good for him now 'cause I can't tote nothin'."

When asked where Uncle Willis was, Rena looked out over the blazing cotton field and called:

"Pap! Oh—pappy! Stop pickin' cotton and come in awhile. Dey's some ladies wants to see you."

Uncle Willis hobbled slowly to the cabin, set in the middle of the cotton patch. He wore clean blue overalls, obviously new. His small, regular features had high cheekbones. There was a tuft of curly white hair on his chin, and his head was covered with a "sundown" hat.

"Mawnin," he said, "I bin sick. So I thought I might git some cotton terday."

Willis thinks he is 101 years old. He said, "I was 35 years old when freedom delcared." He belonged to Dr. Balding Miller, who lived on Rock Creek plantation. Dr. Miller had three or four plantations, Willis said at first, but later stated that the good doctor had five or six places, all in Burke County.

"I wuk in de fiel'," he went on, "and I drove de doctor

thirty years. He owned 300 slaves. I never went to school a day in my life, 'cept Sunday school, but I tuk de doctor's sons fo' miles ev'y day to school. Guess he had so much business in hand he thought the chillun could walk. I used to sit down on de school steps 'till dey turn out. I got way up in de alphabet by listenin', but when I went to courtin' I forgot all dat."

Asked what his regular duties were, Willis answered with pride:

"Marster had a cay'age and a buggy too. My father driv' de cay'age and I driv de doctor. Sometimes I was fixing to go to bed, and had to hitch up my horse and go five or six miles. I had a regular saddle horse, two pairs for cay'age. Doctor were a rich man. Richest man in Burke County. He made his money on his farm. When summertime come, I went wid him to Bath, wheh he had a house on Tena Hill. We driv' down in de cay'age. Sundays we went to church when Dr. Goulding preach. De darkies went in de side do'. I hear him preach many times."

Asked about living conditions on Rock Creek plantation, Willis replied:

"De big house was set in ahalf acre yard. 'Bout fifty yards on one side was my house, and fifty yards on de udder side was de house of granny, a woman that tended de chillun and had charge of de yard when we went to Bath," Willis gestured behind him, "and back yonder was de quarters, a half mile long; dey wuz one room 'crost, and some had shed room. When any of 'em got sick, Marster would go round to see 'em all."

Asked about church and Bible study, Willis said:

"I belongst to Hopeful Church. Church people would have singin' and prayin', and de wicked would have dancin' and singin'. At dat time I was a regular dancer" Willis chuckled. "I cut de pigeon wing high enough! Not many cullud people know de Bible in slavery time. We had dances, and prayers and sing too," he went on, "and we sang a song, 'On Jordan's stormy banks I stand, and cast a wishful eye.'"

"How about marriages?" he was asked.

"Colored preacher marry 'em. You had to get license and give it to the preacher, and he marry 'em. Then de men on our plantation had wives on udder plantations, dey call 'em broad wives."

"Did you give your wife presents when you were courting?" he was asked.

"I went to courtin' and never give her nuthin' till I marry her."

As to punishment, Willis said that slaves were whipped as they needed it, and as a general rule the overseer did the whipping.

"When darky wouldn't take whippin' from de overseer," he said, he had to cay'y dem to de boss; and if we needed any brushin' de marster brush 'em. Why, de darkies would whip de overseer!"

Willis was asked to describe how slaves earned money for personal use, and replied:

"Dey made dey own money. In slavery time, if you wanted four or five acres of land to plant anything on, marster give it to you, and whatever dat land make, it belong to you. You could take dat money and spend it any you wanted to. Still he give you somethin' to eat and clothe you, but dat patch you mek cotton on, sometimes a whole bale, dat money yours."

Willis thought the plantation house was still there, "but it badly wounded," he said. "Dey tell me dere ain't nobody living in it now. It seven miles from Waynesboro, south."

"When de soldiers come thoo'," continued Willis, "dey didn't burn dat place, but dey went in dere and took out ev'thing dey want, and give it to de cullud people. Dey kep' it till dey got free. De soldiers tuk Dr. Millers horses and carry 'em off. Got in de crib and tuk de corn. Got in de smoke'ouse and tuk de meat out. Old Marssa bury his money and silver in a iron chist. Dey tuk it 300 yards away to a clump of trees and bury it. It tuk fo' men to ca'y it. Dere was money without mention in dat chist! After de soldiers pass thoo, de went down and got it back."

"What did you do after freedom was declared?"

Willis straightened up.

"I went down to Augusta to de Freedmen's Bureau to see if twas true we wuz free. I reckon dere was, over a hundred people dere. The man got up and stated to de people, "you is jus' as free as I am. You ain't got no mistis and no marster. Work wheh you want." On Sunday morning old Marster sent de house girl and tell us to all come to de house. He said:

"What I want to send for you all, is to tell you you are free. You hab de privilege to go anywhere you want, but I don't want none of you to leave me now. I wants you-all to stay right wid me. If you stay, you you mus' sign to it' I asked him: "What you want me to sign for?, I is free." 'Dat will hold me to my word, and hold you to yo' word,' he say. All my folks sign it, but I wouldn't sign. Marster call me up and say: 'Willis, why wouldn't you sign?' I say: 'If I already is free, I don't need to sign no paper. If I was working for you, and doing for you befo' I got free, I can do it still, if you want me to stay wid yo'.' My father and mother tried to git me to sign, but I wouldn't sign. My mother said: 'You oughter sign. How you know Marster gwine pay?' I said: 'Den I kin go somewhere else.' Marster pay first class hands $15.00 a month, other hands $10.00, and den on down to five and six dollars. He give rations like dey always. When Christmas come, all come up to be paid off. Den he call me. Ask whar is me? I wus standin' roun' de corner of de house. 'Come up here,' he say, 'you didn't sign dat paper, but I reckon I have to pay you too.' He paid me and my wife $180.000. I said: 'Well, you-all thought he wouldn't pay me, but I got my money too.' I stayed to my marster's place one year after de war den I lef'dere. Nex' year I decided I wuld quit dere and go somewhere else. It was on account of my wife. You see, Marster bought her off, as de highes', and she hadn't seen her mother and father in Waynesboro for 15 years.

When she got free, she went down to see 'em. Waren't willin' to come back. T'was on account Mistis and her. Dey bofe had chilluns, five-six years old. De chillun had disagreement. Mistis slap my girl. My wife sass de Mistis. But my marster, he was as good a man as ever born. I wouldn't have lef' him for anybody, just on account of his wife and her fell out."

"What did your marster say when you told him you were going to leave? Was he sorry?"

"I quit and goes over three miles to another widow lady house, and mek bargain wid her," said Willis. "I pass right by de do'. Old boss sitting on de pi-za. He say: 'Hey, boy, wheh you gwine?' I say; 'I 'cided to go.' I was de fo'man of de plow-han' den. I saw to all de locking up, and things like dat. He say: 'Hold on dere.' He come out to de gate. 'I tell you what I give you to stay on here, I give you five acre of as good land as I got, and $30.00 a month, to stay here and see to my bizness.'"

Willis paused a moment, thinking back on that long distant parting.

"I say," he went on, "I can't, Marster. It don't suit my wife 'round here, and she won't come back, and I can't stay.' He turn on me den, and busted out crying. 'I didn't tho't I could raise up a darky that would talk thataway,' he said to me. Well, I went on off. I got de wagon and come by de house. Marster says: 'Now you gwone off, but don't forget me, boy. Remember me as you always done.' I said: 'All right.'"

Willis chewed his tobacco reflectively for a few minutes, spat into the rosemary bush, and resumed his story:

"I went over to dat widow lady's house and work. Along about May I got sick. She say: 'I going to send for de doctor.' I said: 'Please ma'am, don't do dat.' I thought maybe he kill me 'cause I lef' him. She say: 'Well, I gwine send fo' him.' I in desprut condition. When I know anything, he walk up in de do'. I was laying wid my face toward de do' and I turn over.

"Doctor come up to de bed. 'Boy, how you getting on?' 'I bad off,' I say. He say: 'I see you is. 'yeh.' Lady say: 'Doctor, what you think of him?' 'Mistis, it mos' too late,' he say, 'but I do all I kin.' She say: 'Please do all yo' kin, he 'bout de bes' han' I got.'

"Doctor fix up med'cine and tole her to give it to me. She say: 'Uncle Will, tek dis med'cine.' I 'fraid to tek it, 'fraid he wuz tryin' to kill me. Den two men, John and Charles, come in. Lady say: 'Get dis med'cine in Uncle Will.' One of de men hold my hand, one hold my head, and dey gagged me and put it in me. Nex few days I kin talk, and ax for somethin' to eat, so I git better. I say: 'Well, he didn't kill me when I tuk de Med'cine.'

"I stayed dere wid her. Nex' yar I move right back in two miles other side wheh I always live, wid anudder lady. I stay dere three years. Got along all right. When I lef' from there, I lef' dere wid $300.00 and plenty corn and hog. Everything I want, and three hundred dollars cash in my pocket!"

(It was plain that in his present status of relief ward, Uncle Willis looked back on that sum of money as a small fortune. He thought about it awhile, spat again, and went on:)

"Fourth year I lef' and went down to de John Fryer place on Rock Creek. I stayed dere 33 years in dat one place."

"Uncle Willis, did you ever see the doctor again?"

"He die 'fore I know it," he replied, "I was 'bout fifteen miles from him and be de time I hear of his death, he bury on plantation near Rock Creek."

Willis was asked about superstitions, and answered with great seriousness:

"Eberybody in de worl' have got a spirit what follow 'em roun' and dey kin see diffrunt things. In my sleep I hab vision."

"Pappy, tell de ladies 'bout de hant," urged Aunt Rena from her post in the doorway, and Willis took up the story with eagerness:

"One night I was gwine to a lady's store, riding a horse. De graveyard was 100 yards from de road I wuz passing. De moon was shining bright as day. I saw somethin' coming out of dat graveyard. It come across de road, right befo' me. His tail were dragging on de ground, a long tail. He had hair on both sides of him, laying down on de road. He crep' up. I pull de horse dis way, he move too. I pull him dat way, he move too. I yell out: 'What in de name o' God is dat?' And it turn right straight 'round de graveyard and went back. I went on to de lady's store, and done my shoppin'. I tell you I was skeered, 'cause I was sho' I would see it going back, but I never saw it. De horse was turrible skeered of it. It looked like a Maryno sheep, and it had a long, swishy tail."

Uncle Willis was asked if he had ever seen a person "conjured" and he answered:

"Dey is people in de worl' got sense to kill out de conjur in anybody, but nobuddy ever conjur me. I year 'um say if a person conjur you, you'll git somethin' in you dat would kill you."

Asked to what he attributed his long, healthy life, he raised his head with a preaching look and replied:

"I tell you, Missis, 'zactly what I believe. I bin tryin' to serve God ever since I come to be a man of family. I bin trying to serve de Lawd 79 years, and I live by precepts of de word. Until today nobuddy can turn me away from God business. I am a man studying my gospel. I ain't able to go to church, but I still keep serving God."

A week later Uncle Willis was found standing in the cabin door.

"Do you want to ride to the old plantation to-day?" he was asked. His vitality was almost too low form to grasp the invitation.

"I'se might weak today," he said in a feeble voice. "I don't feel good for much."

"Where is Aunt Rena?" he was asked. "Do you think she would mind your taking an automobile trip?"

"She gone to town on de bus, to see de Fambly Welfare."

"Have you had breakfast?" His weak appearance indicated lack of food.

"I had some coffee, but I ain't eat 'none."

"Well, come on, Uncle Willis. We'll get you some breakfast, and then we'll take you to the plantation and take your picture in the place where you were born 101 years ago."

Uncle Willis appeared to be somewhat in a daze as he padlocked the cabin door, put on his "sundown" hat, took up his stout stick and tottered down the steps. He wore a frayed sweater, with several layers of shirts showing at the cuffs. On the way he recalled the first railroad train that passed through Burke County.

"I kinder scared," he recollected, "we wuz all 'mazed to see dat train flyin' long 'thout any horses. De people wuz all afraid."

"Had you hear of airplanes before you saw one, Uncle Willis?"

"Yes, ma'am. I yeared o' them, but you couldn't gimme dis car full of money to fly, they's too high off de ground. I never is gwine in one."

Uncle Willis was deposited on the porch of one of the remaining slave cabins to eat his "brekkus," while his kidnappers sought over hill and field for "the big house," but only two cabins and the chimney foundation of a large burned dwelling rewarded the search.

He was posed in front of the cabin, just in front of the clay and brick end chimney, and took great pleasure in the ceremony, rearing his head up straight so that his white beard stuck out.

The brutal reality of finding the glories of Rock Creek plantation forever vanished must have been a severe blow for the old man, for several times on the way back he wiped tears from his eyes. Once again at his cabin in the cotton field, his vitality reasserted itself, and he greeted his curious dusky neighbors with the proud statement:

"Dey tuk me wheh I was bred and born. I don't ax no better time."

His farewell words were:

"Goo'bye. I hopes you all gits to Paradise."

United States. Work Projects Administration

FOLKLORE

Interviews obtained from:
MRS. EMMALINE HEARD, 239 Cain St. NE
MRS. ROSA MILLEGAN, 231 Chestnut Ave. NE
MR. JASPER MILLEGAN, 231 Chestnut Ave. NE
Atlanta, Ga.
[Date Stamp: MAY 12 1937]

[MRS. EMMALINE HEARD]

MRS. EMMALINE HEARD

Mrs. Emmaline Heard, who resides at 239 Cain St. NE has proved to be a regular storehouse for conjure and ghost stories. Not only this but she is a firm believer in the practice of conjure. To back up her belief in conjure is her appearance. She is a dark brown-skinned woman of medium height and always wears a dirty towel on her head. The towel which was at one time white gives her the weird look of an old-time fortune teller.

Tuesday, December 8, 1936 a visit was made to her home and the following information was secured:

"There wuz onct a house in McDonough and it wuz owned by the Smiths that wuz slave owners way back yonder. Now, this is the trufe cause it wuz told ter me by old Uncle Joe Turner and he 'spirience it. Nobody could live in this house I don't care how they tried. Dey say this house wuz hanted and anybody that tried to stay there wuz pulled out of bed by a hant. Well, sir, they offered the house and $1,000 to anyone who could stay there over night. Uncle Joe said he decided to try it so sho nuff he got ready one night and went ter this house to stay. After while, says he, something come in the room and started over ter the bed, but fore it got there, he said, "What in the name of the Lord you want with me." It said, 'follow me. There is a pot of gold buried near the chimney; go find it and you won't be worried with me no more.' Der next morning Uncle Joe went out there and begin ter dig and sho nuff he found the gold; and sides that he got the house. Dis here is the trufe. Uncle Joe's house is right there in McDonough now and anybody round there will tell you the same thing cause he wuz well-known. Uncle Joe is dead now.

"Anudder story that happened during slavery time and wuz told ter me by father wuz this; The master had a old man on his plantation named Jimson. Well, Jimson's wife wuz sick and had been fer nearly a year. One day there she wanted some peas, black eyed peas; but old man Harper didn't have none on his plantation, so Jimson planned ter steal off that night and go ter old Marse Daniel's farm, which wuz 4 miles from Marse Harper's farm, and steal a few peas for his wife. Well, between midnight and day he got a sack and started off down the road. Long after while a owl started hootin, sho-o-o are-e-e, who-o-o-o-, and it wounded jest lak someone saying 'who are you.' Jimson got scared, pulled off his cap and run all the way to old man Daniel's farm. As he run he wuz saying, "Sir, dis is me, old Jimson" over and over again. Now, when he got near the farm Old Daniel heard him and got up in the loft ter watch him. Finally old Jimson got dar and started creeping up in the loft. When he got up dar, chile, Marse Daniel grabbed his whip and 'most beat Jimson ter death.

"This here story happened in Mississippi years ago, but den folks that tell it ter me said it wuz the trufe. 'There wuz a woman that wuz sick; her name wuz Mary Jones. Well, she lingered and lingered till she finally died. In them days folks all around would come ter the settin-up if somebody wuz dead. They done sent some men after the casket. Since they had ter go 30 miles they wuz a good while getting back, so the folkses decided ter sing. After while they heard the men come up on the porch and somebody got up ter let 'em in. Chile, jest as they opened the door that 'oman set straight up on that bed; and sech another runnin and getting out of that house you never heard; but some folks realized she wuzn't dead so they got the casket out der way so she wouldn't see it, cause they wuz fraid she would pass out sho nuff; jest the same they wuz fraid of her, too. The man went off and come back with postols, guns, sticks, and everything; and when this 'oman saw 'em she said, 'don't run, I won't bother you.' but, chile, they left there in a big hurry, too. Well, this here Mary went to her sister's house and knocked on the door, and said: 'Let me in. This is Mary. I want to talk to you and tell you where I've been.' The sister's husband opened the door and let her in. This 'oman told 'em that God had brought her to and that she had been in a trance with the Lord. After that every one wuz always afraid of that 'oman and they wouldn't even sit next ter her in the church. They say she is still living.

"This happened right yonder in McDonough years ago. A gal went to a party with her sweet'art and her ma told her not ter go. Well, she went on anyhow in a buggy; when they got ter the railroad crossing a train hit the buggy and killed the gal, but the boy didn't git hurted at all. Well, while they wuz sittin up with this dead gal, the boy comes long there in his buggy with anudder gal, and do you know that horse stopped right in front uv that house and wouldn't budge one inch. No matter how hard he whip that horse it wouldn't move; instid he rared and kicked and jumped about and almost turned the buggy over. The gal in the buggy fainted. Finally a old slavery time man come along and told him to git a quart of whiskey and pour it around the buggy and the hant would go away. So they done that and the sperit let 'em pass. If a hant laked whisky in they lifetime, and you pour it round where they's at, they will go away."

The following are true conjure stories supposedly witnessed by Mrs. Heard: "There wuz a Rev. Dennis that lived below the Federal Prison. Now, he wuz the preacher of the Hardshell Baptist Church in this community. This man stayed sick about a year and kept gittin different doctors and none uv them did him any good. Well, his wife kept on at him till he decided ter go ter see Dr. Geech. His complaint wuz that he felt something run up his legs ter his thighs. Old Dr. Geech told him that he had snakes in his body and they wuz put there by the lady he had been going wid. Dr. Geech give him some medicine ter take and told him that on the 7th day from then that 'oman would come and take the medicine off the shelf and throw it away. Course Rev. Dennis didn't believe a thing he said, so sho nuff she come jest lak Dr. Geech said and took the medicine away. Dr. Geech told him that he would die when the snakes got up in his arm, but if he would do lak he told him he would get all right. Dis 'oman had put this stuff in some whiskey and he drunk it so the snakes breed in his body. After he quit taking the medicine he got bad off and had ter stay in the bed; sho nuff the morning he died you could see the snake in his arm; the print uv it wuz there when he died. The snake stretched out in his arm and died, too.

"I got a son named Jack Heard. Well, somebody fixed him. I wuz in Chicago when that happened and my daughter kept writing ter me ter come home cause Jack wuz acting funny and she thought maybe he wuz losing his mind. They wuz living in Thomasville then and every day he would go sit round the store and laugh and talk, but jest as soon as night would come and he would eat his supper them fits would come on him. He would squeal jest lak a pig and he would get down on his knees and bark jest lak a dog. Well, I come home and went ter see a old conjure doctor. He says ter me, 'that boy is hurt and when you go home you look in the corner of the mattress and you will find it. 'Sho nuff I went home and looked in the corner of the mattress and there the package wuz. It wuz a mixture of his hair and bluestone wrapped up in red flannel with new needles running all through it. When I went back he says ter me, 'Emmaline, have you got 8 dimes?' No, I said, but I got a dollar. 'Well, get that dollar changed into 10 dimes and take 8 of 'em and give 'em ter me. Then he took Jack in a room, took off his clothes and started ter rubbin him down with medicine; all at the same time he wuz saying a ceremony over him; then he took them 8 dimes, put 'em in a bag and tied them around Jack's chest somewhere so that they would hang over his heart. 'Now, wear them always,' says he ter Jack. Jack wore them dimes a long time but he finally drunk 'em up anyway, that doctor cured him cause he sho would a died."

The following aroma [HW: is a] few facts as related by Mrs. Heard concerning an old conjure doctor known as Aunt Barkas [TR: Darkas throughout rest of story].

"Aunt Darkas lived in McDonough, Ga. until a few years ago. She died when she wuz 128 years old; but, chile, lemme tell you that 'oman knowed just what ter do fer you. She wuz blind but she could go ter the woods and pick out any kind of root or herb she wanted. She always said the Lord told her what roots to get and always fore sun-up you would see her in the woods with a short handled pick. She said she had ter pick 'em for sun-up; I don't know why. If you wuz sick all you had ter do wuz go ter see Aunt Darkas and tell her. She had a well and after listening to your complaint she would go out there and draw a bucket of water and set it on the floor, and then she would wave her hand over it and say something. She called this healing the water. After this she would give you a drink of water. As she hand it ter you, she would say, 'now drink, take this and drink.' Honey, I had some of that water myself and blieve me it goes all over you and makes you feel so good. Old Aunt Darkas would give you a supply of water and tell you ter come back fer more when that wuz gone. Old Aunt Darkas said the Lord gave her power and vision, and she used to fast for a week at a time. When she died there wuz a piece in the paper bout her.

"This here is sho the trufe, and if you don't believe it, go out ter Southview Cemetery and see Sid Heard, my oldest son; he been out there over 20 years as sexton and bookkeeper. Yessir, he tole it ter me and I believe it. This happen long ago, 10 or 15 years. There wuz a couple that lived in Macon, Ga., but their home wuz in Atlanta and they had a lot out ter Southview. Well, they had a young baby that tuck sick and died so they had the baby's funeral there in Macon; then they put the coffin in the box, placed the label on the box, then brought it ter Atlanta. Folkes are always buried so that they head faces the east. They say when Judgment Day come and Gabriel blow that trumpet everybody will rise up facing the east. Well, as I wuz saying, they came here. Sid Heard met 'em out yonder and instructed his men fer arrangements fer the grave and everything. A few weeks later the 'oman called Sid Heard up long distance. She said, 'Mr. Heard.' Yesmam, he said. 'I call you ter tell you me and my husband can't rest at all.' 'Why?' he asked. 'Because we can hear our baby crying every night and it is worrying us ter death. Our neighbors next door say our baby must be buried wrong.' Sid Heard said, Well, I buried the baby according ter the way you got the box labeled. 'I am not blaming you, Mr. Heard, but if I pay you will you take my baby up?' Yesmam, I will if you want me to; jest let me know the day you will be here and I'll have everything ready. Alright, said she.

'Well,' said Sid Heard, 'the day she wuz ter come she wuz sick and instead sent a car load of her friends. The men got busy and started digging till they got ter the box; when they took it up sho nuff after they opened it, they found the baby had been buried wrong; the head was facing the west instead of the east. They turned the box around and covered it up. The folks then went on back to Macon. A week later the 'omen called up again. 'Mr. Heard,' she says. Yesmam, says he. 'Well, I haven't heard my baby cry at all in the past week. I wuzn't there but I know the exact date you took my baby up, cause I never heard it cry no more.'

MRS. ROSA MILLEGAN AND MR. JASPER MILLEGAN

On December 10, 1936 Mr. and Mrs. Millegan who reside at 231 Chestnut Ave. NE. were interviewed on the subject of superstitions, signs, conjure, etc. Mrs. Rosa Millegan studied awhile after the facts of the interview were made clear to her. Finally she said; "I kin tell you more bout conjure; that's all I know bout cause I done been hurted myself and every word of it is the trufe.

"Well, it happen lak this. I wuz suffering with rheumatism in my arm and a old man in the neighborhood came ter me and gave me some medicine that he said would help me. Well, I done suffered so I thought mebbe it might help me a little. Chile honey, 'after I done tuck some of that stuff I nearly went crazy. I couldn't talk; couldn't hardly move and my head look lak it bust open. I didn't know what ter do. I called medical doctors and they jest didn't do me no good. Let me tell you right here, when you done been conjured, medical doctors can't do you no good; you got ter get a nudder conjur doctor ter get it off you. Well, one day I says to my daughter, "I'm through wid medical doctors. I'm gwine ter Sam Durham. They say he is good and I go find out. Chile, folks done give me up ter die. I use ter lay in bed and hear 'em say, she won't never get up. Well, I went ter Sam Durham and he looked at me and said: 'You is hurt in the mouth.' He carried me in a small room, put some medicine around my face, and told me ter sit down a while. After while my mouth and face begin ter feel lak it wuz paralyzed, and he begin ter talk. 'That man that give you that medicine is mad wid you about his wife and he fixed you. Now do what I tell you and you will overcome it. He is coming ter your door and is gwine want ter shake your hand. Don't let him touch you, but speak ter him in the name of the Lord and throw your hands over your head; by doing this you will overcome him and the devil.' Anudder thing he says; 'This man is coming from around the back of your house.' Then he give me 5 vials of different lengths and a half cup of pills, and told me ter take all that medicine. He told me too ter get a rooster and let him stay on my porch all the time and he couldn't get ter me no more. Sho nuff, that nigger come jest lak he said he wuz going ter do, but I fixed him. Later on this same man tried ter fix his wife cause he thought she had anudder man. Do you know that oman couldn't drink water in her house? and when he died he wuz nearly crazy; they had ter strap him in the bed; all the while he wuz cussin God and raving."

The next stories were told to the writer by Mr. Jasper Millegan:

"My uncle wuz poisoned. Yes, sir, somebody fixed him in coffee. He lingered and lingered and finally got so he wuz confined ter bed fer good. Somebody put scorpions in him and whenever they would crawl under his skin he would nearly go crazy, and it looked lak his eyes would jest pop out. He waited so long ter go ter the conjure doctors they couldn't do him any good. And the medical doctors ain't no good fer nothing lak that. Yes, sir, them snakes would start in his feet and run up his leg. He nebber did get any better and he died.

"A long time ago I saw a lady that wuz conjured in her feet; somebody put something down fer her ter walk over. Well, anyway she got down with her feet and couldn't travel from her bed ter a chair. Well, she got a old conjure doctor ter come treat her and he rubbed her feet with medicine and after he done that a while he told her that something wuz coming out of her feet. Sho nuff, I see'd them maggots with my own eyes when they come out of her feet; but she got well."

The following are preventatives to use against conjure; also a few home treatments for different sickness.

"Ter keep from being conjured, always use plenty salt and pepper. Always get up soon in the morning so nobody can see you and sprinkle salt and pepper around your door and they sho can't git at you.

"If you think you done been poisoned or conjured, take a bitter gourd and remove the seeds, then beat 'em up and make a tea. You sho will heave all of it up.

"Ef you think you will have a stroke, go to running water and get four flint rocks; heat 'em and lay on all of them, and believe me, it will start your blood circulating and prevent the stroke. Another way to start your blood circulating; heat a brick and (lay) lie on it.

"To get rid of corns, bathe your feet in salt water and take a little salt and put it 'tween your toes."

Mrs. Millegan closed her interview by telling the writer that every morning found her sprinkling her salt and pepper, cause she knows what it means ter be fixed. As the writer started out the door she noticed a horse shoe hanging over the door.

FOLKLORE
(Negro)
Minnie B. Ross

[MRS. CAMILLA JACKSON]

CAMILLA JACKSON

On November 24, 1936 Mrs. Camilla Jackson was interviewed concerning superstitions, signs, etc. Mrs. Jackson, an ex-slave, is about 80 years of age and although advanced in years she is unusually intelligent in her speech and thoughts. The writer was well acquainted with her having previously interviewed her concerning life as a slave.

Mrs. Jackson related to the writer the following signs and incidents:

If a tree is standing in your yard or near your house and an owl lights in it and begins to hoot, some one in the family will die.

If, during the illness of a person, a cat comes in the room, or the house, and whines, the person will die.

Another sure sign of death and one that has been experienced by Mrs. Jackson is as follows: Listen child if a bird flies in your house some one is going to die. My daughter and I were ironing one day and a bird flew in the window right over her head. She looked up and said, "mama that bird came after me or you, but I believe it came for me." One month later my daughter took sick with pneumonia and died.

My mother said before the Civil War ended her mistress owned an old slave woman 100 years old. This old woman was very wicked and the old miss used to visit her cabin and read the Bible to her. Well sir, she died and do you know the horses balked and would go every way but the right way to the grave. They rared and kicked and would turn straight around in the road 'cause the evil spirits were frightening them. It was a long time before they could get the body to the grave.

Mrs. Jackson before relating the following experiences emphatically stated her belief in seeing the dead but only believes that you can see them in a dream.

"Many a night my sister has come to me all dressed in white. I have heard her call me too; but I have never answered. No longer than one night last week old Mr. and Mrs. Tanner came to me in a dream. The old lady came in my room and stood over my bed. Her hair was done up on the top of her head just like she always wore it. She was distressed and spoke about some one being after her. Old Mr. Tanner came and led her away. They really were in my room, you see both of them died in this house years ago."

Mrs. Jackson could not relate any stories of conjuring; but did mention the fact that she had often heard of people wearing money around their legs to keep from being conjured. She also spoke of people keeping a horseshoe over the door for good luck.

During slavery and since that time, if you should go

out doors on a drizzling night for any thing, before you could get back Jack O'lantern would grab you and carry you to the swamps. If you hollowed and some one bring a torch to the door the Jack O'lantern would turn you aloose. Another way to get rid of them is to turn your pockets wrong side out.

One day a man came here selling roots called "John the Conqueror" and sister Blakely there, paid him 10¢ for one of the plants, but she never did plant it. He said the plant would bring good luck.

MRS. ANNA GRANT

On the same day Mrs. Jackson was interviewed, Mrs. Anna Grant told the writer that if she didn't mind she would relate to her a ghost story that was supposed to be true. In her own words the writer gives the following story:

Onst a 'oman, her husband and two chillun wuz travelin'. This 'oman wuz a preacher and only wanted to stop over night. Now this 'oman's husban' wuz a sinner, but she wuz a christian. Well she saw an old empty house setting in a field but when she went ter inquire 'bout it she wuz told that it wuz hanted and no one had ebber been able ter stay there over night. De lady dat owned de house offered her pillows, bed clothes, sheets, etc., if she intended to stay, and even told her that she would give her de house if she could stay there. The woman that owned the house told her butler to go and make a fire for the family and carry the pillows, sheets, etc. Well, they all got there the 'oman built a fire, cooked supper and fed 'em all. Her husband and children went ter bed. The husband wanted to know why his wife wanted him to go to bed and she wanted ter stay up. The wife didn't say nothin', just told him ter go to bed, then she laid the Bible on the table bottom side up and kept looking behind her. The house wuz two story and after while something came ter the top steps and said, "Can I throw down," she said "throw down in the name of the father, son and Holy Ghost." Two thighs and a foot came down. Later the same voice sed, "Can I throw down," and she said, "throw down in the name of the father, son and the Holy

Ghost," and then a whole body came down. The husband woke up when he heard the noise and ran away from the house. The ghost told the 'oman ter follow her, and she picked up her Bible and kept on reading and went on behind the ghost. The ghost showed her where some money was buried near a big oak tree and then vanished. The next morning the 'oman dug and found der money, but the 'oman of the house wouldn't take a penny, said she didn't want it, sides that she gave her the house. They said this wuz a true story and der reason dat house wus hanted wuz 'cause der family dat used to live there got killed about money. Mrs. Grant ended by saying "Deres a horseshoe over my door right now for luck."

MRS. EMMALINE HEARD

Mrs. Emmaline Heard lives on Cain St. between Fort and Butler Sts. She is an ex-slave and on a previous occasion had given the writer an interesting account of slavery as she knew it. When the writer approached her concerning superstitious signs, ghost tales, conjure etc., Mrs. Heard's face became lit with interest and quickly assured the writer that she believed in conjuring, ghosts, and signs. It was not long before our interview began. Mrs. Heard, although seventy or seventy-five years old, is very intelligent in her expression of her different thoughts. This interview, as nearly as possible, was taken in the exact words of the person interviewed.

"If you are eating with a mouthful of food and sneeze, that sho is a true sign of death. I know that 'cause years ago I wuz havin' breakfast with my son Wylie and one other boy and Wylie sneezed and said "Mama I'm so sorry I jist coundn't help it the sneeze came on me so quick." I jist sat there and looked at him and began ter wonder. Two weeks later my brother rode up and announced my mother's death. That is one sign thats true, yes sir.

If a picture falls off the wall some one in the family will die.

If you dream about teeth, if one falls out thats another sign of death.

Another sign of death jest as sho as you live is ter dream of a person naked. I dreamed my son was naked but his body was covered with hair. Three months later he died. Yes sir, that sho is a true sign.

Jest as sho as your left hand itches you will receive money. If fire pops on you from the stove, or fire place, you will get a letter.

If the left side of your nose itches a man is coming to the house. If it itches on the tip, he will come riding.

If the right side of your nose itches a woman is coming to the house.

Following are stories told to Mrs. Heard by her parents, which took place during the period of slavery. They are supposed to be true as they were experienced by the persons who told them.

"My mother told me a story that happened when she was a slave. When her mistress whipped her she would run away ter the woods; but at night she would sneak back to nurse her babies. The plantation was on old McDonough road, so ter get ter the plantation she had ter come by a cemetery and you could see the white stones shining in the moonlight. This cemetery was near a cut in the road that people said was hanted and they still say old McDonough road is hanted. One night, mama said she was on her way to the plantation walking on the middle of the road and the moon was shining very bright. When she reached this cut she heard a noise, Clack! Clack! Clack!, and this noise reminded a person of a lot of machines moving. All at once a big thing as large as a house came down the side of the road. She said it looked like a lot of chains, wheels, posts all mangled together, and it seemed that there were more wheels and chains than anything else. It kept on by making that noise, clack! clack! clack!. She stood right still till it passed and came on ter the farm. On her way back she say she didn't see it any more, but right till ter day that spot is hanted. I have knowed horses to run away right there with people and hurt them. Then sometimes they have rared and kicked and turned to go in the other direction. You see, horses can see hants sometimes when folks can't. Now the reason fer this cut being hanted was because old Dave Copeland used to whip his slaves to death and bury them along there."

The next story was told to Mrs. Heard by her father, who experienced it, as a slave boy.

"My father sed when he wuz a boy him and two more boys run away from the master 'cause the master whipped 'em. They set out and walked till it got dark, and they saw a big old empty house settin' back from der road. Now this house was 3 or 4 miles from any other house. So they went in and made a fire, and laid down 'cause they wuz tired from running from the Pader rollers. Soon they heard something say tap! tap! tap!, down the stairs it came, a loud noise and then "Oh Lordy Master, I aint goin' do it no more; let me off this time." After a while they heard this same noise like a house falling in and the same words "Oh Lordy Master, I ant goin' do it no more. Let me off this time." By this time they had got good and scared, so my pa sed he and his friends looked at each other and got up and ran away from that house jest as fast as they could go. Nobody knowed why this old house wuz hanted; but they believed that some slaves had been killed in it."

The next is a story of the Jack O'lantern as told by Mrs. Heard.

"Old South River on' the Jonesboro road is jest full of swampy land and on a rainy drizzly night Jack O'lanterns will lead you. One night my uncle started out ter see his girl end he had ter go through the woods and the swamps. When he got in der swamp land he had ter cross a branch and the night wuz dark and drizzly, so dark you could hardly see your hand before your face. Way up the creek he saw a little bright light, so he followed it thinking he wuz on his way. All night long he sed he followed this light up and down the swamp, but never got near ter it. When day came he was still in the creek and had not gone any distance at all. He went home and told the folks and they went back ter the swamps and saw his tracks up and down in the mud. Later a group of 'em set out to find the Jack O'lantern and way down the creek they found it on a bush. It looked like soot hanging down from a bush, burnt out. My uncle went ter bed 'cause he wuz sleepy and tired down from walking all night."

The following three stories related by Mrs. Heard deals with practices of conjure. She definitely states that they are true stories; and backs up this statement by saying she is a firm believer in conjure.

"As I told you before, my daddy came from Virginia. He wuz bought there by Old Harper and brought ter McDonough as a slave boy. Well as the speculator drove along south, he learned who the different slaves were. When he got here he wuz told by the master to live with old uncle Ned 'cause he wuz the only bachelor on the plantation. The master said ter old Ned, "Well Ned, I have bought me a fine young plow boy. I want him ter stay with you and you treat him right." Every night uncle Ned would make a pallet on the floor for daddy and make him go to bed. When he got in bed he (uncle Ned) would watch him out of the corner of his eye, but daddy would pretend he wuz asleep and watch old uncle Ned to see what he wuz going ter do. After a while uncle Ned would take a broom and sweep the fireplace clean, then he would get a basket and take out of it a whole lot of little bundles wrapped in white cloth. As he lay out a package he would say "grass hoppers," "spiders", "scorpian," "snake heads", etc., then he, would take the tongs and turn 'em around before the blaze so that they would parch. Night after night he would do this same thing until they had parched enough, then he would beat all of it together and make a powder; then put it up in little bags. My daddy wuz afraid ter ask old uncle Ned what he did with these bags, but heard he conjured folks with 'em. In fact he did conjure a gal 'cause she wouldn't pay him any attention. This gal wuz very young and preferred talking to the younger men, but uncle Ned always tried ter hang around her and help hoe, but she would always tell him to go do his own work 'cause she could do hers. One day he said ter her "All right madam, I'll see you later, you wont notice me now but you'll wish you had. When the dinner came, and they left the field they left their hoes standing so they would know jest where ter start when they got back. When that gal went back ter the field the minute she touched that hoe she fell dead. Some folks say they saw uncle Ned dressing that hoe with conjure.

"My sister Lizzie sho did get fixed, honey, and it took a old conjurer ter get the spell off of her. It wuz like this: Sister Lizzie had a pretty peachtree and one limb spreaded out over the walk and jest as soon as she would walk under this limb, she would stay sick all the time. The funny part 'bout it wuz that while she wuz at other folks house she would feel all right, but the minute she passed under this limb, she would begin ter feel bad. One day she sent fer a conjurer, and he looked under the house, and sho nuff, he found it stuck in the sill. It looked like a bundle of rags, red flannel all stuck up with needles and every thing else. This old conjurer told her that the tree had been dressed for her an t'would be best fer her ter cut it down. It wuz a pretty tree and she sho did hate to cut it down, but she did like he told her. Yes child, I don't know whither I've ever been conjured or not, but sometimes my head hurts and I wonder."

Mrs. Heard asked the writer to return at a later date and she would probably be able to relate more interesting incidents.

United States. Work Projects Administration

FOLKLORE
(Negro)
Edwin Driscoll

[MRS. JULIA RUSH, MR. GEORGE LEONARD, MR. HENRY HOLMES, MR. ELLIS STRICKLAND, MR. SAM STEVENS, JOE (a boy)]

FOLKLORE

The Negro folklore as recounted below was secured from the following persons: Mrs. Julia Rush (an ex-slave) who lives at 878 Coleman Street, S.W.; Mr. George Leonard (a very intelligent elderly person) whose address is 148 Chestnut Avenue N.E.; and Mr. Henry Holmes (an ex-slave); Mr. Ellis Strickland; Mr. Sam Stevens and a young boy known only as Joe. The latter named people can be found at the address of 257 Old Wheat Street, N.E. According to these people this lore represents the sort of thing that their parents and grandparents believed in and at various times they have been heard to tell about these beliefs.

1. Voodoo And Conjure

Mr. Leonard says: "In dem days de old folks b'lieved in witch-craft and conjure and sicha stuff like dat. Dey b'lieved dat an old person could punish anybody by taking a piece of chip and spitting on it and den dey would throw it on 'em. Dey said dat in two weeks time maggots would be in 'em."

"I have seen 'em take a black cat an' put 'im in a sack an' den dey took 'im an' put 'im in a pot of boiling hot water alive. Man de cat would almos' tear dat pot up tryin' to git out. After dey had cooked all de meat off de cat dey took one of his bones (I don't know which one of 'em) and put it crossways in their front teeth while dey mumbled somethin' under their breath an' den dey took dis bone an' throwed it 'cross de right shoulder an' when dey went an' picked it up an' put it in their pocket it was supposed to give 'em de bes' kind of luck. Dey could say or do anything dey wanted to an' ole marster couldn't hit 'em."

Regarding the Black cat's bone Mr. Strickland told the following story which he says he once heard an old man tell his father:

"You goes out in de valley in de woods an' you takes a live black cat an' throws 'im in a pot of boiling water. You boils 'im 'till he gits done all to pieces an' den you takes all de bones an' throws 'em in de creek an' de one dat floats up de creek is de one to use. You takes dis bone an' draws it through your teech an' gits all de meat off an' den you can take dat bone an' do all kinds of majic. You can talk to folks an' dey can't see you. You can even disappear an' come right back. It takes a good 'un to do dat (get a black cat's bone). While you's boilin' de cat dat thunder an' lightnin' look like it goin' tear up de face of de earth—you can even see de wind which is like a red blaze of fire."

Continuing Mr. Strickland says: "Some of de roots dat dey used to bring 'im luck an' to trick folks wid wuz Rattle-Snake Marster, and John de Conquerer. John de Conquerer is supposed to conquer any kind of trouble you gits intuh. Some folks says dat you can tote it in your pocket an' have good luck.

"I once knowed a woman who had some lodestone dat she uster work. She could take men an' dere wives apart an' den put 'em back together again. She say dat she had killed so many folks (by the use of conjure and majic etc.) dat she did'nt know whether she would ever git fit fer forgiveness. She sold She sold herself to de devil fer twenty years."

"Aint nuthin wrong wid folks all de time when dey thinks dey is tricked," says Mr. Strickland. "I had a friend named Joe once an' he uster fool 'roun wid roots an' stuff like dat. One day he heard about a man who had promised to pay five-hundred dollars to anybody dat could cure him of de misery in his stomach. He thought somebody had "tricked" him by puttin' a snake in 'im. Joe stayed wid 'im fer two days an' he did'nt git no better an' so he went out de nex' day an' bought a rubber snake an den he come back an' give de man some medecine to make 'im vomit. When he comited Joe throwed de snake in de can an' den he said to de man: "Dere it is, I knowed somebody had fixed you." De man said: "Dey tol' me somebody had put a snake in me." Joe took de snake an' done away wid it an' de nex' day de man wuz up walkin' 'roun. He never did know how he had been fooled an' Joe made de five-hundred dollars."

According to Mrs. Rush the wife of the colored foreman on her master's plantation was always working with roots. She says "One day I come in fum de field to nurse my baby an' when I got to my house dere was dis woman standing at my door." I said to her: "Name o' God Aunt Candis (dat wus her name) whut is you doin'?" She wus makin' all kings of funny motions when I come up on her. If you aint scared of 'em dey can't do nuthin to you. When I hollered at her de sweat broke out on her face. By dis time I had stayed away fum de field too long an' I knowed I wus goin' to git a whippin' but Candis gimme some of de roots she had in her mouth an' in her pockets. She tol' me to put piece of it in my mouth an' chew it. When I got near de overseer I was to spit some of de juice towars him an' I would'nt git a whippin'. I tied a piece of it 'roun my waist an' put some in my trunk too. I did'nt git a whippin' when I got to de field but when I went to look fer de root 'roun my waist it wus gone. When I went back to de house dat night de other piece was gone too. I aint seed it fum dat day to dis. De rest of de women on de plantation honored Candis but I did'nt. Dey say dat folks like dem can put stuff down fer you to walk in er set in or drink an' dat dey can fix you lie dat. But dey can't do nuthin' wid you if you aint scared of 'em."

"Not so long ago a woman whut uster live back of me tried to do sumpin' to me after we had a fuss. I woke up one mornin' an' looked out by my back fence an' dere wus a lotsa salt an' sulphur an' stuff all 'roun de yard. De other women wus scared fer me but I wus'nt."

Several of my informants say that salt can be used as a weapon of conjure. According to Joe salt may be used to make a gambler lose all of his money. To do this all that is necessary is to stand behind the person to be conjured and then sprinkle a small amount of salt on his back. From that instant on he will lose money. Joe has also seen a woman use the following method to make her male friend remain at home: "She taken some salt an' pepper an' sprinkled it up an' down de steps," says Joe, "an' den she taken a plain eatin' fork an' stuck it under de door steps an' de man stayed right in de house until she moved de fork."

Mr. Stevens says: "If you want to fix somebody all you got to do is to sprinkle some salt an' petter 'roun 'em an' it'll make 'em bus' dere brains out. If you wants to make 'em move you go out to de grave yard an' stick your hand down in de middle of a grave an' git a handful of dat red graveyard dirt an' den you comes back an' sprinkles it 'roun dere door an' dey's gone, dey can't stay dere. Another conjuration is fer a woman to make three waves over a man's head. I saw one do dat once."

Another method used to fix or conjure people, according to Mrs. Rush, is to take a lizard and parch it. The remains must be put in something that the person is to eat and when the food is eaten the individual will be conjured. Mr. Holmes says if a black cat's tail is tied on someone's doorknob it will "cut dey luck off."

Silver money tied around the leg will ward off the effects of conjure. Mrs. Rush says if you are feeling ill and you wish to determine whether or not someone has been trying to conjure you or not just take a silver coin and place it in your mouth. If it turns black somebody is working conjure on you. "I knowed a man who went to Newnan to see his mother who wus sick," stated Mrs. Rush. "She wus so sick dat she could'nt tell whut wus de matter wid her an' so her son took a silver quarter an' put it in her mouth an' it turned as black as a kettle."

Says Mr. Holmes: "If anybody comes to your house an' you don't want 'em dere, when dey leaves you take some salt an' throw it at 'em when dey gits out of hearin' you cuss at 'em an' dey won't never come back again."

Following are some songs that used to be sung about conjure, etc.:

SON:

"Mother, make my bed down
I will freely lie down,
Mother, make my bed down
I will freely lie down"

MOTHER:

"Ransom, my son, what did she give you to eat?
Ransom, my son, what did she give you to eat?

SON:

"Red head (parched lizard) and speckle back
Oh, make my bed down I will freely lie down."
"I'm goin' to pizen (poison) you, I'm goin' to pizen you,
I'm jus' sick an' tired of de way you do,
I'm goin' to sprinkle spider legs 'roun yo' bed
an' you gonna wake up in de mornin' an find yourself dead"
"You beat me an' you kick me an' you black my eyes,

I'm gonna take dis butcher knife an' hew
you down to my size,
You mark my words, my name is Lou,
You mind out what I say, I'm goin' to pizen
you."

2. Positive Cures And Controls

Mrs. Rush says that backache can be cured by rubbing a hot iron up and down the afflicted person's back.

Asafetida tied around the neck will prevent smallpox.

Risings can be cured by rubbing them with a poultice made from House-Leak root.

To prevent a fall while walking from one side of a creek to the other on a log, place a small stick crosswise in the front-teeth and no mishap will result.

Hold the mouth full of water while peeling onions and the onion juice will not get in the eyes.

If a man wishes to make a woman fall in love with him all that he has to do is to take some of her hair, tie it up, and then throw it in running water. In a short while she will fall deeply in love with him.

A man may also cause a woman to fall in love with him by letting her drink whiskey in which he has allowed "Gin-Root" to soak.

If a woman wishes to make a man fall in love with her she has only to take the small bow usually found in the back of a man's cap on the sweatband, or the bow usually found on the band of the man's hat. After this has been secured it must be taken and worn under her clothes next to her body.

3. Witch Riding

Mrs. Betty Brown of 74 Butler Street, N.E. says that when people die angry with someone they usually come back after death in the form of a witch and then they ride the person that they were angry with at the time of their death.

According to Mr. Favors who lives at 78 Raymond Street, when a witch rides anyone it is a sign that a man, a woman, or a dog, is after that person.

Mrs. Julia Rush says: "De old folks uster call witches hags. Dey wus some kind of sperrits (spirits) an' dey would ride anybody. My grandmother uster sleep wid de sissors under her pillow to keep 'em away."

"I once heerd a woman dat a witch come to a house one night an' took her skin off an' went through de key hole. Somebody foun' de skin an' sprinkled salt on it an' when de witch come out she could'nt git in de skin an' she started saying: 'Skinny, Skinny, don't you know me?'"

Regarding witches Mr. Leonard made the following statement: "The old folks b'lieved dat any house a person died in was "hainted" and dat de dead person's spirit was a witch dat would come back at night. They used to put a pan of salt on de corpse to keep it fum purgin' an' to keep de witches away. They burned lamps all night long fer about three weeks after de person was dead an' they sprinkled salt an' pepper 'roun too to keep de witches away."

Another informant claims that if a person sleeps with his or her shoes under the bed the witches are liable to ride him.

Mr. Strickland says that when the witches are riding anyone if that person can say any three words of the Bible such as: "Lord have mercy," or "Jesus save me" the witch will stop riding.

4. Apparitions And Ghosts

Mr. Henry Holmes claims that he has seen the Jack O'Lantern and that at one time he even followed it. He says: "One night me an' two more fellows followed de Jack O'Lantern. It looked like a light in a house or sumpin. We did'nt know where we wus until de nex' mornin' an' when we did find ourselfs we wus at home. All de while we followed it it jus' kep' goin' further an' further until it jus' vanished."

According to Mr. Leonard the Jack O'Lantern is a light that comes out of the swamps at night and after getting in front of a person it will lead him on and on. The old folks also used to think that the vapor seen rising out of the swamps at night were ghosts. One night he and his grandfather were walking down the railroad tracks when suddenly his grandfather said: "Stand back dere George don't you see dat man walkin' 'long dere wid no head?" He says, however, that he himself failed to see any such thing.

According to both Mrs. Brown and Mrs. [Rush?] people who are born with cauls (a kind of a veil) over their eyes are able to see ghosts.

5. Customs Concerning Courtship And Marriage

Mr. Leonard says that a young man wishing to accompany a young woman to her home always spoke in the following manner: "Dear kind Miss, if you have no objection of my being your protection, I'm going in your direction." It was in this manner that he asked her to allow him to escort her home.

For several years after freedom was declared it was the custom for the bride and the groom to jump over the broom together before they were pronounced man and wife.

6. Hunting Lore

The best time to hunt 'possums is on a cloudy night just before the break of day. All of the big ones are out then Mr. Favors claims.

COMPILATION FOLKLORE INTERVIEWS—RICHMOND COUNTY

CONJURATION

Written by:
Louise Oliphant
Federal Writers' Project
Augusta, Georgia

Edited by:
John N. Booth,
District Supervisor,
Residencies 6 & 7,
Federal Writers' Project
Augusta, Georgia

CONJURATION

Richmond County's older colored citizens, particularly the few surviving ex-slaves, are outspoken in their firm belief concerning powers of conjurers and root workers.

"When it comes to conjuration, don't nobody know more 'bout that, and there ain't nobody had as much of it done to 'em as I have," said a wizened old woman. "I know nobody could stand what I have stood. The first I knowed 'bout conjuration was when a woman named Lucinda hurt my sister. She was always a 'big me,' and her chillun was better than anybody elses. Well her oldest child got pregnant and that worried Lucinda nearly to death. She thought everybody she seed was talkin' 'bout her child. One day she passed my sister and another 'oman standin' on the street laughin' and talkin'. Lucinda was so worried 'bout her daughter she thought they was laughin' at her. She got so mad she cussed 'em out right there and told 'em their 'turn was in the mill.' My sister called the other 'oman in the house and shut the door to keep from listenin' at her. That made it wuss.

"'Bout three weeks later my sister started complainin'. Us had two or three doctors with her, but none of 'em done her any good. The more doctors us got the wuss she got. Finally all of the doctors give her up and told us there warn't nothin' they could do. After she had been sick 'bout two months she told us 'bout a strange man comin' to her house a few days 'fore she took sick. She said he had been there three or four times. She 'membered it when he come back after she took sick and offered to do somethin' for her. The doctors hadn't done her no good and she was just 'bout to let him doctor on her when this 'oman that was with her the day Lucinda cussed 'em out told her he was Lucinda's great uncle. She said that everybody called him the greatest root worker in South Carolina. Then my sister thought 'bout how this man had come to her house and asked for water every time. He wouldn't ever let her get the water for him, he always went to the pump and got it hisself. After he had pumped it off real cool he would always offer to get a bucket full for her. She didn't think nothin' 'bout it and she would let him fill her bucket. That's how he got her.

"She stayed sick a long time and Mamie stayed by her bed 'til she died. I noticed Mamie wipin' her mouth every few minutes, so one day I asked her what did she keep wipin' from my sister's mouth. She told me it wasn't nothin' but spit. But I had got very anxious to know so I stood by her head myself. Finally I seed what it was.

Small spiders came crawlin' out of her mouth and nose. Mamie thought it would skeer me, that's why she didn't want me to know.

"That happened on Tuesday and that Friday when she died a small snake come out of her forehead and stood straight up and stuck his tongue out at us. A old man who was sittin' there with us caught the snake, put him in a bottle, and kept him 'bout two weeks before he died.

"Don't think Lucinda didn't have pore Mamie conjured too. Mamie took sick just one month after my sister died. After she found out the doctors couldn't do her no good, she got a real good root worker to doctor on her. He got her up and she stayed up for nearly a year before Lucinda doubled the dose. That time pore Mamie couldn't git up. She suffered and suffered before she died. But Lucinda got her pay for all of it. When Mamie died Lucinda come to see her and said 'some folks was better off dead anyhow'. Mamie's daughter started to jump on her but some of the old folks wouldn't let her.

"Lucinda went a long time, but when she fell she sho' fell hard. She almost went crazy. She stayed sick as long as my sister and Mamie put together. She got so bad off 'til nobody couldn't even go in her house. Everybody said she was reapin' what she sowed. She wouldn't even let her own chillun come in the house. After she got so sick she couldn't get off the bed she would cuss 'em and yell to the top of her voice 'til they left. Nobody didn't feel sorry for her 'cause they knowed she had done too much devilment.

"Just 'fore she died, Lucinda was so sick and everybody was talkin' 'bout it was such a shame for her to have to stay there by herself that her youngest daughter and her husband went to live with her. Her daughter was 'fraid to go by herself. When she died you could stand in the street and hear her cussin' and yellin'. She kept sayin' 'take 'em off of me, I ain't done nothin' to 'em. Tell 'em I didn't hurt 'em, don't let 'em kill me.' And all of a sudden she would start cussin' God and anybody she could think of. When she died it took four men to hold her down in the bed."

"I've been sick so much 'til I can look at other folks when they're sick and tell if its natural sickness or not. Once I seed my face always looked like dirty dish water grease was on it every mornin' 'fore I washed it. Then after I washed it in the places where the grease was would be places that looked like fish scales. Then these places would turn into sores. I went to three doctors and every one of 'em said it was poison grease on my face. I knowed I hadn't put no kind of grease on it, so I couldn't see where it was comin' from. Every time I told my husband 'bout it he got mad, but I never paid too much 'tention to that. Then one day I was tellin' a friend of mine 'bout it, and she told me my husband must be doin' it. I wondered why he would do such a thing and she said he was just 'bout jealous of me.

"The last doctor I went to give me somethin' to put on my face and it really cleared the sores up. But I noticed my husband when my face got clear and he really looked mad. He started grumblin' 'bout every little thing, right or wrong. Then one day he brought me a black hen for dinner. My mind told me not to eat the chicken so I told him I wanted to keep the hen and he got mad 'bout that. 'Bout two or three days later I noticed a big knot on the side of the chicken's head and it bursted inside of that same week. The chicken started drooping 'round and in a week's time that chicken was dead. You see that chicken was poison.

"After that my husband got so fussy I had to start sleepin' in another room. I was still sick, so one day he brought me some medicine he said he got from Dr. Traylor. I tried to take a dose 'cause I knowed if it was from Dr. Traylor it was all right, but that medicine burnt me just like lye. I didn't even try to take no more of it. I got some medicine from the doctor myself and put it in the bottom of the sideboard. I took 'bout three doses out of it and it was doing me good, but when I started to take the fourth dose it had lye in it and I had to throw it away. I went and had the doctor to give me another bottle and I called myself hidin' it, but after I took 'bout six doses, lye was put in it. Then one day a friend of mine, who come from my husband's home, told me he was a root worker and she thought I already knowed it. Well I knowed then how he could find my medicine everytime I hid it. You see he didn't have to do nothin' but run his cards. From then on I carried my medicine 'round in my apron pocket.

"I started sleepin' in the kitchen on a cot 'cause his mother was usin' the other room and I didn't want to sleep with her. Late at night he would come to the window and blow somethin' in there to make me feel real bad. Things can be blowed through the key hole too. I know 'cause I have had it done to me. This kept up for 'bout a year and five or six months. Then 'cause he seed he couldn't do just what he wanted to, he told me to get out. I went 'cause I thought that might help me to git out of my misery. But it didn't 'cause he come where I was every night.

He never did try to come in, but us would hear somebody stumblin' in the yard and whenever us looked out to see who it was us always found it was him. Us told him that us seed him out there, but he always denied it. He does it right now or sometimes he gets other root workers to do it for him. Whenever I go out in the yard my feet always feel like they are twistin' over and I can't stop 'em; my legs and knees feel like somethin' is drawin' 'em, and my head starts swimmin'. I know what's wrong, it just what he had put down for me.

"When I get up in the mornin' I always have to put sulphur and salt and pepper in my shoes to keep down the devilment he puts out for me. A man who can do that kind of work give me somethin' to help me, but I was s'posed to go back in six months and I ain't been back. That's why it's started worryin' me again.

"My sister was conjured by openin' the door and eatin' afterwards without washin' her hands," an 80-year old ex-slave remarked. "She had just come home and opened her front door and went in the house to eat before goin' to church. She et her supper and started to church with another of my sisters. After she had gone 'bout two or three blocks she started feelin' sick and walkin' as if she was drunk. My sister tried to make her go back home but she wouldn't. When they got to church she couldn't hardly get up the steps and they warn't in church over fifteen minutes 'fore she had a stroke. Somebody took a car and carried her home. She couldn't even speak for more than a week. The doctor come and 'xamined her, but he said he didn't see nothin' that would cause her to have a stroke. He treated her for 'bout two weeks but she didn't get no better. A friend told us to try a root worker.

She said she knowed one that was good on such things. Us was afraid at first, but after the three doctors us had tried didn't seem to do her no good, us decided to get the root worker.

"The root worker come that Wednesday mornin' and looked at her, but he never touched her. He told us she had been hurt, but he could have her on her feet in 'bout a week or ten days. He didn't give her no medicine, and he never come back 'til after she was up and walkin' 'round. She got up in 'bout seven days, and started talkin' earlier than that. The root worker told her she had got conjured by puttin' her hands on somethin' and eatin' without washin' 'em.

"She got along fine for 'bout three years, 'til one day she got home from work and found her house open. She thought her son had gone out and forgot to lock the door. When he come home he told her he had not been back since he left that mornin'. She knowed she didn't forget to lock it, so she guessed somebody had jus 'bout gone in through the window and come out the door. But it was too late then 'cause she had et what was left in the house and had drunk some water.

"That night she had her second stroke. Us sent for the same man who had got her up before, but he said he doubted gettin' her up this time 'cause the person had made a good job of it by puttin' somethin' in her water and t'eat. He treated her, and she got strong enough to sit up in the house, but she soon had the third stroke and then he give her up. She died 'bout two months later.

"I know you don't know how folks can really conjure you. I didn't at one time, but I sho' learnt. Everytime somebody gets sick it ain't natchel sickness. I have seed folks die with what the doctors called consumption, and yet they didn't have it. I have seed people die with heart trouble, and they didn't have it. Folks is havin' more strokes now than ever but they ain't natchel. I have seed folks fixed so they would bellow like a cow when they die, and I have seed 'em fixed so you have to tie them down in bed to die. I've got so I hardly trust anybody."

Estella Jones thinks conjurers and root workers are much more skillful now than formerly. "Folks don't kill you like they used to kill you. They used to put most anythin' in you, but now they got so wise or afraid that somebody will know zactly what killed you, 'til they do it slick as a eel.

"Once a man named John tried to go with a girl but her step-pa, Willie, run him away from the house just like he mought be a dog, so John made it up in his mind to conjure Willie. He went to the spring and planted somethin' in the mouth of it, and when Willie went there the next day to get a drink he got the stuff in the water. A little while after he drunk the water he started gettin' sick. He tried to stay up but every day he got wuss and wuss 'til he got flat down in bed.

"In a few days somethin' started growin' in his throat. Every time they tried to give him soup or anythin' to eat, somethin' would come crawlin' up in his throat and choke him. That was what he had drunk in the spring, and he couldn't eat nothin' or drink nothin'. Finally he got so bad off he claimed somethin' was chokin' him to death, and so his wife sont off and got a fortune teller. This fortune teller said it was a turtle in his throat. He 'scribed the man that had conjured Willie but everybody knowed John had done it 'fore the fortune teller told us. It warn't long after that 'fore Willie was dead. That turtle come up in his throat and choked him to death.

"Some folk don't believe me, but I ain't tellin' no tale 'bout it. I have asked root workers to tell me how they does these things, and one told me that it was easy for folks to put snakes, frogs, turtles, spiders, or most anythin' that you couldn't live with crawlin' and eatin' on the inside of you. He said these things was killed and put up to dry and then beat up into dust like. If any of this dust is put in somethin' you have to eat or drink, these things will come alive like they was eggs hatchin' in you. Then the more they grow, the worse off you get.

"My aun't son had took a girl away from another man who was going with her too. As soon as this man heard they was going to marry, he started studyin' some way to stop it. So he went to a root worker and got somethin' and then went to this girl's house one night when he knew my cousin was there. Finally when he got ready to leave, he was smart enough to get my cousin to take a drink with him.

"That next mornin' the boy was feelin' a little bad, but he never paid too much 'tention to it. Next day he felt a little wuss, and everyday from then on he felt wuss and wuss 'til he got too sick to stay up. One day a old lady who lived next door told us to try a root worker who lived on Jones Street. This man came and told us what was wrong, but said us had waited too long to send for him. He give us some thin' to 'lieve the boy of his misery. Us kept givin' this to him 'til he finally got up. Course he warn't well by no means and this medicine didn't help his stomach. His stomach got so big everybody would ask what was wrong. He told everybody that asked him and some who didn't ask him 'bout the frogs in his stomach. The bigger these frogs got, the weaker he got.

"After he had been sick 'bout four months and the frogs had got to be a pretty good size, you could hear 'em holler everytime he opened his mouth. He got to the place where he wouldn't talk much on account of this. His stomach stuck out so far, he looked like he weighed 250 pounds.

"After these frogs started hollerin' in him, he lived 'bout three weeks, and 'fore he died you could see the frogs jumpin' 'bout in him and you could even feel 'em.

"T'ain't no need talkin'; folks can do anythin' to you they wants to. They can run you crazy or they can kill you. Don't you one time believe that every pore pusson they has in the 'sylum is just natchelly crazy. Some was run crazy on account of people not likin' 'em, some 'cause they was gettin' 'long a little too good. Every time a pusson jumps in the river don't think he was just tryin' to kill hisself; most times he just didn't know what he was doin'.

"My daughter was fixed right here under our noses. She was married and had five little chillun and she was the picture of health. But she had a friend that she trusted too much and this friend was single and in love with my daughter's husband. Diff'unt people told Liza 'bout this girl, but she just didn't believe 'em. Every day this girl was at Liza's house 'til time for Lewis to git off from work. She helped Liza wash, clean up, iron and cook, but she always left at the time for Lewis to git off from work.

"This went on for more'n a year, but I kept tellin' Liza to ween off from this girl 'cause I seed she didn't mean her no good. But Liza was grown and nobody couldn't tell her nothin'. I think she had Liza fixed so she would be crazy 'bout her. People can make you love 'em, even marry 'em when if you was in your right mind you wouldn't give 'em a thought. Anyhow Liza went on with the girl 'til one afternoon while she was comin' from the store she seed Lewis and Edna goin' in a house together. He come home 'bout three hours later, and when Liza asked him why he was so late he told her they had to work late. He didn't know she had seed him and she never told him.

"After this she started watchin' him and Edna, and she soon found out what folks had been tellin' her was true. Still she never told Lewis nothin' 'bout it. She told Edna 'bout seein' 'em and asked her to please let Lewis alone. Edna made up some kind of s'cuse but she never let him alone, and she kept goin' to Liza's house. When things finally went too far, Liza spoke to Lewis 'bout it and asked him to leave Edna alone. He did, but that made Edna mad and that's when she 'cided to kill Liza. Lewis really loved Liza and would do anythin' she asked him to.

"One day Edna come to see Liza, after she had stayed away for 'bout three weeks, and she was more lovin' than ever. She hung around 'til she got a chance to put somethin' in the water bucket, then she left. People can put somethin' in things for you and everybody else can eat or drink it, but it won't hurt nobody but the one it's put there for. When Liza drunk water, she said it tasted like it had salt-peter in it. When she went to bed that night, she never got out 'til she was toted out. She suffered and suffered and we never knowed what was wrong 'til Edna told it herself. She took very sick and 'fore she died she told one of her friends 'bout it and this friend told us, but it was too late then, Liza was dead."

COMPILATION RICHMOND COUNTY—EX-SLAVE INTERVIEWS

FOLK REMEDIES AND SUPERSTITION

Written by:
Louise Oliphant
Federal Writers' Project
Augusta, Georgia

Edited by:
John N. Booth
District Supervisor
Federal Writers' Project
Augusta, Georgia

FOLK REMEDIES AND SUPERSTITION

Belief in charms and conjurs is still prevalent among many of Augusta's older Negroes. Signs and omens also play an important part in their lives, as do remedies and cures handed down by word of mouth from generation to generation.

>If a wrestler can get dirt from the head of a fresh grave, sew it up in a sack, and tie it around his waist, no one can throw him.
>To make a person leave town, get some dirt out of one of his tracks, sew it up in a sack, and throw it in running water. The person will keep going as long as the water runs.
>To take a hair out of a person's head and put it in a live fishes mouth will make the person keep traveling as long as the fish swims.

If someone dies and comes back to worry you, nail some new lumber into your house and you won't be bothered any more.

When the hands of a dead person remain limp, some other member of the family will soon follow him in death.

When a spider builds a web in your house, you may expect a visitor the same color as the spider.

A singing fire is a sign of snow.

If a cat takes up at your house it's a sign of good luck; a dog—bad luck.

If a spark of fire pops on you, it is a sign that you will receive some money or a letter.

To dream of muddy water, maggots, or fresh meat is a sign of death. To dream of caskets is also a sign of death. You may expect to hear of as many deaths as there are caskets in the dream.

To dream of blood is a sign of trouble.

To dream of fish is a sign of motherhood.

To dream of eggs is a sign of trouble unless the eggs are broken. If the eggs are broken, your trouble is ended.

To dream of snakes is a sign of enemies. If you kill the snakes, you have conquered your enemies.

To dream of fire is a sign of danger.

To dream of a funeral is a sign of a wedding.

To dream of a wedding is a sign of a funeral.

To dream of silver money is a sign of bad luck; bills—good luck.

To dream of dead folk is a sign of rain.

Wear a raw cotton string tied in nine knots around your waist to cure cramps.
To stop nosebleed or hiccoughs cross two straws on top of your head.
Lick the back of your hand and swallow nine times without stopping to cure hiccoughs.
Tea made from rue is good for stomach worms.
Corn shuck tea is good for measles; fodder tea for asthma.
Goldenrod tea is good for chills and fever.
Richet weed tea is good for a laxative.
Tea made from parched egg shells or green coffee is good for leucorrhoea.
Black snuff, alum, a piece of camphor, and red vaseline mixed together is a sure cure for piles.
To rid yourself of a corn, grease it with a mixture of castor oil and kerosine and then soak the foot in warm water.
Sulphur mixed with lard is good for bad blood.
A cloth heated in melted tallow will give relief when applied to a pain in any part of the body.
Take a pinch of sulphur in the mouth and drink water behind it to cleanse the blood.
Dog fern is good for colds and fever; boneset tea will serve the same purpose.
Catnip tea is good for measles or hives.
If your right shoe comes unlaced, someone is saying good things about you; left shoe— bad things.

If a chunk of fire falls from the fireplace a visitor is coming. If the chunk is short and large the person will be short and fat, etc.
Don't buy new things for a sick person; if you do he will not live to wear it out.
If a person who has money dies without telling where it is, a friend or relative can find it by going to his grave three nights in succession and throwing stones on it. On the fourth night he must go alone, and the person will tell him where the money is hidden.
If a witch rides you, put a sifter under the bed and he will have to count the holes in the sifter before he goes out, thus giving you time to catch him.
Starch your sweetheart's handkerchief and he will love you more.
Don't give your sweetheart a knife. It will cut your love in two.
If it rains while the sun is shining the devil is beating his wife.
To bite your tongue while talking is a sign that you have told a lie.
Persons with gaps between their front teeth are big liars.
Cut your finger nails on Monday, you cut them for news;
 Cut them on Tuesday, get a new pair of shoes;
 Cut them on Wednesday, you cut them for wealth;
 Cut them on Thursday, you cut them for

health;
Cut them on Friday, you cut them for sorrow;
Cut them on Saturday, see your sweetheart tomorrow;
Cut them on Sunday, its safety to seek;
But the devil will have you the rest of the week.

If you start some place and forget something don't turn around without making a cross mark and spitting in it, if you do you will have bad luck.

To stump your right foot is good luck, but to stump your left foot is bad luck. To prevent the bad luck you must turn around three times.

It is bad luck for a black cat to cross you to the left, but good luck if he crosses you to the right.

If a picture of a person falls off the wall it is a sign of death.

To dream of crying is a sign of trouble.

To dream of dancing is a sign of happiness.

If you meet a gray horse pulling a load of hay, a red haired person will soon follow.

If you are eating and drop something when you are about to put it in your mouth someone wishes it.

If a child never sees his father he will make a good doctor.

To dream that your teeth fall out is a sign of death in the family.

To dream of a woman's death is a sign of

some man's death.
To dream of a man's death is the sign of some woman's death.
If a chicken sings early in the morning a hawk will catch him before night.
Always plant corn on the waste of the moon in order for it to yield a good crop. If planted on the growing of the moon there will be more stalk than corn.
When there is a new moon, hold up anything you want and make a wish for it and you will get it.
If you hear a voice call you and you are not sure it is really someone, don't answer because it may be your spirit, and if you answer it will be a sure sign of death.
Cross eyed women are bad luck to other women, but cross eyed men are good luck to women and vice-versa for men.
To wear a dime around your ankle will ward off witch craft.
To put a silver dime in your mouth will determine whether or not you have been bewitched. If the dime turns black, someone has bewitched you, but if it keeps its color, no one has bewitched you.
To take a strand of a person's hair and nail it in a tree will run that person crazy.
If a rooster crows on your back steps you may look for a stranger.
Chinaberries are good for wormy children.
The top of a pine tree and the top of a cedar tree placed over a large coal of fire, just

enough to make a good smoke, will cure chillblain feet.

United States. Work Projects Administration

COMPILATION RICHMOND COUNTY EX-SLAVE INTERVIEWS

MISTREATMENT OF SLAVES

Written by:
Louise Oliphant,
Federal Writers' Project
Augusta, Georgia

Edited by:
John N. Booth,
District Supervisor,
Federal Writers' Project
Augusta, Georgia

MISTREATMENT OF SLAVES

There are many ex-slaves living in Richmond County and Augusta who have vivid recollections of the days when their lives were inseparably bound to those of their masters. These people have a past rich in tradition and sentiment, and their memories of customs, habits of work and play, and the superstitious beliefs, which still govern their actions to a large extent weave a colorful pattern in local history.

Mistreatment at the hands of their masters and the watchdog overseers is outstanding in the memory of most of them. "When I was in slavery, us had what you call good white folk. They warn't rich by no means, but they was good. Us had rather have 'em poor and good than rich and mean. Plenty of white folk mistreated they slaves, but ours never mistreated us. They was a man lived in callin' distance, on the next plantation, who worked his slaves day and night and on Sunday for a rarety. You could hear 'em coming from the field about 12 o'clock at night, and they had to be back in the fields by daylight. They couldn't get off on Saturday nights like everbody else. Whenever he bought their clothes, it was on Sunday when they warn't workin'. He was mean, but he was good about buyin' for 'em, new shoes or a suit or anything of the like they said they needed.

"Marster had overseers, but he wouldn't let 'em whip his slaves unmerciful. They always whipped us just as your mamas whips you now.

"Bob Lampkin was the meanest slave owner I ever knowed. He would beat his slaves and everybody else's he caught in the road. He was so mean 'til God let him freeze to death. He come to town and got drunk and when he was going back home in his buggy, he froze stiff going up Race Creek Hill. White and colored was glad when he died.

"His slaves used to run away whenever they got a chance. I 'member he had a real pretty gal on his place. She was light brown and was built up better than anybody I ever saw. One of the overseers was crazy about her, but her mother had told her not to let any of 'em go with her. So this old overseer would stick close 'round her when they was workin', just so he could get a chance to say somethin' to her. He kept followin' this child and followin' this child until she almost went crazy. Way afterwhile she run away and come to our house and stayed 'bout three days. When my marster found out she was there, he told her she would have to go back, or at least she would have to leave his place. He didn't want no trouble with nobody. When that child left us she stayed in the woods until she got so hungry she just had to go back. This old man was mad with her for leavin', and one day while she was in the field he started at her again and when she told him flat footed she warn't goin' with him he took the big end of his cow hide and struck her in the back so hard it knocked her plumb crazy. It was a big lake of water about ten yards in front of 'em, and if her mother hadn't run and caught her she would have walked right in it and drowned.

"In them times white men went with colored gals and women bold. Any time they saw one and wanted her, she had to go with him, and his wife didn't say nothin' 'bout it. Not only the men, but the women went with colored men too. That's why so many women slave owners wouldn't marry, 'cause they was goin' with one of their slaves. These things that's goin' on now ain't new, they been happenin'. That's why I say you just as well leave 'em alone 'cause they gwine to do what they want to anyhow.

"My marster never did whip any grown folk. He whipped chillun when they did anything wrong. He didn't 'low us to eat plums before breakfus, but all the chillun, his too, would die or do it, so every time he caught us he would whip us."

Another ex-slave recalled that "you had to call all your marster's chillun marster or mistis, even the babies. You never wore enough clothes and you always suffered for comfort. Us warn't even 'lowed to have fire. If you had a fireplace in your house, it was took out and the place closed up. If you was ever caught with fire you was beat 'most to death. Many mothers died in confinement on account of takin' cold 'cause us couldn't have fire.

"My young marster tried to go with me, and 'cause I wouldn't go with him he pretended I had done somethin' and beat me. I fought him back because he had no right to beat me for not goin' with him. His mother got mad with me for fightin' him back and I told her why he had beat me. Well then she sent me to the courthouse to be whipped for fightin' him. They had stocks there where most people would send their slaves to be whipped. These stocks was in the shape of a cross, and they would strap your clothes up around your waist and have nothin' but your naked part out to whip. They didn't care about who saw your nakedness. Anyway they beat me that day until I couldn't sit down. When I went to bed I had to lie on my stomach to sleep. After they finished whippin' me, I told them they needn't think they had done somethin' by strippin' me in front of all them folk 'cause they had also stripped their mamas and sisters. God had made us all, and he made us just alike.

"They never carried me back home after that; they put me in the Nigger Trader's Office to be sold. About two days later I was sold to a man at McBean. When I went to his place everbody told me as soon as I got there how mean he was and they said his wife was still meaner. She was jealous of me because I was light; said she didn't know what her husband wanted to bring that half white nigger there for, and if he didn't get rid of me pretty quick she was goin' to leave. Well he didn't get rid of me and she left about a month after I got there. When he saw she warn't comin' back 'til he got rid of me, he brought me back to the Nigger Trader's Office.

"As long as you warn't sold, your marster was 'sponsible for you, so whenever they put you on the market you had to praise yourself in order to be sold right away. If you didn't praise yourself you got a beatin'. I didn't stay in the market long. A dissipated woman bought me and I done laundry work for her and other dissipated women to pay my board 'til freedom come. They was all very nice to me.

"Whenever you was sold your folk never knowed about it 'til afterwards, and sometimes they never saw you again. They didn't even know who you was sold to or where they was carryin' you, unless you could write back and tell 'em.

"The market was in the middle of Broad and Center Streets. They made a scaffold whenever they was goin' to sell anybody, and would put the person up on this so everybody could see him good. Then they would sell him to the highest bidder. Everybody wanted women who would have children fast. They would always ask you if you was a good breeder, and if so they would buy you at your word, but if you had already had too many chillun, they would say you warn't much good. If you hadn't ever had any chillun, your marster would tell 'em you was strong, healthy, and a fast worker. You had to have somethin' about you to be sold. Now sometimes, if you was a real pretty young gal, somebody would buy you without knowin' anythin' 'bout you, just for yourself. Before my old marster died, he had a pretty gal he was goin' with and he wouldn't let her work nowhere but in the house, and his wife nor nobody else didn't say nothin' 'bout it; they knowed better. She had three chillun for him and when he died his brother come and got the gal and the chillun.

"One white lady that lived near us at McBean slipped

in a colored gal's room and cut her baby's head clean off 'cause it belonged to her husband. He beat her 'bout it and started to kill her, but she begged so I reckon he got to feelin' sorry for her. But he kept goin' with the colored gal and they had more chillun.

"I never will forget how my marster beat a pore old woman so she couldn't even get up. And 'cause she couldn't get up when he told her to, he hit her on the head with a long piece of iron and broke her skull. Then he made one of the other slaves take her to the jail. She suffered in jail all night, and the jailer heard her moanin' and groanin', so the next mornin' he made marster come and get her. He was so mad 'cause he had to take her out of jail that he had water pumped into her skull just as soon as he got back home. Then he dropped her down in a field and she died 'fore night. That was a sad time. You saw your own folk killed and couldn't say a word 'bout it; if you did you would be beat and sometimes killed too.

"A man in callin' distance from our place had a whippin' pole. This man was just as mean as he could be. I know he is in hell now, and he ought to be. A woman on his place had twins and she warn't strong from the beginnin'. The day after the chillun was borned, he told her to go over to his house and scrub it from front to back. She went over to the house and scrubbed two rooms and was so sick she had to lay down on the floor and rest awhile. His wife told her to go on back to her house and get in bed but she was afraid. Finally she got up and scrubbed another room and while she was carryin' the water out she fainted. The mistress had some of the men carry her home and got another slave to finish the scrubbin' so the marster wouldn't beat the pore nigger. She was a good woman but her husband was mean as the devil. He would even beat her. When he got home that night he didn't say nothin' 'cause the house had been scrubbed, but the next mornin' one of the chillun told him about the woman faintin' and the other girl finishin' the scrubbin'. He got mad and said his wife was cloakin' for the slaves, that there was nothin' wrong with the woman, she was just lazy. He beat his wife, then went out and tied the pore colored woman to a whippin' pole and beat her unmerciful. He left her hangin' on the pole and went to church. When he got back she was dead. He had the slaves take her down and bury her in a box. He said that laziness had killed her and that she warn't worth the box she was buried in. The babies died the next day and he said he was glad of it 'cause they would grow up lazy just like their mother.

"My marster had a barrel with nails drove in it that he would put you in when he couldn't think of nothin' else mean enough to do. He would put you in this barrel and roll it down a hill. When you got out you would be in a bad fix, but he didn't care. Sometimes he rolled the barrel in the river and drowned his slaves.

"I had a brother who worked at the acadamy and every night when the teacher had his class he would let my brother come in. He taught him to read and write too. He learned to read and write real well and the teacher said he was the smartest one in the class. Marster passed our window one night and heard him readin'. The next mornin' he called him over to the house and fooled him into readin' and writin', told him he had somethin' he wanted him to do if he could read and write good enough. My brother read everythin' marster give him and wrote with a pencil and ink pen. Marster was so mad that he could read and write better than his own boy that he beat him, took him away from the academy, and put him to work in the blacksmith shop. Marster wouldn't let him wear no shoes in the shop 'cause he wanted the hot cinders to fall on his feet to punish him. When the man in charge of the shop told marster he wouldn't work my brother unless he had on shoes, he bought some brogans that he knowed he couldn't wear, and from then on he made him do the hardest kind of work he could think of.

"My marster never whipped us himself. He had a coachman do all the whippin' and he stood by to see that it was done right. He whipped us until we was blistered and then took a cat-o-nine-tails and busted the blisters. After that he would throw salty water on the raw places. I mean it almost gave you spasms. Whenever they sent you to the courthouse to be whipped the jail keeper's daughter give you a kick after they put you in the stocks. She kicked me once and when they took me out I sho did beat her. I scratched her everwhere I could and I knowed they would beat me again, but I didn't care so long as I had fixed her."

One ex-slave "belonged to an old lady who was a widow. This lady was very good to me. Of course most people said it was 'cause her son was my father. But she was just good to all of us. She did keep me in the house with her. She knowed I was her son's child all right. When I married, I still stayed with my mistress 'til she died. My husband stayed with his marster in the day time and would come and stay with me at night.

"When my mistress died I had to be sold. My husband told me to ask his marster to buy me. He didn't want me to belong to him because I would have to work real hard and I hadn't been use to no hard work, but he was so afraid somebody would buy me and carry me somewhere way off, 'til he decided it was best for his marster to buy me. So his marster bought me and give me and my husband to his son. I kept house and washed for his son as long as he was single. When he married his wife changed me from the house and put me in the field and she put one of the slaves her mother give her when she married, in the kitchen. My marster's wife was very mean to all of us. She didn't like me at all. She sold my oldest child to somebody where I couldn't ever see him any more and kept me. She just did that to hurt me. She took my baby child and put her in the house with her to nurse her baby and make fire. And all while she was in the house with her she had to sleep on the floor.

"Whenever she got mad with us she would take the cow hide, that's what she whipped us with, and whip us 'til the blood ran down. Her house was high off the ground and one night the calf went under the house and made water. The next morning she saw it, so she took two of my sister-in-law's chillun and carried 'em in the kitchen and tied 'em. She did this while her husband was gone. You see if he had been there he wouldn't have let her done that. She took herself a chair and sit down and made one of the slaves she brought there with her whip those chillun so 'til all of the slaves on the place was cryin'. One of the slaves run all the way where our marster was and got him. He come back as quick as he could and tried to make her open the door, but she wouldn't do it so he had to break the door in to make her stop whippin' them chillun. The chillun couldn't even cry when he got there. And when he asked her what she was whippin' them for she told him that they had went under the house and made that water. My master had two of the men to take 'em over to our house, but they was small and neither one ever got over that whippin'. One died two days later and the other one died about a month afterwards. Everybody hated her after that.

"Just before freedom declared, my husband took very sick and she took her husband and come to my house to make him get up. I told her that he was not able to work, but my husband was so scared they would beat me to death 'til he begged me to hush. I expect marster would have if he hadn't been scared of his father. You see his father give me to him. He told me if the legislature set in his behalf he would make me know a nigger's place. You know it was near freedom. I told him if he made my husband get out of bed as sick as he was and go to work, I would tell his father if he killed me afterwards. And that's one time I was goin' to fight with 'em. I never was scared of none of 'em, so I told 'em if they touched my husband they wouldn't touch nothin' else. They wouldn't give us nothin' to eat that whole day.

"Course we never did have much to eat. At night they would give us a teacup of meal and a slice of bacon a piece for breakfus' the next mornin'. If you had chillun they would give you a teacup of meal for two chillun. By day light the next mornin' the overseer was at your house to see if you was out, and if you hadn't cooked and eat and got out of that house he would take that bull whip, and whip you nearly to death. He carried that bull whip with him everywhere he went.

"Those folks killed one of my husband's brothers. He was kind of crack-brained, and 'cause he was half crazy, they beat him all the time. The last time they beat him we was in the field and this overseer beat him with that bull hide all across the head and everywhere. He beat him until he fell down on his knees and couldn't even say a word. And do you know he wouldn't even let a one of us go to see about him. He stayed stretched out in the the field 'til us went home. The next mornin' he was found dead right where he had beat him that evenin'.

"'Bout two or three weeks later than that they told one of the slaves they was goin' to beat him after we quit work that evenin'. His name was Josh.

"When the overseer went to the other end of the field Josh dropped his hoe and walked off. Nobody saw him anymore for about three weeks. He was the best hand us had and us sho' did need him. Our master went everywhere he could think of, lookin' for Josh, but he couldn't find him and we was glad of it. After he looked and looked and couldn't find him he told all of us to tell Josh to come back if we knowed where he was. He said if Josh would come back he wouldn't whip him, wouldn't let the overseer whip him. My husband knowed where he was but he warn't goin' to tell nobody. Josh would come to our house every night and us would give him some of what us had for dinner and supper. Us always saved it for him. Us would eat breakfus' at our house, but all of us et dinner and supper at the mess house together. Everyday when I et dinner and supper I would take a part of mine and my husband would take a part of his and us would carry it to our house for pore Josh. 'Bout 'leven o'clock at night, when everybody was sleep, Josh would come to the side window and get what us had for him. It's really a shame the way that pore man had to hide about just to keep from bein' beat to death 'bout nothin'. Josh said the first day he left he went in the woods and looked and looked for a place to hide. Later he saw a tree that the wind had blowed the top off and left 'bout ten feet standin'. This was rather a big tree and all of the insides had rotted out. I reckon you have seen trees like that. Well that's the way this one was. So Josh climbed up this tree and got down inside of it. He didn't know there was nothin' down in that tree, but there was some little baby bears in there. Then there he was down there with no way to come out, and knowin' all the time that the mama bear was comin' back. So he thought and thought and thought. After while he thought 'bout a knife he had in his pocket. You see he couldn't climb out of the tree, it was too tall. When he heard the bear climbin' up the tree he opened his knife. Have you ever seen a bear comin' down a tree? Well he comes down backwards. So when this bear started down inside of the tree he went down backwards, and Josh had his knife open and just caught him by the tail and begin stickin' him with the knife. That's the way Josh got out of that tree. When he stuck the bear with the knife the bear went back up the tree, and that pulled Josh up. And when the bear got to the top of the tree Josh caught a hold of the tree and pulled himself on out, but the bear fell and broke his neck. Well Josh had to find him somewhere else to hide. In them times there was big caves in the woods, not only the woods but all over the country, and that's where pore Josh hid all while he was away. Josh stayed there in that cave a long time then he come on back home. He didn't get a whippin' either."

Childhood memories were recalled by an old woman who said: "When I was about nine years old, for about six months, I slept on a crocus bag sheet in order to get up and nurse the babies when they cried. Do you see this finger? You wonder why its broke? Well one night the babies cried and I didn't wake up right away to 'tend to 'em and my mistress jumped out of bed, grabbed the piece of iron that was used to push up the fire and began beatin' me with it. That's the night this finger got broke, she hit me on it. I have two more fingers she broke beatin' me at diff'unt times. She made me break this leg too. You see they would put the women in stocks and beat 'em whenever they done somethin' wrong. That's the way my leg was broke. You see us had to call all of our marster's chillun 'mistess' or 'marster.' One day I forgot to call one of my young mistesses, 'miss.' She was about eight or nine months old. My mistress heard me and put me in a stock and beat me. While she was beatin' me, I turned my leg by some means and broke it. Don't you think she quit beatin' me 'cause I had broke my leg. No, that made no diff'unce to her. That's been years ago, but it still worries me now. Now other times when you called your marster's chillun by their names, they would strip you and let the child beat you. It didn't matter whether the child was large or small, and they always beat you 'til the blood ran down.

"Have you ever slept in the grave yard? I know you haven't but I have. Many a time when I was told that I was goin' to get a beatin', I would hide away in the cemetery where I stayed all night layin' in gullies between graves prayin'. All night long I could see little lights runnin' all over the grave yard, and I could see ha'nts, and hear 'em sayin' 'Uh, Uh, Uh, Uh, Uh,' which meant they were pityin' my case.

"When they whipped the men, all their clothes was

took off, their hands was fastened together and then they wound 'em up in the air to a post and tied their feet to the bottom of the post. They would begin whippin' 'em at sundown, and sometimes they would be whippin' 'em as late as 'leven o'clock at night. You could hear 'em cryin' and prayin' a long ways off. When they prayed for the Lord to have mercy, their marster would cuss the Lord and tell 'em they better not call his name again."

The whipping pole, as described by Lizzie, was a long post several feet in diameter to which was attached a long rope through a pulley. On one end was a device, similiar to the modern handcuff—the other end was used to draw the hand to an upward position, thereby, rendering the individual helpless. At the base of the pole was a clamp like instrument which held the feet in a motionless position.

Roy Redfield recalls going to the courthouse and seeing the older slaves whipped. "When I would go there with my young marster I would see 'em whippin' the slaves. You see they had stocks there then, and they wouldn't put you in jail like they do now. Your marster or mistess would send you to the courthouse with a note and they would put you in them stocks and beat you, then they would give you a note and send you back. They never did beat me, if they had my old mistess would have raised sand with 'em. Whenever I was whipped my mother did it. I warn't no slave and my ma neither, but my pa was.

"When they whipped you they would strap you down in them stocks, then a man would wind the whippin' machine and beat you 'til they had given you the number of lashes your boss had on the note. I didn't see them whippin' any women there, so I can't say they did and I can't say they didn't.

"My master wouldn't let us go to school, but his chillun would slip 'round and teach us what they could out of their books. They would also give us books to read. Whenever their pa or ma caught them tryin' to teach us they always whipped them. I learned to read and write from 'em and I'll never forget how hard it was for 'em to get a chance to teach me. But if they caught you tryin' to write they would cut your finger off and if they caught you again they would cut your head off.

"When I was a young man, a old man stole the head and pluck (pluck is the liver and lites) out of the hog (some people call it the haslet) and hid it up in the loft of his house. When his marster missed it he went to this man's house lookin' for it. The man told him that he didn't have it. He had already told his wife if his marster come not to own it either. Well his master kept askin' him over and over 'bout the head and pluck, but they denied having it. The marster told 'em if they didn't give it to him and that quick he was goin' to give 'em a thousand lashes each, if less didn't kill 'em. This woman's husband told her not to own it. He told her to take three thousand lashes and don't own it. So their marster whipped her and whipped her, but she wouldn't own it. Finally he quit whippin' her and started whippin' the old man. Just as soon as he started whippin' the man he told his wife to go up in the loft of the house and throw the head and pluck down 'cause he didn't want it.

"You always had to get a pass when goin' out. Sometimes, when you wouldn't be thinking, a patter roller would step up to the door and ask who was there. If any visitor was there they would ask 'em to show their pass. If you didn't have a pass they would take you out and beat you, then make you go home and when you got home, your marster would take you to the barn, strip you buck naked, tie you to a post and beat you. Us didn't have to get passes whenever us wanted to go visitin'. All us had to do was tell 'em who us belonged to, and they always let us by. They knowed our marster would let us go 'thout passes.

"Us used to go to barn dances all the time. I never will forget the fellow who played the fiddle for them dances. He had run away from his marster seven years before. He lived in a cave he had dug in the ground. He stayed in this cave all day and would come out at night. This cave was in the swamp. He stole just 'bout everythin' he et. His marster had been tryin' to catch him for a long time. Well they found out he was playin' for these dances and one night us saw some strange lookin' men come in but us didn't pay it much 'tention. Us always made a big oak fire and thats where us got mos' of our light from. Well these men danced with the girls a good while and after a while they started goin' out one by one. Way after while they all came back in together, they had washed the blackenin' off their faces, and us seen they was white. This man had a song he would always sing. 'Fooled my marster seven years—expect to fool him seven more.' So when these men came in they went to him and told him maybe he had fooled 'em for seven years, but he wouldn't fool 'em seven more. When they started to grab him he just reached in the fire and got a piece of wood that was burnin' good on one end and waved it all around (in a circle) until he set three of 'em on fire. While they was puttin' this fire out he run out in the swamp and back in his cave. They tried to catch him again. They painted their faces and done just like they did the first time, but this time they carried pistols. When they pulled their pistols on him he did just like he did the first time, and they never did catch him. He stopped comin' to play for the dances after they was straight after him. Dogs couldn't trail him 'cause he kept his feet rubbed with onions.

"I have seen some marsters make their slaves walk in snow knee deep, barefooted. Their heels would be cracked open jus' like corn bread.

"The only real mean thing they did to us when I was young was to sell my father when our marster died. They sold him to somebody way off, and they promised to bring him back to see us, but they never did. We always wished he would come, but until this day us hasn't laid eyes on him again. My mother worried 'bout him 'til she died.

"Chillun didn't know what shoes was 'til they was 'bout fifteen years old. They would go a mile or a mile and a half in the snow for water anytime, and the only thin' they ever had on their feet would be somethin' made out of home-spun. You don't hardly hear of chilblain feet now, but then most every child you saw had cracked heels. The first pair of shoes I ever wore, I was sixteen years old, was too small for me and I pulled 'em off and throwed 'em in the fire."

United States. Work Projects Administration

[HW: Dist. #2
Ex. Slave #99]

SLAVERY
by
RUBY LORRAINE RADFORD

COMPILATION MADE FROM
INTERVIEWS WITH 30 SLAVES
AND INFORMATION FROM SLAVERY
LAWS AND OLD NEWSPAPER FILES
[Date Stamp: MAY 8 1937]

SLAVERY

The ex-slaves interviewed ranged in ages from 75 to 100 years old. Out of about thirty-five negroes contacted only two seemed to feel bitter over memories of slave days. All the others spoke with much feeling and gratitude of the good old days when they were so well cared for by their masters. Without exception the manners of these old men and women were gentle and courteous. The younger ones could pass on to us only traditional memories of slavery times, as given them by their parents; on some points a few were vague, while others could give clear-cut and vivid pictures.

Practically all the Negroes interviewed seemed to be of pure African blood, with black or dark brown skin, Negroid features, and kinky, tightly wrapped wool. Most of the women were small and thin. We found one who had a strain of Indian blood, a woman named Mary, who belonged to John Roof. Her grandfather was an Indian, and her grandmother was part Indian, having migrated into South Carolina from Virginia.

Sarah Ray, who was born on the Curtis Lowe place in McDuffie County was one of the few ex-slaves contacted, who was admittedly half-white. Although now wrinkled and weazened with age she has no definite Negroid features. Her eyes are light hazel and her hair fluffs about her face in soft ringlets instead of the tight kinks of the pure Negro.

"My father was a white man, de overseer," said Sarah. "Leastways, dey laid me to him."

Sarah was brought up like the Negro children on the plantation. She had no hard work to do. Her mother was a field hand, and they lived in a little house in the quarters. "De ve'y fust thing I kin remember is ridin' down de road in de ox cart wid my mammy," she said. "Ole man Eli wus drivin'. We wus goin' to Miss Meg's on de odder side o' Hart's Branch. Marster had give us to Miss Meg when she married Mr. Obediah Cloud."

HOUSING CONDITIONS

The slave houses were called "quarters," which consisted generally of a double row of houses facing each other in a grove of trees behind the "big house." On prosperous plantations each of these cabins had a garden plot and a chicken yard. Some of them were built of logs, but many were of planks. Most of them were large, one-room, unceiled, with open fireplaces at one end for cooking. When families grew too large a shed room would be "drap down on de back." Another type of slave cabin was called the "Double-pen" house. This was a large two-room cabin, with a chimney between the two rooms, and accommodating two families. On the more prosperous plantations the slave quarters were whitewashed at intervals.

On plantations housing arrangements were left entirely to the discretion of the owner, but in the cities strict rules were made. Among the ordinances of the City Council of Augusta, dated from August 10th, 1820-July 8, 1829, Section 14, is the following law concerning the housing of slaves:

"No person of color shall occupy any house but that of some white person by whom he or she is owned or hired without a license from the City Council. If this license is required application must first be made for permission to take it out. If granted the applicant shall give bond with approved security, not exceeding the sum of $100.00 for his or her good behavior. On execution of charge the Clerk shall issue the license. Any person renting a house, or tenement contrary to this section or permitting the occupancy of one, may be fined in a sum not exceeding $50.00."

Descriptions were given of housing conditions by quite a number of slaves interviewed. Fannie Fulcher, who was a slave on Dr. Balding Miller's plantation in Burke County described the slave quarters thus: "Houses wus built in rows, one on dat side, one on dis side—open space in de middle, and de overseer's house at de end, wid a wide hall right through it. (Fannie was evidently referring to the breezeway or dogtrot, down the middle of many small plantation houses). We cook on de fireplace in de house. We used to have pots hanging right up in de chimbley. When dere wus lots of chillun it wus crowded. But sometimes dey took some of 'em to de house for house girls. Some slep' on de flo' and some on de bed. Two-three houses had shed rooms at de back. Dey had a patch sometime. My father, he used to have a patch. He clean it up hisself at night in de swamp."

Susie Brown, of the Evans Plantation on Little River in Columbia County said, in describing the Quarters, "Dey look like dis street." She indicated the unpaved street with its rows of unpainted shacks. "Some of dem wus plank houses and some wus log houses, two rooms and a shed room. And we had good beds, too—high tester beds wid good corn shuck and hay mattresses."

On the plantation of John Roof the slave cabins were of logs. Large families had two or three rooms; smaller ones one or two rooms.

Susannah Wyman, who was a slave on the Starling Freeman place near Troy, S.C. said, "Our houses wus made outer logs. We didn't have nothin' much nohow, but my mammy she had plenty o' room fer her chillun. We didn't sleep on de flo', we had bed. De people in de plantachun all had bed."

Others described mattresses made of straw and corn shucks. Another said, "Yas'm, we had good cotton mattresses. Marster let us go to de gin house and git all de cotton we need."

Another described the sleeping conditions thus, "Chillun pretty much slep' on de flo' and old folks had beds. Dey wus made out o' boards nailed togedder wid a rope strung across it instead o' springs, and a cotton mattress across it."

FOOD

Many of the Negroes with whom we talked looked back on those days of plenty with longing. Rations of meal, bacon and syrup were given out once a week by the overseer. Vegetables, eggs and chickens raised in the little plots back of the cabins were added to these staples.

Ellen Campbell, who was owned by Mr. William Eve of Richmond County said, "My boss would feed 'em good. He was killin' hogs stidy fum Jinuary to March. He had two smokehouses. Dere wus four cows. At night de folks on one side de row o' cabins go wid de piggins fer milk, and in de mawnin's, dose on de odder side go fer de piggins o' milk."

"And did you have plenty of other good things to eat?" we asked.

"Law, yas'm. Rations wus give out to de slaves; meal, meat, and jugs o' syrup. Dey give us white flour at Christmas. Every slave family had de gyarden patch and chickens. Marster buy eggs and chickens fum us at market prices."

Another slave told us that when the slaves got hungry before dinner time they would ask the nursing mothers to bring them back hoe-cake when they went to nurse the babies. Those hot hoe-cakes were eaten in mid-morning, "to hold us till dinner-time."

On one plantation where the mother was the cook for the owner, her children were fed from the big kitchen.

A piece of iron crossed the fireplace, and the pots hung down on hooks. "Us cooked corn dodgers," one ex-slave recalled, "the hearth would be swept clean, the ash cakes wrapped up into corn shucks and cooked brown. They sure was good!"

TYPES OF WORK

The large plantations were really industrial centers in which almost everything necessary to the life of the white family and the large retinue of slaves was grown or manufactured. On estates where there were many slaves there were always trained blacksmiths, coopers, carpenters, tanners, shoemakers, seamstresses, laundresses, weavers, spinners, cooks and house servants; all employed in the interest of the community life of the plantation. Those who could not learn to do any of this skilled work were turned into the fields and called, "hands". Both men and women were employed in the fields where cotton, corn, rice and tobacco were cultivated. House servants ware always considered superior to field hands.

Melinda Mitchell, who was born a slave in Edgefield, S.C., said, "My family wasn't fiel' hands. We wus all house servants. My father wus de butler, and he weighed out de rations fer de slaves. My mammy wus de house 'oman and her mother and sister wus de cooks. Marster wouldn't sell none of his slaves, and when he wanted to buy one he'd buy de whole fambly to keep fum havin' 'em separated."

At an early age Melinda and her younger sister were given to the two young ladies of the house as their personal maids. "I wus given to Miss Nettie," Melinda said, "Our young Mistresses visited, too, and wherever dey went my sister and me went erlong. My own mammy took long trips with ole Mistis to de Blue Ridge Mountains and sometimes over de big water."

Susannah Wyman of the Starling Freeman plantation in South Carolina said, "The house servants wuz trained to cook, clean up, de man wuz trained to make shoes. I don't think us had carpenters. I toted water in de field, hoed some. I wuz quite young. I spun but I didn't weave. Dere wuz a lady dey had on de place did de weavin'. I had many a striped dress woven on dat big loom and dey wuz pretty, too."

Susie Brown, who used to live on the Evans plantation on Little River in Columbia County was too little to do any hard work during slavery times. "I jus' stayed at home and 'tend de baby," she said. "But my mother was a cook and my father a blacksmith."

Mary's mother was a plantation weaver. "Mistis would cut out dresses out of homespun. We had purple dyed checks. They was pretty. I had to sew seams. Marster had to buy shoes for us, he give us good-soled ones."

Easter Jones, who had only bitter memories of the slavery period said, "Sometimes we eben had to pull fodder on Sunday. But what I used to hate worse'n anything was wipin' dishes. Dey'd make me take de dish out de scaldin' water, den if I drap it dey whip me. Dey whip you so hard your back bleed, den dey pour salt and water on it. And your shirt stick to your back, and you hadder get somebody to grease it 'fore you kin take it off."

Ellen Campbell, who used to belong to Mr. William Eve said she did only simple jobs about the plantation in childhood, "When I was 'bout ten years old dey started me totin' water—you know ca'yin' water to de hands in de field. 'Bout two years later I got my first field job 'tending sheep. When I wus fifteen year old Missus gib me to Miss Eva, you know she de one marry Colonel Jones. My young Mistus was fixin' to git married, but she couldn't on account de war, so she brought me to town and rented me out to a lady runnin' a boarding house. De rent wus paid to my Mistus. One day I was takin' a tray from de out-door kitchen to de house when I stumbled and dropped it. De food spill all over de ground. Da lady got so mad she picked up de butcher knife and chop me in de haid. I went runnin' till I come to da place where mah white folks live. Miss Eva took me and wash de blood out mah head and put medicine on it, and she wrote a note to de lady and she say, 'Ellen is my slave, give to me by my mother. I wouldn't had dis happen to her no more dan to me. She won't come back dere no more.'"

Willis Bennefield, who was a slave on Dr. Balding Miller's plantation in Burke County, said, "I wuk in de fiel' and I drove him 30 years. He was a doctor. He had a ca'iage and a buggy, too. My father driv de ca'iage. I driv de doctor. Sometimes I was fixin' to go to bed and had to hitch up my horse and go five or six miles. He had regular saddle horses, two pair o' horses fer de ca'iage. He was a rich man—riches' man in Burke County—had three hundred slaves. He made his money on de plantachuns, not doctorin'."

Fannie Fulcher, who was also one of Dr. Miller's slaves, and Willis Bennefield's sister gives this account of the slaves' work in earning extra money. "De marster give 'em ev'y day work clothes, but dey bought de res' deyselves. Some raise pumpkins, squashes, potatoes, all sich things like dat in dey patches; sell 'em to different stores. Jus' like somebody want ground clear up, dey git big torches fer light, clean up de new groun' at night, dat money b'long to dem. I year my mother and father say de slaves made baskets and quilts and things and sell 'em for they-selves."

EDUCATION

The following appears in the Statue Laws of Georgia for 1845 concerning educating negroes, under Section II, Minor Offences.

"Punishment for teaching slaves or free persons of color to read. If any slave, negro, or free person of color, or any white person, shall teach any other slave, negro or free person of color, to read or write either written or printed characters, the said free person of color or slave shall be punished by fine and whipping, or fine or whipping, at the direction of the court."

Among the ordinances passed by the City of Augusta, effective between August 10th, 1820 and July 8th, 1829, was the following concerning the teaching of negroes:

"No person shall teach a negro or person of color to read or cause any one to be taught within the limits of the City, nor shall any person suffer a school for the instruction of negroes, or persons of color to be kept on his or her lot."

None of the ex-slaves whom we interviewed could either read or write. Old Willis Bennefield, who used to accompany his young master to school, said he "larned something then. I got way up in my A B Cs, but atter I got to thinkin' 'bout gals I fergit all 'bout dat."

Another slave said, "We had a school on our plantation and a Negro teacher named, Mathis, but they couldn't make me learn nothin'. I sure is sorry now."

Easter Jones, who was once a slave of Lawyer Bennet, on a plantation about ten miles from Waynesboro, said, when we asked if she had been to school, "Chillun didn't know whut a book wus in dem days—dey didn't teach 'em nothin' but wuk. Dey didn' learn me nothin' but to churn and clean up house, and 'tend to dat boy and spin and cyard de roll."

RELIGION

Most of the ex-slaves interviewed received their early religious training in the churches of their masters. Many churches which have slave sections in this district are still standing. Sometimes the slaves sat in pews partitioned off at the back of the church, and sometimes there was a gallery with a side entrance.

The old Bath Presbyterian Church had a gallery and private entrance of this kind. Sunday Schools were often conducted for the slaves on the plantation.

Among the ordinances passed by the City of Augusta, February 7, 1862, was section forty-seven, which concerned negro preaching and teaching:

> "No slave or free person of color shall be allowed to preach, exhort or teach, in any meeting of slaves or free persons of color, for public worship or religious instruction in this city, but except at funerals or sitting up with the dead, without a license in writing from the Inferior Court of Richmond County, and Mayor of the City, regularly granted under the Act of the General Assembly of this State, passed on the 23rd day of December, 1843.
> "No colored preacher residing out of the County of Richmond, shall preach, exhort, or teach, until he has produced his license granted under the Act aforesaid, and had the same countersigned by the Mayor of this

City, or in his absence by two members of Council.

"Persons qualified as aforesaid, may hold meetings in this city for the purpose aforesaid, at any time during the Sabbath day, and on Sunday, Tuesday, and Thursday nights. No other meetings of slaves or free persons of color for religious purposes shall be held, except by permission of Council.

"No meeting of slaves or free persons of color for the purpose aforesaid, shall continue at any time later than 10:30 at night, and all such meetings shall be superintended by one or more citizens, appointed by the ministers in charge of their respective denominations, and approved by the Mayor. All slaves or free persons of color attending such meetings, after that hour, shall be arrested, and punished, under the Section, whether with or without tickets from their owners; and all such persons returning from such meetings after the ringing of the Market Bell, without tickets, shall be arrested and punished as in other cases.

"Every offense against this section shall be punished by whipping, not exceeding 39 lashes, or fined not exceeding $50.00."

Harriet White, who told us some of her father's slavery experiences said, "Yas'm, dey let'em go to chu'ch, but de colored folks hadder sit behind a boarded up place, so dey hadder stretch dey neck to see de preacher, and den day hadder jine de Master's chu'ch—de Methodis'

Chu'ch. De spirit done tole my father to jine da Baptis' Chu'ch—dat de right t'ing, but he hadder jine de Methodis', 'cause his Master was Methodis'. But when he come to Augusta he wus baptise in de river. He say he gwine ca'y God's point."

We asked Ellen Campbell of the Eve Plantation in Richmond County about church going. She replied, "Yas'm, we used to go to town. But de Padderolas wus ridin' in dem days, and you couldn' go off de plantachun widout a pass. So my boss he built a brick chu'ch on de plantachun, and de D'Laigles built a chu'ch on dere's."

Susie Brown, who was a slave on the Evans Plantation in Columbia County, said, in speaking of her mother getting religion, "My Maw and Paw wasn't married till after freedom. When my Maw got 'ligion dey wouldn' let her be baptise till she was married." She stated that her mother had seven children then. Aunt Susie had had eight children herself, but her husband was now dead. When asked why she didn't get married again, she replied, "Whut I wanner git married fer? I ain' able to wuk fer myself let alone a man!"

Augustus Burden, who was born a slave on General Walker's plantation at Windsor Springs, Ga., said, "We had no churches on our place. We went to the white people's church at Hale's Gate. Then after they stopped the colored people going there to church, they had their little meetings right at home. We had one preacher, a real fine preacher, named Ned Walker, who was my uncle by marriage."

Fannie Fulcher, a former slave on Dr. Miller's plantation in Burke County, gave this unique account of the slave children's early religious trainings: "Dey had a ole lady stay in de quarters who tuk care o' de chillun whilst de mother wus in de fiel'. Den dey met at her house at dark, and a man name, Hickman, had prayers. Dey all kneel down. Den de chillun couln' talk till dey got home—if you talk you git a whippin' frum de ole lady nex' night. Ole granny whip 'em."

Fannie said the slaves went to the "white folks church," and that "white folks baptise 'em at Farmer's Bridge or Rock Creek." A white preacher also married the slaves.

DISCIPLINE

In 1757 the Patrol System was organized. This was done as a result of continual threats of uprisings among the slaves. All white male citizens living in each district, between the ages of 16 and 45 were eligible for this service. The better class of people paid fines to avoid this duty. Members of the patrol group could commit no violence, but had power to search Negro houses and premises, and break up illegal gatherings. They were on duty from nine at night until dawn.

By 1845 there were many laws on the Statute books of Georgia concerning the duties of patrols. The justice of the peace in each captain's district of the state was empowered to decide who was eligible to patrol duty and to appoint the patrol. Every member of the patrol was required to carry a pistol while on duty. They were required to arrest all slaves found outside their master's domain without a pass, or who was not in company with some white person. He was empowered to whip such slave with twenty lashes. He also had power to search for offensive weapons and fugitive slaves. Every time a person evaded patrol duty he was required to pay the sum of five dollars fine.

The entire life of the slave was hedged about with rules and regulations. Beside those passed by individual masters for their own plantations there were many city and state laws. Severe punishment, such as whipping on the bare skin, was the exception rather than the rule, though some slaves have told of treatment that was actually inhuman.

In 1845 the following laws had been passed in Georgia, the violation of which brought the death penalty:

"Capital crimes when punished with death: The following shall be considered as capital offenses, when committed by a slave or free person of color: insurrection or an attempt to excite it; committing a rape, or attempting it on a free white female; murder of a free white person, or murder of a slave or free person of color, or poisoning a human being; every and each of these offenses shall, on conviction, be punished with death."

There were severe punishments for a slave striking a white person, burning or attempting to burn a house, for circulating documents to incite insurrection, conspiracy or resistance of slaves. It was against the law for slaves to harbor other fugitive slaves, to preach without a license, or to kill or brand cattle without instructions.

In Section Forty-Five of the Ordinances of the City of Augusta, passed on Feb. 7, 1862, were the following restrictions:

"Any slave or free person of color found riding or driving about the city, not having a written pass from his or her owner, hirer, or guardian, expressing the date of such pass, the name of the negro to whom it is given, the place or places to which he or she is going, how long he or she is to be absent, and in the case of a slave, that such slave is in the services of the person before the Recorder's Court by which he or she shall be tried, and on conviction shall be punished by whipping not to exceed 39 lashes.

"No slave or free person of color, other than Ministers of the Gospel, having charge of churches, in the discharge of their duties, and funeral processions, shall be allowed to ride or drive within the limits of the city, on the Sabbath, without written permission from his or her owner, or employer, stating that such slave or free parson of color is on business of such owners or employer.

"Every slave or free person of color not excepted as aforesaid, who shall be found riding or driving in the city on the Sabbath, without such permission from his or her owner or employer shall be arrested and taken to Recorder's Court; and if such slave or free person of color was actually engaged in the business of said owner or employer, the said slave or free person of color shall be convicted and punished by whipping, not to exceed 39 lashes, which punishment in no case be commuted by a fine.

"It shall be the duty of the officer making the arrest of such slave or free person of color as aforesaid, to take into his possession the horse or horse and vehicle, or horses and vehicles, so used by such slave or free person of color, which property may be redeemed by the owner, if white, upon the payment of $10.00, and if the owner of such property is a slave or free person of color, he or she shall be punished by whipping not less than 15 lashes."

"No slave or free person of color shall be allowed to attend military parades, or any procession of citizens, or at the markethouse on public sale days under the penalty of receiving not exceeding 15 lashes, for each and every offense, to be inflicted by the Chief of Police, Captain or any lieutenant; provided no person shall be prevented from having the attendance of his own servant on such occasions."

"No slave or free person of color shall walk with a cane, club, or stick, except such slave or free person of color be blind or infirm; nor smoke a pipe or cigar in any street, lane, alley or other public place, under a penalty of not exceeding 25 lashes, to be inflicted by any officer of the City, by order of the Recorder's Court."

Section Forty-Third

"No slave or free person of color shall play upon any instrument of music after sunset, without permission from the mayor or two members of Council, unless employed in the house of some citizen. No slave or free person of color shall be absent from his or her house 15 minutes after the bell shall have been rung, without a sufficient pass, under the penalty of 25 lashes, to be inflicted by the Chief of Police, or any officer of the City, and be confined in the Guard-Room for further examination, if found under suspicious circumstances. No slave or person of color shall keep lights in the house which they occupy after 10:00 at night, unless in case of necessity."

Section Forty-Four

"No slave or free person of color shall in the streets or alleys, fight, quarrel, riot, or otherwise, act in a disorderly manner, under the penalty of chastisement by any officer of the city, not exceeding 25 lashes, and in all cases of conviction before the Recorder's Court, he or she shall be punished by whipping, not exceeding 75 lashes.
"No slave or free person of color, shall be allowed to keep a shop or shops for the sale of beer, cake, fruit, soda water, or any similar articles on their own account or for the benefit of any other person whomsoever. Any slave or slaves, or free person of color, found keeping a shop and selling, bartering, or trading in any way, shall be taken up and punished by whipping, with not more than 30 lashes for each and every offense, and shall stand committed until the officer's fees are paid."

Most of the slaves interviewed were too young during the slavery period to have experienced any of the more cruel punishments, though some remembered hearing tales of brutal beatings. Most of the punishments inflicted were mild chastisements or restrictions.

Susie Brown, who was a slave on the Evans' plantation on Little River in Columbia, said, "My Marster wus good to me, good as he could be—only thing he whup me fer wus usin' snuff. And when he go to whup me, Mistis beg him to stop, and he only gib me a lick or two. And if

Mistis try to whup me, he make her stop. No, dey didn't had to do much whuppin'. Dey wus good to de hand." When asked about her overseer she replied, "Dere wus a overseer, but I disremember his name."

Most of these old ex-slaves' recollections had to do with the "Patterolas", as the Patrol was called. One of them said about the Patrol, "Oh yes, ma'm, I seed da Patterolas, but I never heard no song about 'em. Dey wus all white mens. Jus' like now you want to go off your Marster's place to another man's place, you had to get a pass from your boss man. If you didn't have dat pass, de Patterolas would whip you."

A woman who lived on the Roof plantation said, "I worked under four overseers, one of 'em was mean, and he had a big deep voice. When the niggers was at the feed lot, the place where they carried the dinner they brought to the fields, he would hardly give 'em time to eat before he hollered out, 'Git up and go back to work!'"

She also said that Mars. Thomas, the red-haired young master, was mean about slaves over-staying pass time. "If they want off and stayed too long, when they came back, he'd strip them stark, mother nekked, tie 'em to a tree, and whip 'em good. But old Marster, he didn't believe in whipping. It was different when the boys took possession after he died."

Very few slaves ran away, but when they did the master hunted them with dogs.

When Carrie Lewis, who belonged to Captain Ward, was asked if the slaves were ever whipped on their plantation, she replied, "No ma'm, de Marster say to de overseer, 'If you whup dem, I whup you.' No ma'm, he wouldn't keep a overseer dat wus mean to us—Cap'n Ward wus good to us. He wouldn't let de little ones call him 'Marster', dey had to call him and de Missus, 'Grampa' and 'Gramma'. My folks didn't mistreat de slaves. I'd be better off now if it wus dem times now."

We asked Ellen Campbell, a Richmond County slave if her master was good to her and she replied, "I'll say fer Mr. William Eve—he de bes' white man anywhere round here on any dese plantachuns. Dey all own slaves. Sometimes de overseer whup 'em—make 'em strip off dey shirt and whup 'em on de bare skin. My boss had a white overseer and two colored men dey call drivers. If dey didn't done right dey dus whup 'em and turn 'em loose."

It was said that those who refused to take whippings were generally negroes of African royal blood, or their descendants.

Edward Glenn of the Clinton Brown plantation in Forsythe County, Ga., said, "My father would not take a whipping. He would die before he would take a whipping. The Marster thought so much of him, he made young Marster Clinton promise he would never sell him or put a stripe on him. Once, when he wanted to punish him, he give him a horse and bridle and fifty dollars. 'Go on off somewhere and get somebody to buy you.' My father stayed away a month. One day he come home, he had been off about 100 miles. He brought with him a man who wanted to buy him. Marster put the man up for the night, fed his horse, and father went on out to mother. Next day when the man made him a price on father, Marster said, 'I was just foolin'. I wouldn't sell him for nothing. I was trying to punish him. He is true and honest, but he won't take a whipping.'

"Sometimes a slave was treated so bad by his owners he was glad if they put him up to be sold. If he was a bad man, they handcuffed him, put him on a stand, like for preachings and auctioned him off to the highest bidder.

"When runaway slave was brought back they was punished. Once in Alabama I saw a woman stripped naked, laid over a stump in a field with her head hangin' down on one side, her feet on the other, and tied to the stump. Then they whipped her hard, and you could hear her hollering far off, 'Oh, Lawd a'musay! Lawd a-musay!'."

Another punishment Edward said, was called the "Gameron Stick", (sometimes called the Gamlin stick, or Spanish Buck). The slave's arms were bound around the bent knees and fastened to a stick run beneath them. This was called the "Spanish Buck" punishment. They stripped the slave, who was unable to stand up, and rolled him on one side and whipped him till the blood came. They called the whip the "cowhide". Slaves were whipped for small things, such as forgetting orders or spilling food.

OVERSEERS

The most important person in the disciplining of negro slaves was the overseer. However, he occupied an unfortunate position socially. He was not regarded as the equal of the owner's family, and was not allowed to mix socially with the slaves. His was a hard lot, and consequently this position was generally filled by men of inferior grade. However, he was supposed to have an education so that he could handle the finances of the plantation accurately, and to be possessed of a good moral character in order to enforce the regulations. On most Georgia plantations overseers were given a house near the slave quarters. In some instances he lived in the house with the plantation owner. The average pay for overseers was from three to five hundred dollars a year.

Next in authority to the overseer was the driver, who directed the work in the fields. Every morning the driver blew the horn or rang the plantation bell to summon slaves to their work. Next to him was some trusted slave, who carried the keys to the smokehouse and commissary, and helped to give out rations once a week.

Many of the overseers were naturally cruel and inclined to treat the slaves harshly. Often strict rules and regulations had to be made to hold them in check. Overseers were generally made to sign these regulations on receiving their appointments.

In 1840 the Southern Cultivator and Monthly Journal published the following rules of the plantation:

Rules Of The Plantation

Rule 1st. The overseer will not be expected to work in the crop, but he must constantly with the hands, when not otherwise engaged in the employer's business, and will be required to attend on occasions to any pecuniary transactions connected with the plantation.
Rule 2nd. The overseer is not expected to be absent from the plantation unless actual necessity compels him, Sundays excepted, and then it is expected that he will, on all occasions, be at home by night.
Rule 3rd. He will attend, morning, noon and night, at the stable, and see that the mules and horses are ordered, curried, and fed.
Rule 4th. He will see that every negro is out by daylight in the morning—a signal being given by a blast of the horn, the first horn will be blown half an hour before day. He will also visit the negro cabins at least once or twice a week, at night, to see that all are in. No negro must be out of his house after ten oclock in summer and eleven in winter.
Rule 5th. The overseer is not to give passes to the negroes without the employer's consent. The families the negroes are allowed to visit will be specified by the employer; also those allowed to visit the premises. Nor is any negro allowed to visit the place without showing himself to the employer or overseer.

Rule 6th. The overseer is required not to chat with the negroes, except on business, nor to encourage tale bearing, nor is any tale to be told to him or employer, by any negro, unless he has a witness to his statements, nor are they allowed, in any instance, to quarrel and fight. But the employer will question any negro, if confidence can be placed in him, without giving him cause of suspicion, about all matters connected with the plantation, if he has any reason to believe that all things are not going on right.

Rule 7th. As the employer pays the overseer for his time and attention, it is not to be expected he will receive much company.

Rule 8th. As the employer employs an overseer, not to please himself, but the employer, it will be expected that he will attend strictly to all his instructions. His opinion will be frequently asked relative to plantation matters, and respectfully listened to, but it is required they be given in a polite and respectful manner, and not urged, or insisted upon; and if not adopted, he must carry into effect the views of the employer, and with a sincere desire to produce a successful result. He is expected to carry on all experiments faithfully and carefully note the results, and he must, when required by the employer, give a fair trial to all new methods of culture, and new implements of agriculture.

Rule 9th. As the whole stock will be under

immediate charge of the overseer, it is expected he will give his personal attention to it, and will accompany the hog feeder once a week and feed them, and count and keep a correct number of the same. The hog feeder is required to attend to feeding them every morning.

Rule 10th. The negroes must be made to obey, and to work, which may be done by an overseer who attends regularly to his business, with very little whipping; for much whipping indicates a bad tempered or an inattentive manager. He must never, on any occasion, unless in self-defense, kick a negro, or strike him with his fist, or butt end of his whip. No unusual punishment must be resorted to without the employer's consent. He is not expected to punish the foreman, except on some extraordinary emergency that will not allow of delay, until the employer is consulted. Of this rule the foreman is to be kept in entire ignorance.

Rule 11th. The sick must be attended to. When sick they are to make known the fact to him; if in the field, he is requested to send them to the employer, if at home; and if not, the overseer is expected to attend to them in person, or send for a physician if necessary. Suckling and pregnant women must be indulged more than others. Sucklers are to be allowed time to visit their children, morning, noon and evening, until they are eight months old, and twice a day from thence until they are twelve months old—they are to be kept working near their children. No lifting, pulling fodder, or hard work is expected of pregnant women.

Rule 12th. The negroes are to appear in the field on Monday mornings cleanly clad. To carry out said rule they are to be allowed time (say one hour by sun) every Saturday evening for the purpose of washing their clothes.

Rule 13th. The overseer is particularly required to keep the negroes as much as possible out of the rain, and from all kind of exposure.

Rule 14th. It will be expected of a good manager, that he will constantly arrange the daily work of the negroes, so that no negro may wait to know what to go to doing. Small jobs that will not reasonably admit of delay must be forthwith attended to.

Rule 15th. It is required of him, to keep the tools, ploughs, hoes &c. out of the weather and have all collected after they are done using them. The wagon and cart must be kept under a shed. He is expected to keep good gates, bars and fences.

Rule 16th. The employer will give him a list of all the tools and farming utensils and place the same in his care, and he is to return them at the years' end to the employer; if any are broke, the pieces are expected to be returned.

Rule 17th. He is not to keep a horse or dog

against the employer's approbation—and dogs kept for the purpose of catching negroes will not be allowed under any consideration.

Rule 18th. He is required to come to his meals at the blowing of the horn. It is not expected he will leave the field at night before the hands quit their work.

Rule 19th. It will be expected he will not speak of the employer's pecuniary business, his domestic affairs, or his arrangements to any one. He will be expected to inform the employer of anything going on that may concern his interest.

Rule 20th. He is to have no control whatever over the employer's domestic affairs; nor to take any privileges in the way of using himself, or loaning the employers property to others.

Rule 21st. He is expected to be guilty of no disrespectful language in the employer's presence—such as vulgarity, swearing &c; nor is he expected to be guilty of any indecencies, such as spitting on the floor, wearing his hat in the house, sitting at the table with his coat off, or whistling or singing in the house (Such habits are frequently indulged in, in Bachelor establishments in the South). His room will be appropriated to him, and he will not be expected to obtrude upon the employer's private chamber, except on business.

Rule 22nd. It will be expected of him that he

will not get drunk, and if he returns home in that state he will be immediately discharged. He will also be immediately discharged, if it is ascertained he is too intimate with any of the negro women.

Rule 23rd. It is distinctly understood, in the agreement with every overseer, should they separate, from death or other cause—and either is at liberty to separate from the other whenever dissatisfied—without giving his reasons for so doing; in said event the employer, upon settlement, is not expected to pay the cash nor settle for the year, but for the time only he remained in the employer's service, by note, due January next (with interest) pro rata, he was to pay for the year.

AMUSEMENTS

In spite of the many restrictions that hedged the slaves about there were many good times on the plantation. Old Mary of the Roof plantation described their frolics thus:

"We would sing and there was always a fiddle. I never could put up to dance much but nobody could beat me runnin' 'Peep Squirrel'. That was a game we made up on the plantation. The girls peeped out, then ran by the men, and they'd be caught and twirled around. They said I was like a kildee bird, I was so little and could run so fast. When we growed up we walked the boys to death! They used to say we walked the heels off their boots. We would have dances every Christmas, on different plantations. I tell my grandchildren sometimes that my brother-in-law would carry us to dances and wouldn' allow us to sleep, we'd dance all night long. We had a good time, us girls!"

When the negroes got married long tables were set under the trees in the back yard and the people from the big house came down to see how the slaves were dressed and to wish them well.

Concerning her own marriage Mary said, "They say I was married when I was 17 years old. I know it was after freedom. I married a boy who belonged to the Childs plantation. I had the finest kind of marrying dress, my father bought it for me. It had great big grapes hanging down from the sleeves and around the skirt." She sighed and a shadow passed over her placid old face, as she added, "I wish't I had a kep' it for my children to saw."

A slave from the Starling Freeman plantation in South Carolina said, "When cullud people wus married, white people give a supper. A cullud man whut lives on de place marries 'em."

"I used to sing good myself," continued Susannah, "you could hear the echo of my voice way out yonder, but I can't sing no more." Here Susannah stuck out her legs, covered with long-ribbed pink stockings. "My legs got de misery in 'em now, and my voice gone. In my mother's house dey never trained us to sing things like the mos' o' people. We sung the good old hymns, like, 'A Charge to Keep I have, a God to Glorify.'"

Old Tim, who used to live on a plantation in Virginia, said in speaking of good times before the war, "Sho', we had plenty o' banjo pickers! They was 'lowed to play banjos and guitars at night, if de Patterolas didn' interfere. At home de owners wouldn' 'low de Patterolas to tech their folks. We used to run mighty fast to git home after de frolics! Patterolas wus a club of men who'd go around and catch slaves on strange plantations and break up frolics, and whip 'em sometimes."

We asked Aunt Ellen Campbell, who was a slave on the Eve plantation in Richmond County, about good times in slavery days. She laughed delightedly and said, "When anybody gwine be married dey tell de boss and he have a cake fix. Den when Sunday come, after dey be married she put on de white dress she be married in and dey go up to town so de boss can see de young couple."

She was thoughtful a moment, then continued, "Den sometimes on Sadday night we have a big frolic. De nigger fum Hammond's place and Phinizy place, Eve place, Clayton place, D'Laigle place, all git together fer a big dance and frolic. A lot o' de young sports used to come dere and push de young nigger bucks aside and dance wid de wenches."

"We used to have big parties sometime," said Fannie Fulcher, a former slave on Dr. Miller's plantation in Burke County. "No white folks—jus' de overseer come round to see how dey git erlong. I 'member dey have a fiddle. I had a cousin who played fer frolics, and fer de white folks, too."

According to Melinda Mitchell, who lived on the plantation of Rev. Allen Dozier in Edgefield County, South Carolina, the field hands and house servants forgot cares in merriment and dancing after the day's work was over. When asked about her master, a Baptist preacher, condoning dancing Melinda replied with the simple statement, "He wasn't only a preacher, he was a religious man. De slaves danced at de house of a man who 'tended de stack, way off in de fiel' away fum de big house." They danced to the tunes of banjos and a homemade instrument termed, "Quill", evidently some kind of reed. It was fairly certain that the noise of merriment must have been heard at the big house, but the slaves were not interrupted in their frolic.

"My mammy wus de bes' dancer on de plantachun," Melinda said proudly. "She could dance so sturdy she could balance a glass o' water on her head an never spill a drop." She recalls watching the dancers late into the night until she fell asleep.

She could tell of dances and good times in the big house as well as in the quarters. The young ladies were belles. They were constantly entertaining. One day a wandering fortune-teller came on the piazza where a crowd of young people were gathered, and asked to tell the young ladies' fortunes. Everything was satisfactory until he told Miss Nettie she would marry a one-armed man. At this the young belle was so indignant that the man was driven off and the dogs set on him. "But de fortune teller told true-true," Melinda said. A faint ominous note crept into her voice and her eyes seemed to be seeing events that had transpired almost three-quarters of a century ago. "After de war Miss Nettie did marry a one-arm man, like de fortune-teller said, a Confederate officer, Captain Shelton, who had come back wid his sleeve empty."

SLAVE SALES

There were two legal places for selling slaves in Augusta; the Lower Market, at the corner of Fifth and Broad Street, and the Upper Market at the corner of Broad and Marbury Streets. The old slave quarters are still standing in Hamburg, S.C., directly across the Savannah River from the Lower Market in Augusta. Slaves who were to be put up for sale were kept there until the legal days of sales.

Advertisements in the newspapers of that day seem to point to the fact that most slave sales were the results of the death of the master, and the consequent settlement of estates, or a result of the foreclosure of mortgages.

In the Thirty-Seventh Section of the Ordinances of the City of Augusta, August 10, 1820-July 8, 1829, is the following concerning Vendue Masters:

> "If any person acts as a Vendue Master within the limits of this City without a license from the City Council, he shall be fined in a sum not exceeding $1,000.00. There shall not be more than four Vendue Masters for this city. They shall be appointed by ballot, and their license shall expire on the day proceeding the 1st Saturday in October of every year. No license shall be issued to a Vendue Master until he has given bond, with securities according to the laws of this State, and also a bond with approved security to the Council for the faithful discharge of his duties in the sum of

$5,000.00."

The newspapers of the time regularly carried advertisements concerning the sale of slaves. The following is a fair sample:

> "Would sell slaves: With this farm will be sold about Thirty Likely Negroes mostly country born, among them a very good bricklayer, and driver, and two sawyers, 17 of them are fit for field or boat work, and the rest fine, thriving children."

The following advertisement appeared in *The Georgia Constitutionalist* on January 17, 1769: "To be sold in Savannah on Thursday the 15th. inst. a cargo of 140 Prime Slaves, chiefly men. Just arrived in the Scow Gambia Captain Nicholas Doyle after a passage of six weeks directly from the River Gambia." by Inglis and Hall.

Most of the advertisements gave descriptions of each slave, with his age and the type of work he could do. They were generally advertised along with other property belonging to the slave owner.

The following appeared in the Chronicle and Sentinel of Augusta on December 23rd, 1864: "Negro Sales. At an auction in Columbus the annexed prices were obtained: a boy 16 years old, $3,625.

"At a late sale in Wilmington the annexed prices were obtained: a girl 14 years old $5,400; a girl 22 years old, $4,850; a girl 13 years $3,500; a negro boy, 22 years old $4,900."

Very few of the slaves interviewed had passed through the bitter experience of being sold. Janie Satterwhite, who was born on a Carolina plantation, and was about thirteen years old when she was freed, remembered very distinctly when she was sold away from her parents.

"Yes'm, my Mama died in slavery, and I was sold when I was a little tot," she said. "I 'member when dey put me on de block."

"Were you separated from your family?" we asked.

"Yes'm. We wus scattered eberywhere. Some went to Florida and some to odder places. De Missus she die and we wus all sold at one time. Atter dat nobody could do nothin' on de ole plantachun fer a year—till all wus settled up. My brudder he wasn't happy den. He run away fer five years."

"Where was he all that time?"

"Lawd knows, honey. Hidin', I reckon, hidin in de swamp."

"Did you like your new master?"

"Honey, I wus too little to have any sense. When dat man bought me—dat Dr. Henry, he put me in a buggy to take me off. I kin see it all right now, and I say to Mama and Papa, 'Good-bye, I'll be back in de mawnin'.' And dey all feel sorry fer me and say, 'She don' know whut happenin'.'"

"Did you ever see your family again?"

"Yes'm. Dey wusn't so far away. When Christmas come de Marster say I can stay wid Mama de whole week."

Easter Jones, who had many bitter memories of slavery days back on the Bennet plantation near Waynesboro, said, when asked if she was ever sold into slavery, "Dey had me up fer sale once, but de horse run away and broke de neck o' de man whut gwine buy me."

Harriet White, whose father was a slave, gives this account of his sale, "Yas'm, he tell me many times 'bout when he wus put up for sale on Warren Block (in Augusta). Father say dey put him on de block down here. De gemmen whut bought him name Mr. Tom Crew. But when dey tryin' to sell him—dat right durin' de war, one man say, 'No, I don' want him—he know too much.' He'd done been down to Savannah wid de Yankees. Den my father say, 'If you buy me you can't take me oudder de state of Georgia, 'cause de Yankees all around."

Carrie Lewis, who was owned by Captain Phillip Ward and lived on a plantation down in Richmond County said, "No'm, I wasn't never sold, but my Mama was sold fum me. See, I belonged to de young girl and old Marster fool Missus away fum de house so he git to sell my Mama."

"Did you ever see your mother afterwards?" we asked.

"No, ma'm. I wouldn' know my Mammy no more den you would."

"But were you happy on the plantation?"

A smile brightened her wrinkled old face as she replied, "I'd be a heap better off if it was dem times now."

When we asked Ellen Campbell if she was ever sold during slavery times she replied, "No'm. I wa'n't sold, but I know dem whut wus. Jedge Robinson he kept a nigger trade office over in Hamburg."

"Oh yes, we remember—the old brick building."

"Yas'm, dat it. Well, all de colored people whut gonner be sold was kept dere. Den dey brung 'em over to de market and put 'em up fer sale. Anybody fixin' to buy 'em, 'zamines 'em to see if day all right. Looks at de teef to tell 'bout de age."

Laura Steward, who was a slave in a Baptist preacher's family in Augusta told some interesting things about slave sales here: "Slaves were sold at the Augusta market, in spite of what white ladies say." She stated that there was a long house with porches on Ellis between 7th and 8th, where a garage now stands. In this building slaves were herded for market. "Dey would line 'em up like horses or cows," said Laura, "and look in de mouf at dey teef; den dey march 'em down togedder to market in crowds, first Tuesday sale day."

Old Mary used to live on the Roof plantation with her mother, while her father lived on a nearby plantation. She said her father tried for a long time to have his owner buy his wife and children, until finally, "One day Mr. Tom Perry sont his son-in-law to buy us in. You had to get up on what they called the block, but we just stood on some steps. The bidder stood on the ground and called out the prices. There was always a speculator at the sales. We wus bought all right and moved over to the Perry place. I had another young marster there. He had his own hands and didn't sell them at all. Wouldn't none of us been sold from the Roof place, except for my father beggin' Mr. Perry to buy us, so we wouldn't be separated."

Susannah Wyman of the Freeman plantation in South Carolina said, "Once de Marster tried to sell my brudder and anodder youngster fer a pair o' mules, and our Mistis said, 'No! You don' sell my chillun for no mules!' And he didn't sell us neider. They never sold anybody off our plantation. But people did sell women, old like I am now—or if they didn't have no chillun. The fus' spec-lator come along and wants to buy 'em, he kin have 'em. De Marster say, 'Bring me han's in. I want han's!'"

Eugene Smith, who used to belong to Mr. Steadman Clark of Augusta said, "I read in the papers where a lady said slaves were never sold here in Augusta at the old market, but I saw 'em selling slaves myself. They put 'em up on something like a table, bid 'em off just like you would do horses or cows. Dere wus two men. I kin recollect. I know one was call Mr. Tom Heckle. He used to buy slaves, speculatin'. The other was name Wilson. They would sell a mother from her children. That's why so many colored people married their sisters and brothers, not knowin' till they got to talking 'bout it. One would say: 'I remember my grandmother,' and another would say, 'that's *my* grandmother!' Then they'd find out they were sister and brother."

WAR MEMORIES

Most of the ex-slaves interviewed were too young to have taken any part in war activities, though many of them remembered that the best slaves were picked and sent from each plantation to help build breastworks for the defense of Waynesboro. On some places the Yankees were encamped and on others the southern soldiers were entertained.

"De Yankees come through de plantation on Sunday," said Hannah Murphy, a former slave on a Georgia plantation. "I'll never forgit dat! Dey wus singin' Dixie, 'I wisht I wus in Dixie, look away!' Dey wus all dress in blue. Dey sot de gin house afire, and den dey went in de lot and got all de mules and de horses and ca'y 'em wid 'em. Dey didn't bother de smoke house where de food wuz, and dey didn't tek no hogs. But dey did go to de long dairy and thowed out all de milk and cream and butter and stuff. Dey didn' bother us none. Some o' de cullard folks went wid de Yankees. De white folks had yeared dey wuz comin' and dey had lef'—after de Yankees all gone away, de white folks come back. De cullud folks stayed dere a while, but de owners of de place declaimed dey wuz free, and sont de people off. I know dat my mother and father and a lot o' people come heah to Augusta."

Old Tim, from a plantation in Virginia, remembers when Lee was fighting near Danville, and how frightened the negroes were at the sound of the cannon. "They cay'd the wounded by the 'bacco factory," he said, "on de way to de horspittle."

The northern troops came to the William Morris plantation in Burke County. Eliza Morris, a slave, who was her master's, "right hand bough" was entrusted with burying the family silver. "There was a battle over by Waynesboro," Eliza's daughter explained to us. "I hear my mother speak many times about how the Yankees come to our place." It seems that some of the other slaves were jealous of Eliza because of her being so favored by her master. "Some of the niggers told the soldiers that my mother had hidden the silver, but she wouldn' tell the hidin' place. The others were always jealous of my mother, and now they tried to made the Yankees shoot her because she wouldn' tell where the silver was hidden. My mother was a good cook and she fixed food for the Yankees camped on the place, and this softened the soldiers' hearts. They burned both the plantation houses, but they give my mother a horse and plenty of food to last for some time after they left."

"What did your mother do after the war?" we asked.

"She spent the rest of her life cookin' for her young Mistis, Mrs. Dr. Madden in Jacksonville. She was Cap'n Bill's daughter. That was her home till shortly after the World War when she died."

"Did your Master live through the war?"

"Yas'm. He come home. Some of the old slaves had stayed on at the plantation; others followed the Yankees off. Long time afterward some of 'em drifted back—half starved and in bad shape."

"'Let'em come home'", Marster said. "And them that he couldn' hire he give patches of land to farm."

"'Member de war? Course I do!" said Easter Jones, "My Marster went to Savannah, and dey put him in prison somewhere. He died atter he come back, it done him so bad. I 'member my brudder was born dat Sunday when Lee surrender. Dey name him Richmond. But I was sick de day dey came and 'nounced freedom."

Augustus Burden, a former slave on General Walker's plantation at Windsor Springs, Ga., served as valet for his master, said, "Master was killed at Chickamauga. When the war ceased they brought us home—our old master's home. My old Mistis was living and we came back to the old lady."

When the Yankees came through Georgia the Walkers and Schleys asked for protection from gunfire. Because of school associations with Northern officers nothing on the plantation was disturbed.

"Mrs. Jefferson Davis came there to visit the Schleys," said Augustus, and his face lit up with enthusiasm, "She was a mighty pretty woman—a big lady, very beautiful. She seemed to be real merry amongst the white folks, and Miss Winnie was a pretty little baby. She was talking then."

Louis Jones was seven years old when he was freed. He said, "I kin 'member de Yankees comin'. I wasn't skeered. I wanted to see 'em. I hung on de fence corners, and nearabouts some sich place. After freedom my Ma didn't go 'way. She stayed on de plantation till she could make more money cookin' some udder place. I don't think dey did anything to de plantation whar I wus. I yeared dey cay'd out de silver and mebbe hid it in places whar de Yankees couldn't find it."

When Ellen Campbell of the Eve plantation in Richmond County, was asked if she remembered anything about the Yankees coming through this part of the country, she replied:

"Yas'm, I seen 'em comin' down de street. Every one had er canteen on de side, a blanket on de shoulder, caps cocked on one side de haid. De Cavalry had boots on, and spurros on de boots. First dey sot de niggers free on Dead River, den dey come on here and sot us free. Dey march straight up Broad Street to de Planters Hotel, den dey camped on de river. Dey stayed here six months till dey sot dis place free. When dey campin' on de river bank we go down dere and wash dey clo'se fer a good price. Day had hard tack to eat. Dey gib us hard tack and tell us to soak it in water, and fry it in meat gravy. I ain't taste nothin' so good since. Dey say, 'Dis hard tack whut we hadder lib on while we fightin' to sot you free.'"

FREEDOM

Although the Emancipation Proclamation was delivered on January 1st, 1863 it was not until Lee's final surrender that most of the negroes knew they were free. The Freedman's Bureau in Augusta gave out the news officially to the negroes, but in most cases the plantation owners themselves summoned their slaves and told them they were free. Many negroes stayed right with their masters.

Carrie Lewis, a slave on Captain Ward's plantation in Richmond County, said, when asked where she went when freedom came, "Me? I didn't went nowhere. Da niggers come 'long wid de babies and dey backs, and say I wus free, and I tell 'em I was free already. Didn't make no diffunce to me—freedom."

Old Susannah from the Freeman plantation said, "When freedom come I got mad at Marster. He cut off my hair. I was free so I come from Ca'lina to Augusta to sue him. I walk myself to death! Den I found I couldn't sue him over here in Georgia! I had to go back. He was jus' nachally mad 'cause we was free. Soon as I got here, dere was a lady on de street, she tole me to come in, tek a seat. I stayed dere. Nex' mornin' I couldn't stand up. My limbs was hurtin' all over."

Tim from the plantation in Virginia remembers distinctly when freedom came to his people. "When we wus about to have freedom," he said, "they thought the Yankees was a-goin' to take all the slaves so they put us on trains and run us down south. I went to a place whut they call 'Butler' in Georgia, then they sent me on down to the Chattahoochee, where they were cuttin' a piece of railroad, then to Quincy, then to Tallahassee. When the war ended I weren't 'xactly in 'Gusta, I was in Irwinville, where they caught Mars. Jeff Davis. Folks said he had de money train, but I never seed no gold, nor nobody whut had any. I come on up to 'Gusta and jined de Bush Arbor Springfield Church.

"When freedom came they called all the white people to the court house first, and told them the darkies ware free. Then on a certain day they called all the colored people down to the parade ground. They had a big stand," explained Eugene Wesley Smith, whose father was a slave in Augusta. "All the Yankees and some of our leading colored men got up there and spoke, and told the negroes: "You are free. Don't steal! Now work and make a living. Do honest work, make an honest living and support yourself and children. There are no more masters. You are free!"

"When the colored troops came in, they came in playing:

> 'Don't you see the lightning?
> Don't you hear the thunder?
> It isn't the lightning,
> It isn't the thunder
> But the buttons on the Negro uniform!'

"The negroes shouted and carried on when they heard they were free."

This story of freedom was told by Edward Glenn of Forsythe County: "A local preacher, Walter Raleigh, used to wait by the road for me every day, and read the paper before I give it to Mistis. One day he was waiting for me, and instead of handing it back to me he tho'wed it down and hollered, 'I'm free as a frog!' He ran away. I tuk the paper to Mistis. She read it and went to cryin'. I didn't say no more. That was during the week. On Sunday morning I was talking to my brother's wife, who was the cook. We were talking about the Yankees. Mistis come in and say, 'Come out in the garden with me.' When we got outside Mistis said: 'Ed, you suppose them Yankees would spill their blood to come down here to free you niggers?'

"I said, 'I dunno, but I'se free anyhow, Miss Mary.'"

"'Shut up, sir, I'll mash your mouth!"

"That day Marster was eating, and he said, 'Doc' (they called me Doc, 'cause I was the seventh son). 'You have been a good boy. What did you tell your Mistis?'"

"I said, 'I told her the truth, that I knowed I was free.'

"He said, 'Well, Doc, you aren't really free. You are free from me, but you aren't of age yet, and you still belong to your father and mother.'

"One morning I saw a blue cloud of Yankees coming down the road. The leader was waving his arms and singing:

> 'Ha, ha, ha! Trabble all the day!
> I'm in the Rebel's Happy Land of Caanan.
> Needn't mind the weather,
> Jump over double trouble,
> I'm in the Rebel's Happy Land of Caanan.'

"The Yankee captain, Captain Brown, gathered all us negroes in the fair ground, July or August after freedom, and he made a speech. Lawsy! I can see that crowd yet, a-yelling and a-stomping! And the captain waving his arms and shouting!

"'We have achieved the victory over the South. Today you are all free men and free women!'

"We had everybody shouting and jumping, and my father and mother shouted along with the others. Everybody was happy."

Janie Satterwhite's memories were very vivid about freedom. "Oh yas'm," she said, "my brudder comed fer me. He say, 'Jane, you free now. You wanna go home and see Papa?' But old Mars say, 'Son, I don' know you and you don' know me. You better let Jane stay here a while.' So he went off, but pretty soon I slip off. I had my little black bonnet in my hand, and de shoes Papa give me, and I started off 'Ticht, ticht; crost dat bridge.

"I kept on till I got to my sister's. But when I got to de bridge de river wus risin'. And I hadder go down de swamp road. When I got dere, wus I dirty? And my sister say, 'How come you here all by yourself?' Den she took off my clo'es and put me to bed. And I remember de next mornin' when I got up it wus Sunday and she had my clo'es all wash and iron. De fus' Sunday atter freedom."

Folk Lore

As most of the ex-slaves interviewed were mere children during the slavery period they remembered only tales that were told them by their parents. Two bits of folk lore were outstanding as they were repeated with many variations by several old women. One of these stories may be a relic of race memory, dating back to the dawn of the race in Africa. Several negroes of the locality gave different versions of this story of the woman who got out of her skin every night. Hannah Murphy, who was once a slave and now lives in Augusta gives this version:

"Dere was a big pon' on de plantation, and I yeared de ole folks tell a story 'bout dat pon', how one time dere was a white Mistis what would go out ev'y evenin' in her cay'age and mek de driver tak her to de pon'. She would stay out a long time. De driver kep' a wonderin' whut she do here. One night he saw her go thu' de bushes, and he crep' behin' her. He saw her step out o' her skin. Da skin jus' roll up and lay down on de groun', and den de Mistis disappear. De driver wus too skeered to move. In a little while he yeared her voice sayin', 'Skinny, Skinny, don't you know me? Den de skin jump up and dere she wus again, ez big as life. He watch her like dat for a lot o' nights, and den he went and tole de Marster. De Marster wus so skeered o' her he run away frum de plantation and quit her."

Laura Stewart, who was born a slave in Virginia, gives this verson of the same story:

"Dey always tole me de story 'bout de ole witch who git out her skin. I ain't know it all. In dem days I guess dose kinder things went on. Dey said while she was out ridin' wid de ole witch she lef' her skin behind her, and when she come back, de other woman had put salt and pepper on it; and whan she say, 'Skinny, Skinny, don't you know me?' de ole skin wouldn't jump up, so she ain't had no skin a-tall."

"Granny," Laura's granddaughter called to her, "tell the ladies about the Mistis what got bury."

"Oh yes," Laura recalled, "dey didn' bury her so far. A bad man went dere to git her gold ring off her finger. She make a sound like 'Shs' like her bref comin' out, and de man got skeered. He run off. She got up direckly and come to de house. Dey was skeered o' dat Mistis de res' o' her life and say she were a hant."

Interesting Customs

On one southern plantation soap was made at a certain time of the year and left in the hollowed-out trough of a big log.

Indigo was planted for blueing. Starch was made out of wheat bran put in soak. The bran was squeezed out and used to feed the hogs, and the starch was saved for clothes.

A hollow stump was filled with apples when cider was to be made. A hole was bored in the middle, and a lever put inside, which would crush the apples. As Mary put it, "you put the apples in the top, pressed the lever, the cider come out the spout, and my, it was good!"

Dress

Most of the old ex-slave women interviewed wore long full skirts, and flat loose shoes. In spite of what tradition and story claim, few of the older negroes of this district wear head clothes. Most of them wear their wooly hair "wropped" with string. The women often wear men's discarded slouch hats. Though many of the old woman were interviewed in mid-summer, they wore several waists and seemed absolutely unaware of the heat.

One man, wearing the typical dress of the poverty-stricken old person of this district, is Tim Thornton, who used to live on the Virginia plantation of Mrs. Lavinia Tinsley. His ragged pants are sewed up with cord, and on his coat nails are used where buttons used to be. In the edges of his "salt and pepper" hair are stuck matches, convenient for lighting his pipe. His beard is bushy and his lower lip pendulous and long, showing strong yellow teeth. His manner is kindly, and he is known as "Old Singing Tim" because he hums spirituals all day long as he stumps around town leaning on a stick.

NUMBER OF SLAVES

Plantations owned by Dr. Balding Miller in Burke County had about eight hundred slaves. Governor Pickens of South Carolina was said to have had about four hundred on his various plantations. The William Morris plantations in Burke County had about five hundred slaves.

BIBLIOGRAPHY

Flanders, Ralph Betts
Plantation Slavery in Georgia.
Chapel Hill: The University Press of N.C.,
326 pages,
p. 1933, c. 1933, pp. 254-279.

Hotchkiss, William A.
Statute Laws of Georgia and State Papers;
Savannah, Ga.; John M. Cooper, pub., 990
pages, p. 1845, c. 1845,
pp. 810, 817, 838, 839, 840.

Rutherford, John
Acts of the General Assembly of the State of Georgia
Savannah, Ga.: Samuel T. Chapman, State Printer,
620 pages, p. 1854, c. 1854, p. 103.

Jones, J.W., Editor,
Southern Cultivator
Augusta, Ga.: J.W. and W.S. Jones, pubs., Vol. 1, 1843.

Ordinances of the City Council of Augusta.
August 10, 1820; July 8, 1829; Feb. 7, 1862.

The Daily Chronicle & Sentinel
Vol. XXVIII. No. 306.
Augusta, Ga., Dec. 23, 1864.

Clipping.

United States. Work Projects Administration

COMPILATION RICHMOND COUNTY EX-SLAVE INTERVIEWS

WORK, PLAY, FOOD, CLOTHING, MARRIAGE, etc.

Written by:
Louise Oliphant
Federal Writers' Project
Augusta, Ga.

Edited by:
John N. Booth
District Supervisor,
Federal Writers' Project
Augusta, Ga.

WORK, PLAY, FOOD, CLOTHING, MARRIAGE, etc.

In recalling habits of work and play, marriage customs, and like memories of Southern life before the Civil War, Richmond County's ex-slaves tell varied stories. One said: "I didn't start workin' 'til I was 'bout nine years old. Before that I had watched chickens, carried in wood, gathered eggs and such light work as that. But when I was nine I started workin' in the field. I didn't plow then because I was too small, but I hoed and did other light jobs.

"Our marster made our shoes for us out of raw cow hide. Us got two pairs of shoes a year, one for every day and one for Sunday. Us made everythin' us needed. The old women, who couldn't work in the field, would make cloth on the looms and the spinnin' wheels. Us didn't have chairs; us made benches and stools to sit on. Us didn't know what swings was. Us used to tie ropes in trees and swing in 'em.

"Everybody had his own tin plate and tin cup to eat out of. On Saturday they would give everybody three pounds of meat, twelve pounds of flour, twelve pounds of meal, and one quart of syrup. This was to last a week. Us always had plenty to eat 'til the war started, then us went hungry many a day because they took the food and carried it to the soldiers. Us stole stuff from everybody durin' that time.

"They always blowed a horn for you to go to work by and get off for dinner by and stop work in the evening by. When that horn blowed, you couldn't get them mules to plow another foot. They just wouldn't do it. Us always et dinner out in the yard, in the summer time, at a long bench. In cold weather us always went inside to eat. Whenever us didn't have enough to eat us would tell the overseer and he seed to it that us got plenty. Our overseers was colored."

Another old woman said she "started working at the age of seven as a nurse. I nursed, made fire in the house and around the wash pots 'til I was old enough to go to work in the fields. When I got big enough I hoed and later plowed. Us didn't wait 'til sun up to start workin', us started as soon as it was light enough. When it come to field work, you couldn't tell the women from the men. Of course my marster had two old women on the place and he never made them work hard, and he never did whip' em. They always took care of the cookin' and the little chillun.

"I'll tell you one thing, they had better doctors then than they do now. When folks had high blood pressure the doctors would cut you in your head or your arm and folks would get over it then. They took better care of themselves. Whenever anybody was caught in the rain they had to go to the marster's house and take some medicine. They had somethin' that looks like black draught looks now, and they would put it in a gallon jug, fill it a little over half full of boiling water, and finish fillin' it with whiskey. It was real bitter, but it was good for colds. Young folk didn't die then like they do now. Whenever anybody died it was a old person.

"I know more about conjuration than I'll ever be able to tell. I didn't believe in it at one time, but I've seen so much of it that I can almost look at a sick person and tell whether he is conjured or not. I wouldn't believe it now if I hadn't looked at snakes come out of my own sister's daughter. She married a man that had been goin' 'round with a old woman who wasn't nothin'. Well one day this woman and my niece got in a fight 'bout him, and my niece whipped her. She was already mad with my niece 'bout him, and after she found she couldn't whip her she decided to get her some way and she just conjured her.

"My niece was sick a long time and we had 'bout seven or eight diff'unt doctors with her, but none of 'em done her any good. One day us was sittin' on the porch and a man walked up. Us hadn't never seen him before, and he said he wanted to talk with the lady of the house. I 'vited him in and he asked to speak to me alone. So I went in the front room and told him to come on in there. When he got there he said just like this: 'You have sickness don't you?' I said, 'yes.' Then he said: 'I know it, and I come by here to tell you I could cure her. All I want is a chance, and you don't have to pay me a cent 'til I get her back on her feet, and if I don't put her back on her feet you won't be out one cent. Just promise you'll pay me when the work is done.' I told him to come back the next day 'cause I would have to talk with her husband and her mother 'fore I could tell him anythin'.

"Us all agreed to let him doctor on her since nobody else had did her any good. Two days later he brought her some medicine to take and told us to have her say: 'relieve me of this misery and send it back where it come from.' Seven days from the day she started takin' this medicine she was up and walkin' 'round the room. 'Fore that time she had been in bed for more than five weeks without puttin' her feet on the floor. Well three days after she took the first medicine, she told us she felt like she wanted to heave. So we gave her the bucket and that's what come out of her. I know they was snakes because I know snakes when I see 'em. One was about six inches long, but the others was smaller. He had told us not to be scared 'bout nothin' us saw, so I wasn't, but my sister was. After that day my niece started to get better fast. I put the snakes in a bottle and kept 'em 'til the man come back and showed 'em to him. He took 'em with him. It was 'bout three weeks after this that the other woman took sick and didn't live but 'bout a month."

Roy Redfield recalls that "when a person died several people would come in and bathe the body and dress it. Then somebody would knock up some kind of box for 'em to be buried in. They would have the funeral and then put the body on a wagon and all the family and friends would walk to the cemetery behind the wagon. They didn't have graves like they does now; they would dig some kind of hole and put you in it, then cover you up.

"In olden times there was only a few undertakers, and of course there warn't any in the country; so when a person died he was bathed and dressed by friends of the family. Then he was laid on a ironing board and covered with a sheet.

"For a long while us knowed that for some cause a part of the person's nose or lips had been et off, but nobody could find out why. Finally somebody caught a cat in the very act. Most people didn't believe a cat would do this, but everybody started watchin' and later found out it was so. So from then on, 'til the caskets come into use, a crowd of folks stayed awake all night sittin' up with the dead."

One old woman lived on a plantation where "every Saturday they would give you your week's 'lowance. They would give you a plenty to eat so you could keep strong and work. They weighed your meat, flour, meal and things like that, but you got all the potatoes, lard and other things you wanted. You got your groceries and washed and ironed on Saturday evenin' and on Saturday night everybody used that for frolicin'. Us would have quiltin's, candy pullin's, play, or dance. Us done whatever us wanted to. On these nights our mist'ess would give us chickens or somethin' else so us could have somethin' extra. Well, us would dance, quilt, or do whatever us had made up to do for 'bout three hours then us would all stop and eat. When us finished eatin' us would tell tales or somethin' for a while, then everybody would go home. Course us have stayed there 'til almost day when us was havin' a good time.

"My marster wanted his slaves to have plenty of chillun. He never would make you do much work when you had a lot of chillun, and had them fast. My ma had nineteen chillun, and it looked like she had one every ten months. My marster said he didn't care if she never worked if she kept havin' chillun like that for him. He put ma in the kitchen to cook for the slaves who didn't have families.

"People who didn't have families would live in a house together, but whenever you married you lived in a house to yourself. You could fix up your house to suit yourself. The house where everybody lived that warn't married, had 'bout a dozen and a half beds in it. Sometimes as many as three and four slept in a bed together when it was cold. The others had to sleep on the floor, but they had plenty of cover. Us didn't have anythin' in this house but what was made by some of us. There warn't but one room to this house with one fire place in it. Us never et in this room, us had another house where everybody from this house and from the house for the men who warn't married, et. Our beds was diff'unt from these you see now. They was made by the slaves out of rough lumber. Our marster seed to it that all the chillun had beds to sleep in. They was taken good care of. Us had no such things as dressers or the like. Us didn't have but a very few chairs 'cause the men didn't have time to waste makin' chairs, but us had plenty of benches. Our trunks was made by the men.

"People who had families lived by theyselves, but they didn't have but one room to their houses. They had to cook and sleep in this one room, and as their chillun got old enough they was sent over to the big house. Everybody called it that. The house you lived in with your family was small. It had a fire place and was only big enough to hold two beds and a bench and maybe a chair. Sometimes, if you had chillun fast enough, five and six had to sleep in that other bed together. Mothers didn't stay in after their chillun was born then like they do now. Whenever a child was born the mother come out in three days afterwards if she was healthy, but nobody stayed in over a week. They never stayed in bed but one day.

"When they called you to breakfast it would be dark as night. They did this so you could begin workin' at daybreak. At twelve o'clock they blowed the horn for dinner, but they didn't have to 'cause everybody knowed when it was dinner time. Us could tell time by the sun. Whenever the sun was over us so us could almost step in our shadow it was time to eat. When us went in to eat all the victuals was on the table and the plates was stacked on the table. You got your plate and fork, then got your dinner. Some would sit on the floor, some in chairs, and some would sit on the steps, but mos' everybody held their plates in their laps. Whenever any of the slaves had company for dinner, us was allowed to set the table and you and your company would eat at the table. In our dinin'-room, we called it mess house, us only had one long table, one small table, a stove, some benches, a few chairs, and stools. Whenever us got out of forks the men would make some out of wood to be used 'til some more could be bought. The food we got on Saturday would be turned over to the cook.

"When you married, your husband didn't stay with you like they do now. You had to stay with your marster and he had to stay with his. He was 'lowed to come every Saturday night and stay with you and the chillun 'til

Monday mornin'. If he was smart enough to have a little garden or to make little things like little chairs for his chillun to sit in or tables for 'em to eat on and wanted you to have 'em 'fore he could get back to see you, they would be sent by the runner. They had one boy they always used just to go from one place to the other, and they called him a runner. The runner wouldn't do anythin' else but that.

"Us made everythin' us wore. Us knitted our socks and stockin's. Things was much better then than they are now. Shoes lasted two and three years, and clothes didn't tear or wear out as easy as they do now. Us made all our cloth at night or mos' times durin' the winter time when us didn't have so much other work to do.

"When a person died he was buried the same day, and the funeral would be preached one year later. The slaves made your coffin and painted it with any kind of paint they could find, but they usually painted the outside box black.

"The slaves 'tended church with their marsters and after their service was over they would let the slaves hold service. They always left their pastor to preach for us and sometimes they would leave one of their deacons. When they left a deacon with us one of our preachers would preach. They only had two kinds of song books: Baptist Cluster, and Methodist Cluster. I kept one of these 'til a few years ago. Our preachers could read some, but only a very few other slaves could read and write. If you found one that could you might know some of his marster's chillun had slipped and learned it to him 'cause one thing they didn't 'low was no colored folk to learn to read and write. Us had singin' classes on Sunday, and at that time everybody could really sing. People can't sing now."

Slave Narratives

www.ingramcontent.com/pod-product-compliance
Lightning Source LLC
Chambersburg PA
CBHW071647160426
43195CB00012B/1376